Sidgwick's *The Methods of Ethics*

OXFORD GUIDES TO PHILOSOPHY

Series Editors
Rebecca Copenhaver, Washington University St. Louis
Christopher Shields, University of Notre Dame
Mark Timmons, University of Arizona

Advisory Board
Michael Beaney, Ursula Coope, Karen Detlefsen, Lisa Downing,
Tom Hurka, Pauline Kleingeld, Robert Pasnau, Dominik Perler,
Houston Smit, Allen Wood

Oxford Guides to Philosophy presents concise introductions to the most important primary texts in the history of philosophy. Written by top scholars, the volumes in the series are designed to present up-to-date scholarship in an accessible manner, in order to guide readers through these challenging texts.

Anscombe's Intention: A Guide
John Schwenkler

Kant's Doctrine of Virtue: A Guide
Mark C. Timmons

Sidgwick's *The Methods of Ethics*: A Guide
David Phillips

Sidgwick's *The Methods of Ethics*

A Guide

DAVID PHILLIPS

OXFORD
UNIVERSITY PRESS

Oxford University Press is a department of the University of Oxford. It furthers the University's objective of excellence in research, scholarship, and education by publishing worldwide. Oxford is a registered trade mark of Oxford University Press in the UK and certain other countries.

Published in the United States of America by Oxford University Press
198 Madison Avenue, New York, NY 10016, United States of America.

© Oxford University Press 2022

All rights reserved. No part of this publication may be reproduced, stored in a retrieval system, or transmitted, in any form or by any means, without the prior permission in writing of Oxford University Press, or as expressly permitted by law, by license, or under terms agreed with the appropriate reproduction rights organization. Inquiries concerning reproduction outside the scope of the above should be sent to the Rights Department, Oxford University Press, at the address above.

You must not circulate this work in any other form
and you must impose this same condition on any acquirer.

Library of Congress Control Number: 2022930023
ISBN 978-0-19-753962-0 (pbk.)
ISBN 978-0-19-753961-3 (hbk.)

DOI: 10.1093/oso/9780197539613.001.0001

1 3 5 7 9 8 6 4 2

Paperback printed by Marquis, Canada
Hardback printed by Bridgeport National Bindery, Inc., United States of America

For Sarah, Sam, Mary, and Max.

Contents

Preface ix
Acknowledgments xi

1. Introduction (*Methods* Prefaces) 1
2. Sidgwick's Project and the Three Methods (*Methods* I.I and I.VI) 20
3. Meaning, Motivation, and Free Will (*Methods* I.III, I.IV, and I.V) 41
4. Intuitionism and Goodness (*Methods* I.VIII and I.IX) 59
5. The Method of Egoism (*Methods* I.VII and Book II) 80
6. The Critique of Common-Sense Morality (*Methods* III.I–III.XI) 96
7. Philosophical Intuitionism (*Methods* III.XIII) 120
8. Hedonism (*Methods* III.XIV) 145
9. Utilitarianism: Meaning and Proof (*Methods* IV.I and IV.II) 162
10. Utilitarianism and Common-Sense Morality (*Methods* IV.III, IV.IV, and IV.V) 188
11. The Dualism of Practical Reason (*Methods* Concluding Chapter) 210

Guide to Terminology 233
Bibliography 239
Index 245

Preface

This book, included in the Oxford Guides series, is a concise guide to Henry Sidgwick's masterpiece, *The Methods of Ethics*. I have written the book to be read alongside Sidgwick's text. I aim to help readers to navigate through the text, and to raise the most significant interpretive and philosophical issues about Sidgwick's views and arguments.

I highlight throughout the important connections between the work of Sidgwick and that of others in contemporary moral philosophy and in the history of moral philosophy. I pay particular attention to his relations to predecessors he discusses, including Immanuel Kant and John Stuart Mill, and to G. E. Moore and W. D. Ross, his most celebrated successors in the British intuitionist tradition he revitalized.

At the end of the first eight chapters I give brief suggestions for further reading. At the end of the final three chapters, when I have covered all relevant parts of the *Methods*, I provide more substantial overviews of the secondary literature on the aspects of Sidgwick's work that have generated the most interest among his commentators: metaethics and moral epistemology; consequentialism versus deontology; and egoism and the dualism of practical reason.

Acknowledgments

I am very grateful for the help I have received with this project. Mark Timmons was a model of flexibility and good sense in allowing me to come to the right decision about which volume in the series I should try to write. Peter Ohlin was characteristically responsive, professional, and helpful throughout. Justin Coates gave very useful feedback on Chapter 3. Tom Hurka provided enormously valuable comments on the entire draft in record time. Over the years it has been a great boon and a great pleasure to learn from Tom and from other Sidgwickians including Roger Crisp, Kasia de Lazari-Radek, Tyler Paytas, Rob Shaver, Peter Singer, and Anthony Skelton. And, last but certainly not least, I owe a great deal to the generations of students at the University of Houston with whom I have had the privilege of discussing the *Methods*, and to those in my Fall 2020 seminar who were the first to read most of this material.

1
Introduction (*Methods* Prefaces)

1.1. Sidgwick's Life and Work

Henry Sidgwick lived his entire life during the reign of Queen Victoria. He was born on May 31, 1838, less than a year after she became queen; he died on August 28, 1900, some five months before she did. The first edition of *The Methods of Ethics* was published in 1874, at about the high point of Britain's global power. In his later years Sidgwick was an extraordinarily well-connected member of the British establishment. He held the highest philosophy position at Cambridge, the Knightsbridge Professorship of Moral Philosophy. One of his brothers-in-law, Edward White Benson, was Archbishop of Canterbury. Another, the Conservative politician Arthur Balfour, would in 1902 become prime minister. Sidgwick and his wife entertained Queen Victoria; he stayed with the most famous Victorian statesman, W. E. Gladstone, at his north Wales stately home, Hawarden; and he made multiple visits to the Isle of Wight home of the poet laureate, Alfred Lord Tennyson, whose work he loved.

His background was educated and middle-class, at a time when the educated middle class was a much smaller proportion of the population than it is in developed countries today. He was born in Skipton in Yorkshire where his father, a Church of England clergyman, was headmaster of the grammar school. As was then all too common his childhood was marked by early death. Two of his five siblings did not survive childhood. When his father died in 1841 his mother left Yorkshire seeking cures for her ailing older daughter. After that daughter's death, the family, consisting now of Henry's mother, older brother William, younger brother Arthur, and sister Mary, settled first near Bristol then at Rugby. Sidgwick attended Rugby School, one of England's most important private schools (and the place where rugby football was invented; Sidgwick himself had little aptitude for sports). There he fell under the influence of his older cousin, Edward White Benson, then a young master at the school (who would later become Archbishop of Canterbury). Benson went on to marry Sidgwick's sister Mary.

The Church of England was an extraordinarily powerful institution in early Victorian England. The sovereign was officially its head; it controlled a great deal of wealth; the major function of the two ancient universities in England, Oxford and Cambridge, was to train its clergymen; and in various ways those who were not members were less than first-class citizens. One of these ways had particular importance for Sidgwick: subscribing to the thirty-nine articles of the Church of England was a requirement for holding a fellowship at Oxford and Cambridge.

Sidgwick grew up during a period of intense intellectual and social ferment, when the justification for the position of the Church of England in particular and of Christianity in general was challenged from a number of directions. The Oxford Movement of the 1840s questioned the claim of the Church of England to a special historical authenticity; its most important leader, John Henry Newman, and a number of other prominent figures converted to Catholicism. Historical scholarship brought the divine origin of the Bible into question. Work in geology began to show that the Earth was far older than the Bible said it was. And the publication and dissemination of Darwin's theory of evolution in 1859 undermined the major remaining argument for the existence of God, the argument from design. The crisis of faith these developments brought on was a defining feature of Victorian intellectual life and of Sidgwick's life in particular. The economist John Maynard Keynes famously wrote of the memoir of Sidgwick compiled by his wife and brother:

[It is] very important as a historical document dealing with the mind of the Victorian period [...] [Sidgwick] never did anything but wonder whether Christianity was true and prove that it wasn't and hope that it was.[1]

This is quite unfair as an assessment of Sidgwick's intellectual achievements but very revealing about their deepest motivation.

Sidgwick entered Trinity College Cambridge in 1855. As an undergraduate he studied classics and mathematics, which at that time were the two subjects in which almost all Cambridge undergraduates took their degrees. It was possible to study just one of the two, but many especially able undergraduates studied both. Sidgwick did very well in mathematics, but it was classics in which he excelled, winning the most important prizes in the subject. He retained a great fondness for literature in general and for poetry in particular. He knew so much poetry that, in order to combat seasickness, he once managed to recite from memory without repetition for an entire voyage across the English Channel. And he continued well into his career as a philosopher to write literary criticism, in which he still retains a significant reputation.

Anyone with Sidgwick's intellect and temperament would have been drawn into the intellectual and theological controversies of his time. But Sidgwick was drawn into them in a special way. During his undergraduate years he joined the elite semi-secret discussion society known as the Cambridge Apostles.[2] In an autobiographical fragment dictated in his last days, he says:

> In the Michaelmas term of my second year an event occurred which had more effect on my intellectual life than any one thing that happened to me afterwards: I became a member of a discussion society—old and possessing historical traditions—which went by the name of "The Apostles" [... Its spirit] absorbed and dominated me. I can only describe it as the spirit of the pursuit of truth with absolute devotion and unreserve by a group of intimate

friends, who were perfectly frank with each other, and indulged in any amount of humorous sarcasm and playful banter, and yet each respects the other, and when he discourses tries to learn from him and see what he sees [. . .] It came to seem to me that no part of my life at Cambridge was so real to me as the Saturday evenings on which the apostolic debates were held; and the tie of attachment to the society is much the strongest corporate bond which I have known in my life. I think, then, that my admission into this society and the enthusiastic way in which I came to idealise it really determined or revealed that the deepest bent of my nature was towards the life of thought—thought exercised on the central problems of human life.[3]

After completing his undergraduate degree, Sidgwick was offered and accepted a faculty position—a fellowship—at Trinity. His interests were by this time primarily in philosophy and theology. But there were no fellowships in those subjects, so he took the fellowship he was offered in classics. In the early 1860s he studied philosophy and theology in his spare time while being employed as a classicist. His pursuits during these years included significant study of Hebrew and Arabic, with a view to researching biblical history. In 1865 he accepted a position as examiner for the small and relatively new moral sciences tripos (the Cambridge term for a degree program) which included philosophy among its subjects. And in 1867 Trinity allowed him to switch from lecturing in classics to lecturing in philosophy. But as his theological views moved further away from those of the Church of England, he was increasingly uncomfortable about continuing officially to subscribe to the thirty-nine articles. In June 1869 he resigned his fellowship, thus imperiling his future academic career. His doing so was one part of a movement of academic reform that resulted in the removal of the subscription requirement. His college came to his aid initially by appointing him as a lecturer in moral sciences rather than a fellow. His income was reduced, but his career preserved. In 1875, with subscription no longer required, he was appointed College Praelector of Moral and Political Philosophy, a permanent position with a larger income. And in 1883 he was elected Knightsbridge Professor of Moral Philosophy.

Sidgwick became a central figure in moral sciences at Cambridge. As it was then constituted, moral sciences encompassed philosophy, politics, psychology, and economics.[4] Though philosophy was his most important academic interest, Sidgwick published books that ranged across the moral sciences. The first edition of *The Methods of Ethics* was published in 1874 (with five further editions between then and 1901). The first edition of his *Principles of Political Economy* (as economics was then known) came out in 1883. His book on political theory, *The Elements of Politics*, appeared in 1891. At the time of his death he was working on a book on political history, *The Development of European Polity*. Like a number of his courses of lectures, it was published posthumously.

With the energy characteristic of great Victorians, Sidgwick's projects and pursuits did not end there. Working with his wife, Eleanor Mildred (née Balfour, known as "Nora"), whom he married in 1876, Sidgwick devoted much time to two other endeavors: women's higher education and psychical research. When Sidgwick arrived at Cambridge there were no colleges for women and it was not possible for women to take Cambridge degrees. The Sidgwicks worked tirelessly to open the doors of Cambridge to women students. They were among the founders of Newnham College, one of the first two Cambridge colleges for women, and Eleanor Sidgwick served as the college's second principal. In the last years of Henry Sidgwick's life, from 1894 on, he lived with his wife at Newnham in rooms in a new building whose construction they had helped to finance.

Sidgwick had been interested in ghost stories and the paranormal since childhood. Motivated by religious doubts and the desire for evidence of an afterlife and other spiritual phenomena, he and his wife became part of a very distinguished group that sought scientific evidence of their reality. He was the first president of the Society for Psychical Research, founded in 1882,

> with the declared object of "making an organized and systematic attempt to investigate that large group of debatable phenomena designated by such terms as mesmeric, psychical, and spiritualistic."[5]

They spent much time investigating mediums, almost all of whom they ended up exposing as frauds. One of them was an Italian named Eusapia Palladino (one of the photographs of Sidgwick owned by the National Portrait Gallery shows him with Palladino).

In the history of moral philosophy Sidgwick tends to be grouped with other philosophers in one of two ways, both illuminating. The first and more traditional classification scheme makes him the last of the three great classical utilitarians: Jeremy Bentham (1748–1832), John Stuart Mill (1806–1873), and Sidgwick (1838–1900). The second classification scheme places him not at the end but at the beginning of a tradition: as the founder of a group of philosophers who broadly agreed about metaethics but disagreed about moral theory that Thomas Hurka has called "the Sidgwick to Ewing school."[6] Other than Sidgwick, the best-known figures in the Sidgwick to Ewing school are his pupil G. E. Moore (1873–1958), whose most celebrated work in ethics is *Principia Ethica* (1903), and W. D. Ross (1877–1971), whose most famous ethical work is *The Right and the Good* (1930).

At the time of his death Sidgwick was widely regarded as at least one of and perhaps the most important Anglophone moral philosopher of the late nineteenth century. But in the first decades of the twentieth century his reputation declined significantly and his work was no longer widely read. One cause of this decline was the influence of Moore. Though there are more references to Sidgwick in the index to *Principia Ethica* than there are to any other philosopher, and though Moore himself, while not personally warm about Sidgwick, properly acknowledged his influence,[7] other philosophers under Moore's spell in the early twentieth century tended to ignore Sidgwick's contribution, influenced by what Hurka calls *Principia*'s "rhetoric of the clean break."[8] This history can still arouse strong feelings among philosophers who are Sidgwick enthusiasts. In a footnote to *On What Matters*, Volume 1 (2011a), Derek Parfit wrote:

> When Moore's clouds, for many decades, hid the light from Sidgwick's sun, that was in part because, unlike the judicious Sidgwick, Moore writes with the extremism that makes Kant's texts so compelling. With the exception of the 'doctrine of organic unities', every interesting claim in Moore's *Principia* is either taken from Sidgwick or [. . .] obviously false.[9]

1.2. The *Methods*: An Introductory Sketch

The part of the Prefaces to the *Methods* of most value to contemporary students is what is sometimes called the "short intellectual autobiography" that Sidgwick's literary executor, E. E. Constance Jones, included in the preface to the sixth edition (pp. xvii–xxiii).[10] As she says, the material comprises notes for a lecture that Sidgwick gave late in his life, in which he explained how he arrived at the ethical view set out in the *Methods*. It is a very helpful introduction to the *Methods* for three reasons. First, it gives a succinct presentation of Sidgwick's overall position. Second, like many of Sidgwick's papers, the style is more direct and accessible than the style of much of the *Methods*. Third, it locates Sidgwick's thought by reference to figures in the history of philosophy most of whom are still well-known and widely read. Three of them, Aristotle, Kant, and Mill, are among the most celebrated figures in the history of ethics. Of the other two, Joseph Butler is still read, though he is not nearly as influential today as he was in the nineteenth century. Only William Whewell is now quite obscure.[11]

The standard mid-Victorian menu in moral philosophy that Sidgwick and others inherited featured just two options: the empirical utilitarianism of Mill and the intuitive anti-utilitarianism of Whewell. The opposition between them encompassed both questions in normative ethics (of what you ought to do) and questions in metaethics (of how you know what you ought to do). Utilitarians like Mill thought that what you ought to do is whatever will bring about the greatest amount of happiness for everybody, and they thought that you know this through experience. Intuitionists like Whewell thought that what you ought to do is to always follow absolute, non-utilitarian moral rules, and they thought that you know what these rules are because they are self-evident, in the same way that mathematical truths like $2 + 2 = 4$ are self-evident.

Sidgwick tells us that his early sympathies were with Mill, describing his "antagonism" to Whewell's intuitionism. But he came to be concerned about an incoherence in Mill's view. On the one hand, Mill was a psychological hedonist: he held that each person in fact seeks his or her own happiness. On the other hand, he was an ethical utilitarian: he held that each person ought to seek the general happiness. There was thus a conflict between interest and duty. It is possible that that conflict is of no practical importance because doing what best promotes the general happiness is always in fact in each person's individual interest. But Sidgwick thought that this kind of harmony between duty and interest could not be demonstrated on the basis of ordinary experience. So what was needed instead to resolve the conflict was a fundamental ethical intuition.

At this point he read Kant again and saw Kant identifying a fundamental ethical intuition: the formula of universal law. As Sidgwick frames it, this fundamental principle tells you to "Act from a principle or maxim that you can will to be a universal law."

Sidgwick thought that Kant, unlike Whewell, had identified a genuine intuition: a self-evident principle with real ethical import.[12] But in two other ways he disagreed with what he took to be Kant's view about his principle. First, he took Kant to think that the universal law formula provided complete ethical guidance: that every duty could be deduced from it. Sidgwick thought otherwise: "the fundamental principle seemed to me inadequate for the construction of a system of duties" (xix). Second, Sidgwick rejected Kant's idea that there was a crucial connection between his fundamental principle and the philosophical question of free will, Kant's "resting of morality on freedom." Furthermore, and crucially, the Kantian principle did not resolve the conflict between interest and duty he had found in Mill. The rational egoist "might accept the Kantian principle and remain an egoist," holding that it is a universal law that each of us ought to aim exclusively at our own individual happiness.

Sidgwick was then "a disciple on the loose" (xx), not having found a solution to the conflict between interest and duty in either of his two "masters," Mill or Kant. At this point, "the influence of Butler came in." Sidgwick found in Butler ("with pleasure and surprise") the view he had come to independently in thinking about Mill and Kant: that there is a rational stand-off between duty and interest, a dualism of the practical reason.

> It was on this side—if I may so say—that I entered into Butler's system and came under the influence of his powerful and cautious intellect. (xxi)

Butler's influence led Sidgwick to two further important changes of view. First, it led him to reject Mill's psychological hedonism and to hold instead that human motivation includes disinterested as well as self-interested impulses. Second, it led him to reconsider his antipathy to intuitional ethics. He had already accepted Kant's view that there was one ethical intuition, the universal law formula. And he had come to think that there was also an intuition that supported utilitarianism:

> The axiom [...] that a rational agent is bound to aim at Universal Happiness. (xxi)

Should he not then countenance the possibility that there were more intuitions, that Whewell's view that there is a plurality of intuitive ethical principles was correct even if Whewell himself had not properly developed that view?

"In this state of mind," Sidgwick tells us, he "had to read Aristotle again." In doing so, he came to see Aristotle as providing a model for what Sidgwick himself needed to do to determine whether there was a plurality of genuine ethical intuitions. Aristotle had given

> [t]he Common-Sense Morality of Greece, reduced to consistency by careful comparison[.] (xxi)

Sidgwick set out to do the same for the common-sense morality of Victorian England, in order to determine whether it could be regarded as a system of genuine intuitions. But his conclusion after doing so was still negative:

> The result of the examination was to bring out with fresh force and vividness the difference between the Maxims of Common-Sense Morality [...] and the intuitions which I had already attained, i.e., the Kantian principle [...] and the Fundamental Principle of Utilitarianism. (xxii)

Thus resulted Sidgwick's own distinctive philosophical position:

> I was then a Utilitarian again, but on an Intuitional basis. (xxii)

Sidgwick ends the lecture by summarizing his view on the two key conflicts, between utilitarianism and intuitionism and between utilitarianism and egoism. The conflict between utilitarianism and intuitionism can be resolved. As to the source of our moral knowledge, the intuitionists are right. As to its content, the utilitarians are right. But there are sufficient practical difficulties in applying the utilitarian method that it is usefully supplemented by commonsense morality. The rules of common-sense morality are then to be regarded not as themselves fundamental intuitions but instead as useful practical guides that generally lead us to do what utilitarianism says is correct. By contrast, the conflict between utilitarianism and egoism has not been resolved:

> There was indeed a fundamental opposition between the individual's interest and either morality, which I could not solve by any method I had yet found trustworthy, without the assumption of the moral government of the world. (xxii)

1.3. Reasons to Read Sidgwick

Reasons to read Sidgwick are suggested by the two philosophers who arguably did the most to restore and enhance his reputation after its early twentieth-century decline: C. D. Broad (1887–1973) and Derek Parfit (1942–2017). At the beginning of the long chapter on Sidgwick in *Five Types of Ethical Theory* (1930)[13], Broad writes:

> Sidgwick's *Methods of Ethics* seems to me to be on the whole the best treatise on moral theory that has ever been written, and to be one of the English philosophical classics. This does not of course imply that Sidgwick was a better man or an acuter thinker than the other writers with whose theories we have been dealing; for he inherited the results of their labours, and he thus had over them an advantage of the kind which any contemporary student of mathematics or physics has over Newton and Faraday. But, even when this advantage has been discounted, Sidgwick must continue to rank extremely high. He combined deep moral

earnestness with complete coolness and absence of moral fanaticism. His capacity for seeing all sides of a question and estimating their relative importance was unrivalled; his power of analysis was very great; and he never allowed the natural desire to make up one's mind on important questions to hurry him into a decision where the evidence seemed inadequate or conflicting.

In the Preface to *On What Matters*, Volume 1 (2011a), Parfit concurs:

> Sidgwick's *Methods* is, I believe, the best book on ethics ever written. There are some books that are greater achievements, such as Plato's *Republic* and Aristotle's *Ethics*. But Sidgwick's book contains the largest number of true and important claims [. . .] In the *Methods*, as Broad claims, 'almost all the main problems of ethics are discussed with extreme acuteness'. And Sidgwick gets very many things right. He gives the best critical accounts of three of the main subjects in ancient and modern ethics: hedonism, egoism, and consequentialism. And in the longest of the book's four parts, he also gives the best critical account of pluralistic non-consequentialist common-sense morality. Though Sidgwick makes mistakes [. . .] he does not, I believe, make many. These facts make Sidgwick's *Methods* the book that it would be best for everyone interested in ethics to read, remember, and be able to assume that others have read.[14]

1.4. Challenges in Reading Sidgwick

Immediately after the passage just quoted, Broad famously identifies some challenges facing a reader of the *Methods*:

> [Sidgwick] has grave defects as a writer which have certainly detracted from his fame. His style is heavy and involved, and

he seldom allowed that strong sense of humour, which is said to have made him a delightful conversationalist, to relieve the uniform dull dignity of his writing. He incessantly refines, qualifies, raises objections, answers them, and then finds further objections to the answers. Each of these objections, rebuttals, rejoinders, and surrejoinders is in itself admirable, and does infinite credit to the acuteness and candor of the author. But the reader is apt to become impatient; to lose the thread of the argument; and to rise from his desk finding that he has read a great deal with constant admiration and now remembers little or nothing.[15]

Twenty-first-century philosophy students are liable also to be struck by how long many of Sidgwick's sentences are. This is a feature of Victorian writing in general, not just of Sidgwick's writing in the *Methods*. Even allowing for this, it is often very hard to quote a short key passage from the *Methods*. Sidgwick's thoughts are normally clearly and acutely expressed. But (as Broad implies) they are typically embedded in quite complex grammatical and argumentative structures and often resist the effort to remove them from those structures.

The main thing I hope to do in this Guide is to help readers keep track of what Broad calls "the thread of the argument." It can be hard to do this both within individual chapters of the *Methods* and in the book as a whole. Sidgwick himself supplied one very helpful aid: the analytical table of contents, pages xxv to xxxviii. It is always well worth consulting the summary Sidgwick gives there before and after reading a chapter of the *Methods*.

I will aim to provide much further such aid. I will consistently try to highlight the central conclusions of each part of the *Methods* I discuss, and to focus on the central parts of the arguments for those conclusions. In doing that, there will inevitably be much interesting detail I can't discuss. The *Methods* is a long book containing acute discussions of a very wide range of ethical questions. No text the size of this Guide can track all of Sidgwick's discussion. The reader I am primarily writing for is someone who needs help navigating through the text, not someone who already has a secure sense of its geography.

That most important part of my aim is a matter of bringing out as clearly as I can what is central in the text. Sometimes I will also need to supplement the text. Thomas Hurka has remarked that "the more important something is, the less Sidgwick says about it." There is something clearly right about this critical observation. To mention two important instances: In Book I Chapter VIII, Sidgwick gives a general argument for epistemic intuitionism. That argument is absolutely crucial to his distinctive view, "utilitarianism on an intuitional basis." But it is introduced halfway through a paragraph, and the analytical table of contents does not tell a reader it is there. In Book III Chapter XI, Sidgwick introduces four conditions or tests that putative axioms have to meet. These conditions are crucial to his critical assessment of common-sense morality. Despite the fact that the *Methods* is 509 pages long, the conditions are introduced quite abruptly with no background discussion. A reader can learn more about them from Sidgwick's few short papers in epistemology than from the text of the *Methods*. In cases like these, I will aim not merely to highlight the key parts of the text but also to supplement it.

I will aim also to locate Sidgwick's thought in relation to contemporary moral philosophy and to the history of moral philosophy. Where I think it will be helpful, I will relate Sidgwick's views and arguments to those in ethics today. And I will also aim to locate Sidgwick's views in relation to other key figures in the history of moral philosophy: to predecessors, particularly celebrated philosophers like Aristotle, Kant, and Mill whose influence he discusses in the short intellectual autobiography; and to successors, particularly philosophers like Moore and Ross in the British intuitionist tradition Sidgwick revitalized.

1.5. The Structure of the *Methods* and the Plan of this Guide

The *Methods* is divided into four books. The apparent plan is clear enough: Book I is introductory, while the other three books focus in turn on the three methods Sidgwick distinguishes: Book II on egoism, Book III on intuitionism, and Book IV on utilitarianism. But the apparent plan might lead a reader to have false expectations: to expect that Book II is only relevant to egoism and that everything important Sidgwick wants to say about egoism is to be found in Book II; that Book III is only relevant to intuitionism and that everything important Sidgwick wants to say about intuitionism is to be found in Book III; and that Book IV is only relevant to utilitarianism and that everything important Sidgwick wants to say about utilitarianism is to be found in Book IV.

None of these expectations are fulfilled. Book II is not only relevant to egoism: it contains Sidgwick's main discussions of the nature and measurement of happiness and so is essential to his treatment of utilitarianism. And not everything important Sidgwick wants to say about egoism is to be found in Book II: crucial material about egoism is contained in III.XIII, IV.II, and the Concluding Chapter. Again, Book III is not only relevant to intuitionism: III.XIII and III.XIV in particular contain material absolutely central to Sidgwick's views on egoism and utilitarianism as well as to his views on intuitionism. And not everything important Sidgwick wants to say about intuitionism can be found in Book III; crucial material about intuitionism is to be found in II.V and in much of Book IV, particularly IV.II and the Concluding Chapter, as well as in Book III. Again, Book IV is not only relevant to utilitarianism: more or less the whole of it is directly relevant to Sidgwick's views on intuitionism as well as to his views on utilitarianism, and, as just noted, IV.II and the Concluding Chapter are crucial to his views on egoism. And not everything important Sidgwick wants to say about utilitarianism is to be found in Book IV: his views on utilitarianism cannot be understood without taking into account much of Book II, and III.XIII and III.XIV, as well as the material in Book IV.

One of Sidgwick's criticisms of himself was that his work was "ill-arranged."[16] His contemporary admirers often agree. Few of them think that the *Methods*' organization is one of its strengths. But, for better or worse, readers of the *Methods* will encounter, most likely in the excellent and inexpensive Hackett edition, the prefatory material and 509 pages of text arranged as Sidgwick arranged it. It seemed to me that, in writing this Guide, the most straightforward option was to take the material in its original order (with a couple of small exceptions). This is the normal approach for Guides in this series, and an approach not employed in any of the recent monographs on Sidgwick referred to below. Both seem good reasons to try it. Its disadvantage is that I will follow Sidgwick in discussing some important topics in more than one place. I hope to mitigate this disadvantage in two ways. One is that I will provide cross-references within my text to earlier and later treatments of related themes. The other is that in the final three chapters, when I have covered all the parts of the *Methods* relevant to understanding and assessing Sidgwick's views on key issues, I will give an overview of the secondary literature on those issues.[17] There will be three such overview discussions, on the aspects of Sidgwick that have generated the most philosophical interest among his commentators: metaethics and moral epistemology; consequentialism versus deontology; and egoism and the dualism of practical reason.

Though I will discuss the material in the *Methods* largely in the order in which it appears in the original, I will not be able to devote equal amounts of space to all its chapters. This Guide is roughly one third of the length of the *Methods*. And not all of the chapters in the *Methods* are equally important. A short list of the most important chapters might be: I.I, I.III, I.VIII, I.IX, II.V, III.XI, III.XIII, III.XIV, IV.II, and the Concluding Chapter. While I will be able to say something about most chapters of the *Methods*, I will need to say the most about these crucial chapters. Accordingly, I won't cover the same amount of the original in each of my chapters.[18] When I am discussing parts of the *Methods* whose details are less crucial to the overall argument, I will cover a lot of its pages quickly. When I am discussing parts of the *Methods* whose details are central to its overall argument, my discussion will be much more fine-grained.

While this Guide is designed to help readers planning to work through the whole of the *Methods*, it comports well with some obvious, rather less ambitious, alternative plans. One such alternative plan is to omit Chapter II of Book I, to read only Chapters II and V of Book II, and to read only Chapters I, XI, XIII, and XIV of Book III. This reduces the number of pages one reads in the body of the *Methods* from 509 to just over 300. A variant of this plan would involve reading slightly more of Book III: picking one of Chapters II through X with the aim of focusing on one element of the common-sense morality Sidgwick there discusses. No such cut will be costless. But for some readers such a scaled-back plan might well be on balance the best option.

Notes

1. Quoted on p. 118 of Regan 1986.
2. Many famous Cambridge-educated figures were Apostles before, during, and after Sidgwick's time. They include Alfred Lord Tennyson, Bertrand Russell, G. E. Moore, John Maynard Keynes, Lytton Strachey, and several of the Cambridge spies who passed secrets to the Soviet Union between the 1930s and 1950s.
3. Sidgwick and Sidgwick 1906, 34–35.
4. Economics split off from moral sciences in 1903. The degree program most comparable to nineteenth-century Cambridge moral sciences in the later history of Oxford and Cambridge is the politics, philosophy, and economics (PPE) degree, which has been a central part of undergraduate education at Oxford since the 1920s.
5. Sidgwick and Sidgwick 1906, 358.

6. For his fullest treatment, see Hurka 2014a.
7. Moore 1942, 16–17.
8. Hurka 2003.
9. Parfit 2011a, 464–65.
10. All page references in the text are to the seventh edition of the *Methods* (Sidgwick 1907). As E. E. Constance Jones (Sidgwick's literary executor) explains in the preface to the sixth edition, Sidgwick himself managed the revisions of about the first half of the sixth edition (1901); Constance Jones finished the work. There are almost no changes between the sixth and the seventh editions.
11. By contrast, the course of lectures on ethics that Sidgwick standardly gave in his later years at Cambridge (and which Moore among others attended) focused on contemporaries of his, all of whom are now quite obscure: T. H. Green, Herbert Spencer, and Jacques Martineau. These lectures were posthumously published (Sidgwick 1902).
12. We will consider the question whether Sidgwick was right in thinking this in Chapter 7, Section 2.
13. Broad 1930, 143.
14. Parfit 2011a, xxxiii–xl.
15. Broad 1930, 143–44.
16. Sidgwick and Sidgwick 1906, 177.
17. In those chapters the overview discussions will replace the (less detailed) suggestions for further reading to be found at the end of each of the first eight chapters.
18. I will use Roman numerals for chapters in the *Methods*, for which I will normally give both book and chapter number (for example, "I.III" signifies Book I Chapter III). Roman numerals can be a nuisance to read. But this Guide is designed to be read along with the text of the *Methods*, and Sidgwick uses Roman numerals throughout. And using Roman numerals for chapters in the *Methods* allows me to be very clear in distinguishing references to chapters in the *Methods* from references to chapters in this Guide. I will always use Arabic numbers to refer to chapters in this Guide.

Further Reading

For Sidgwick's life the two most important sources are the memoir compiled by his wife and his brother (Sidgwick and Sidgwick 1906), much of which consists of passages from Sidgwick's own letters and diaries, and Bart Schultz's magisterial intellectual biography (Schultz 2004).

Overall assessments of the importance of the *Methods* are Broad 1930, 143–144, and Parfit 2011a, xxxii–xlv. A more general introduction to Sidgwick's intellectual life is Schultz 2004, Chapter 1.

For a long period after Sidgwick's death there was little secondary literature on the *Methods*. The two crucial exceptions are Broad 1930 and Schneewind 1977.

The past twenty years or so have seen growing philosophical interest in Sidgwick. Books exclusively focused on Sidgwick are Schultz 2004, Phillips 2011, Nakano-Okuno 2011, Lazari-Radek and Singer 2014, and Crisp 2015. Important treatments of Sidgwick in books with broader foci are Shaver 1999, Irwin 2009, Parfit 2011a, and Hurka 2014a.

2
Sidgwick's Project and the Three Methods (*Methods* I.I and I.VI)

2.1. Sidgwick's Project

In the final section of I.I Sidgwick writes:

> My object, then, in the present work, is to expound as clearly and fully as my limits will allow the different methods of Ethics that I find implicit in our common moral reasoning; to point out their mutual relations; and where they seem to conflict, to define the issue as much as possible. In the course of this endeavour I am led to discuss the considerations which should, in my opinion, be decisive in determining the adoption of ethical first principles; but it is not my primary aim to establish such principles[.] (14)

The kind of project Sidgwick describes here will not seem at all surprising to anyone who has taken an introductory ethics course. Lots of introductory texts in moral philosophy discuss different competing moral theories. They have perhaps a chapter on each of these theories, explaining how the theory works and considering key problems or difficulties with it. Often they do something at the end to try to decide which of the competing moral theories is correct, or to try to reconcile the differences between them. Though some of Sidgwick's terminology is not widely used today—philosophers these days tend to talk about "moral theories" not "methods of ethics," and don't tend to talk much about "first principles"—there is nothing surprising about a project of this general kind.

Nor is there much that is surprising about the methods of ethics (or moral theories) Sidgwick considers. Utilitarianism is pretty much always one of the moral theories that are addressed in introductory ethics texts. The same is true of the theory Sidgwick calls "intuitionism." Here again, we need to avoid being misled by his terminology. In a way whose history, as we will see in Chapter 4, has a lot to do with Sidgwick, the moral theory he calls "intuitionism" is today instead called "deontology." Like Sidgwick, introductory ethics texts today very often focus a good deal of attention on the conflict between utilitarianism and deontology. Egoism is trickier. For reasons which Sidgwick himself was quite sensitive to, though egoism is not uncommonly considered in introductory ethics texts today, it is likely to be treated as (as Derek Parfit puts it) an "external rival to" morality, rather than as itself a moral theory.[1]

The major questions about Sidgwick's project are not, then, the result of his framework being alien or of his inclusion among his methods of ethics of views that would not be taken seriously today. They are rather matters of the crucial detail first laid out in Chapters I and VI of Book I of the *Methods*. Some key questions are (1) Whether Sidgwick omits important moral theories, either culpably because he failed to note the independent importance of some moral theory that had already been articulated in his time, or non-culpably because the later history of moral philosophy revealed the importance of further independent theories he did not consider; (2) Whether the different terminology Sidgwick uses—of methods of ethics and of first principles—makes any important difference to the way he proceeds as compared to contemporary philosophers who talk instead about moral theories; (3) Whether anything about the initial setup of the *Methods* gives grounds for the suspicion a number of his contemporaries expressed that he was not, as he claimed, fairly and impartially treating each of the three methods but instead setting out to argue against one or more of them.

2.2. The Three Methods

It may be helpful at this point to give very preliminary characterizations of the three methods. The egoist method of determining what you ought to do is to consider the consequences of the possible actions open to you, and to choose the action that will produce the greatest balance of pleasure over pain for you. The utilitarian method agrees with the egoist method that you should consider consequences and that pleasure and pain are the only things that are intrinsically good and bad. But it differs from the egoist method about whose pain or pleasure you should consider. According to egoism, you should consider only your own; according to utilitarianism, you should consider everyone's.

The intuitionist method is quite different. Instead of looking at consequences, according to intuitionism, when you are deciding what to do you should follow a set of absolute moral rules that you can see to be correct. For a simple model of an intuitionist moral theory, start with the Judeo-Christian Ten Commandments. Subtract the ones that seem to you to be theological rather than moral. Then consider a moral theory that says: the only thing that you ought to do is always to obey all of these commandments.

2.3. Why Are There Just Three Methods?

The main places in which Sidgwick argues that there are just three methods are in Chapters I and VI of Book I. The initial argument is in Section 4 of Chapter I. The argument has two stages: a first, less controversial stage which yields five methods, then a second, much more controversial, stage that reduces the five to three.

SIDGWICK'S PROJECT AND THE THREE METHODS

The first stage of the argument occupies the bulk of Section 4, up to the last paragraph. Sidgwick identifies distinct methods by connecting them with what in Chapter VI he calls "valid ultimate reasons for action," and what he here calls "practical principles" that are "ultimate":

> What then are these different methods? What are the different practical principles which the common sense of mankind is *prima facie* prepared to accept as ultimate? (6)

Four of the five methods he initially identifies are connected to ends or goods. The question is what ends

> the common sense of mankind is prepared to accept as rational ultimate ends[.] (9)

Sidgwick answers that there are just two such ends: happiness on the one hand, and perfection or excellence on the other. We don't need to say more here about Sidgwick's conception of happiness. It will be a topic particularly in Chapters 5 and 8. It is helpful to quote what he says in introducing perfection or excellence:

> By 'Excellence' [I mean] not primarily superiority to others, but a partial realization of, or approximation to, an ideal type of human Perfection. (9)

Each of these ultimate ends appears initially to generate two distinct methods. For in the case of happiness there seem to be two distinct methods corresponding to two distinct ultimate principles. One tells you that the ultimate reason for action is to secure happiness for yourself. This is egoism. The other tells you that the ultimate reason for action is to secure happiness for everyone. This is utilitarianism. And it initially appears that the same can be said for perfection or excellence: one view might be that the ultimate reason for action is to secure perfection or excellence for yourself, another that the ultimate reason for action is to secure perfection or excellence for everyone. This gets us—apparently—to four methods. The fifth method is intuitionism.

The second and much more controversial stage of the argument is the reduction from five methods to three. It all takes place initially in a single paragraph that runs from page 10 to page 11. There are two key moves in the paragraph. The first move reduces the five methods to four. Sidgwick says that, while there may seem to be the same alternatives for perfection or excellence as there are for happiness, namely a requirement to pursue it for yourself or a requirement to pursue it for everyone, no one in fact thinks you should sacrifice your own excellence to further the excellence of others. So there is really only one method connected with perfection or excellence as an end. The ultimate reason for action is your own perfection or excellence.

This first move is very questionable. It may be that many writers before Sidgwick who took perfection or excellence to be the ultimate end thought each of us bound to seek only his or her own perfection. But that is not true of all the views Sidgwick himself goes on to consider. As we will see in Chapter 8, in III.XIV Sidgwick considers two perfectionist alternatives to hedonism. One of these alternatives, a pluralistic perfectionist alternative, has it that, in addition to pleasure, "cognition of truth," "contemplation of beauty," and "free or virtuous action" are intrinsically good (400). And Sidgwick clearly envisages a view according to which we are directed to pursue these goods "for mankind generally," not just for ourselves. Later philosophers who reject hedonism, including Moore and Ross and many of their intellectual successors, similarly combine a pluralistic perfectionist view of the good with the idea that you should pursue perfection for everyone, not just for yourself.

The second move in the paragraph is at least equally questionable. It gets us from four to three methods by identifying the method that tells you to pursue your own perfection or excellence with intuitionism. The move is made in a single sentence:

> And since virtue is commonly conceived as the most valuable element of human Excellence—and an element essentially preferable to any other element that can come into competition with it as an alternative for rational choice—any method which takes Perfection or Excellence of human nature as ultimate End will *prima facie* coincide to a great extent with that based on what I called the Intuitional view: and I have accordingly decided to treat it as a special form of the latter. (11)

This move involves at least three debatable ideas. The first is the idea that excellence or perfection can properly be understood as basically a matter just of *moral* excellence or perfection. The second is the idea that moral excellence or perfection—virtue—is a matter of following absolute moral rules. Third, this is a place at which Sidgwick needs to lean very heavily on the distinction between methods and first principles. If we focus on first principles, the idea that the reason to follow moral rules is that doing so promotes your own excellence seems very different from the idea that the reason to follow moral rules is that they are absolute requirements. It is only by emphasizing methods and deemphasizing first principles that Sidgwick can get these ideas to seem largely to coincide.

After considering reason, motivation, and free will in I.III, I.IV, and I.V, Sidgwick returns in I.VI to methods and principles. He first raises again the question whether there are just three methods. Now the focus is not primarily on the reduction from five methods to three, but on whether there are further first principles or valid ultimate reasons for action that he has not yet properly accounted for.

> What then do we commonly regard as valid ultimate reasons for acting or abstaining? This, as was said, is the starting-point for the discussions of the present treatise, which is not primarily

concerned with proving or disproving the validity of any such reasons, but rather with the critical exposition of the different 'methods'—or rational procedures for determining right conduct in any particular case—which are logically connected with the different ultimate reasons widely accepted. In the first chapter we found that such reasons were supplied by the notions of Happiness and Excellence or Perfection (including Virtue or Moral Perfection as a prominent element), regarded as ultimate ends, and Duty as prescribed by unconditional rules [. . .] It may seem, however, that these notions by no means exhaust the list of reasons which are widely accepted as ultimate grounds for action. Many religious persons think that the highest reason for doing anything is that it is God's Will: while to others 'Self-Realisation' or 'Self-Development,' and to others, again, 'Life according to nature' appear the really ultimate ends. (78–79)

We can focus here on what Sidgwick says about the view that the highest reason for doing anything is that it is God's will. Of the three alternative conceptions he considers, it is the most likely to seem to readers today a genuine alternative to egoism, intuitionism, and utilitarianism. Sidgwick argues that it is not a genuine alternative within ethics. The question is how God's will is ascertained. If it is by revelation, we have moved beyond the sphere of the ethical into the sphere of the theological. If not, we need to determine God's will by the exercise of reason. If we do that, we don't end up generating any new methods. We end up instead thinking of one of the methods we have already articulated in a new way. We end up, that is, thinking that God desires people's happiness, so with a divine form of egoism or utilitarianism. Or we end up thinking God desires our perfection, so with a divine form of perfectionism. Or we end up thinking that the rules of intuitional morality are God's laws, so with a divine form of intuitionism. In any event, we end up, Sidgwick argues, with one of the three methods already considered in a new form, not with a genuinely new method.

It would be unreasonable to expect Sidgwick, writing at the time he did, fully to anticipate the range of alternative moral theories that contemporary philosophers are apt to consider. It is nonetheless worth thinking a bit more about where the main differences are between the options considered by Sidgwick and the options considered by later moral philosophers. No way of quickly dividing up the terrain of moral theories will be uncontroversial. But, for our purposes, a simple and useful division is between consequentialist and non-consequentialist moral theories. According to consequentialist theories, the rightness or wrongness of an action is always determined by its tendency to produce good or bad consequences. Non-consequentialist theories reject this key consequentialist claim. On this way of dividing things up, egoism and utilitarianism will be consequentialist theories. And so will views that tell us to promote or maximize our own perfection or excellence or the perfection or excellence of everyone.

Sidgwick's coverage of consequentialist theories is quite comprehensive. He considers egoism as well as utilitarianism. And while he argues for hedonism in Book III Chapter XIV, he takes perfectionist alternatives to hedonism very seriously.

It is on the non-consequentialist side that Sidgwick is more apt to seem to be missing something that contemporary moral philosophers take to be important. The major alternative to consequentialism that he considers is absolutist deontology, according to which there are a number of absolute moral rules. He misses the possibility of other versions of deontology. As we will see in Chapters 6 and 7, he regrettably does not anticipate Ross's most famous idea, that there are a number of moral rules but that they are not absolute principles but instead principles of *prima facie* duty. Most deontologists today agree with Ross: they don't regard moral rules as absolute. And Sidgwick doesn't do much to consider monistic deontological theories. A significant number of contemporary philosophers think that Kant provides the basis for a monistic deontological theory: that somewhere among his formulations of the categorical imperative there is a single key principle that unifies morality. As we saw in Chapter 1, Sidgwick did consider one possible version of this view, the idea that it is the universal law formulation of the categorical imperative that unifies morality, but he did not think it a workable idea.

Sidgwick also misses the possibility of theories that are neither consequentialist nor deontological. In contemporary moral philosophy, virtue ethics is quite often taken to be a third way, an alternative both to consequentialism and to deontology. We will be in a position to say more about Sidgwick and virtue theory in Chapter 8, after considering his treatment of virtue in Book III. But a preliminary verdict is that Sidgwick doesn't really consider virtue ethics. He says a lot about virtue and about particular virtues. But he doesn't treat virtue as supplying a new basis for systematizing ethics. He always treats it instead either in a deontological way as a matter of following absolute rules or in a consequentialist way as a matter of character traits that promote the good. Other non-consequentialist views that are much discussed in contemporary moral philosophy are also missing. One influential such idea is contractualism, the idea that in some way morality is to be understood as the product of an agreement.[2] Sidgwick does not really consider this kind of view.

It is not surprising that a work written in the late nineteenth century should fail to anticipate later developments in moral theory; that it does so is not necessarily a criticism of Sidgwick. One response would be to build on Sidgwick's work by undertaking a kind of Sidgwickian critical examination and attempted synthesis of some of these further moral theories. And, indeed, just this project was undertaken by one of Sidgwick's most important later admirers, Derek Parfit, in Volumes I and II of *On What Matters* (2011). Parfit's project has a strikingly Sidgwickian flavor, though Parfit claims more success in his project that Sidgwick claimed in his. Both consider three main competing theories and try to synthesize them. Sidgwick considers utilitarianism, intuitionism, and egoism; he thinks he can synthesize utilitarianism and intuitionism, but not utilitarianism and egoism. Parfit considers utilitarianism, Kantianism, and contractualism. He thinks he can achieve a full synthesis: a "triple theory" that combines all three of them.[3]

2.4. Methods of Ethics, First Principles, and Moral Theories

Thus far I have basically assumed that Sidgwick's term "method of ethics" means the same as the more familiar contemporary term "moral theory." And I have not highlighted Sidgwick's distinction between methods of ethics and first principles. In this section I address the questions I have so far neglected: What exactly does Sidgwick mean by the terms "method of ethics" and "first principle"? How much (if any) difference does it make if you think, as Sidgwick does, in terms of methods of ethics and first principles, rather than in terms of moral theories?

Sidgwick introduces the term "method of ethics" in the very first sentence of the book:

[A] 'Method of Ethics' is [...] any rational procedure by which we determine what individual human beings 'ought'—or what it is 'right' for them—to do, or to seek to realise by voluntary action. (1)

Three things are worth noting about this definition. First, a method of ethics is a rational *procedure*. The emphasis is important for Sidgwick. As we have seen he claims to focus mainly on procedures rather than on the ultimate reasons or first principles that justify them. Second, and more straightforwardly: the focus on what *individual* human beings ought to do distinguishes ethics from politics, politics being concerned with what groups of human beings ought to do. Third, the concept of a method of ethics is defined by reference to what Sidgwick in I.3 calls "the fundamental notion represented by the words 'ought' or 'right.'" (25).

The implications of defining a method of ethics in terms of this fundamental concept require more extended treatment. There are questions about Sidgwick's metaethical views: what does he think is meant by claims about rightness; does he think we can know their truth; does he think they are objective? In the paragraph that runs from page 1 to page 2, Sidgwick offers a first sketch of his metaethical position. He thinks we can reasonably hope to obtain objective knowledge about what is right.

> The student of Ethics seeks to attain systematic and precise general knowledge of what ought to be, and in this sense his aims and methods may properly be termed 'scientific'[.] (1)

But he thinks that such knowledge belongs in a fundamentally different category from ordinary factual knowledge. He says he prefers to call ethics a "study" not a "science" because it does not "have some department of actual existence for its subject matter" (2). Sidgwick says significantly more about these matters in the most important metaethical chapter in the *Methods*, I.III. We can defer further discussion until we turn to I.III in the next chapter. Sidgwick's view that there is a single fundamental ethical concept, the concept expressed by "right" or "ought," also has important implications for normative ethics. We will explore some of those implications in Section 6.

Sidgwick distinguishes methods of ethics from ultimate or first principles. It is worth reflecting more on this distinction. He does not give a definition of the term "first principle" in the way he does of the term "method of ethics." Unlike "method of ethics," "first principle" is not a piece of terminology Sidgwick invented. The terminology goes back as far as Aristotle, was used by key predecessors like Mill, and was commonplace in ethical writing in Sidgwick's time (so that among the places in which he felt no need to define it was his important brief 1879 *Mind* article, "The Establishment of Ethical First Principles").[4] Still, it is important to bring out what is involved in the conception of an ethical first principle. Jerome Schneewind plausibly suggests the following:

> Roughly speaking, a principle asserts that some property which acts may or may not possess is an ultimate reason for the rightness of acts.[5]

The picture that goes along with this conception of an ethical first principle, then, is this: there is a relatively small number of properties that are ultimate right-making properties—the properties that make acts right. (According to utilitarians, for instance, there is only one such property: the property of producing a greater balance of pleasure over pain than any possible alternative action.) If any other properties of acts have moral significance, their significance is derivative. It is a matter not of their own moral significance but of their relationship to the properties that are ultimately right-making.

This way of understanding what first principles are emphasizes their metaphysical significance. To put it in the terms Ross uses in the title of his most famous chapter, first principles answer the question: what makes right acts right?[6] But, as we will see in Chapter 9 when we discuss *Methods* IV.II, the concept of a first principle is also epistemically important. The epistemic picture associated with the idea of a first principle is that there are some propositions—the first principles—that are the foundations of our knowledge. When we justify—or prove—propositions other than first principles, we do so by deducing them from the first principles. It is then in the nature of first principles that they themselves cannot be proved.

Armed with these further reflections on Sidgwick's key concepts, return to the question whether it makes a significant difference to think as Sidgwick does in terms of methods of ethics rather than, as contemporary philosophers do, in terms of moral theories. One point seems relatively clear: contemporary philosophers don't usually make a distinction like that between method of ethics and first principle. So to the extent that Sidgwick's terminology tracks contemporary terminology, the thing in Sidgwick that is the equivalent of what these days would be called a "moral theory" is not a method of ethics as distinguished from a first principle, but rather a method of ethics plus a first principle. So the equivalent in Sidgwick's terminology for "the utilitarian moral theory" would be "the first principle plus the method of utilitarianism," the equivalent in Sidgwick's terminology of "the egoist moral theory" would be "the first principle plus the method of egoism," and the equivalent in Sidgwick's terminology of "the intuitionist moral theory" would be "the first principles plus the method of intuitionism."

Making the method/first principle distinction also introduces complications that are not introduced in the same way by the terminology of moral theories. Talk of a singular method of utilitarianism, one of intuitionism, and one of egoism suggests a one-to-one correspondence between methods and first principles. But there are significant reasons to think it is not that simple. One is that there are passages where Sidgwick explicitly denies that there is any such straightforward one-to-one correspondence, in particular the following from I.VI:

> Indeed we find that almost any method may be connected with almost any ultimate reason by means of some—often plausible—assumption. (83)

Another is that, as we will see in Chapter 5, Sidgwick in Book II distinguishes three different egoist methods.

2.5. The Relations Between the Three Methods

In Section 3 of I.VI there is an important preliminary discussion of the relations between the three methods. Characteristically,

Sidgwick focuses on the relations between utilitarianism and egoism, and between utilitarianism and intuitionism. While there are places in the *Methods*—most importantly Book II Chapter V—where the main focus is instead on the relation between intuitionism and egoism, those places are much rarer.

He begins with the affinities between utilitarianism and egoism, noting the important structural parallels:

> In the first place, they agree in prescribing actions as a means to an end distinct from, and lying outside the actions; so that they both lay down rules which are not absolute but relative, and only valid if they conduce to the end. Again, the ultimate end is according to both methods the same in quality, *i.e.* pleasure; or, more strictly, the maximum of pleasure attainable, pains being subtracted. (84)

He notes that under most circumstances they will coincide in the actions they require. And he discusses the ways in which the earlier utilitarians, Bentham and Mill, tended to combine psychological hedonism and utilitarianism. Despite these affinities, he argues that

> the practical affinity between Utilitarianism and Intuitionism is really much greater than that between the two forms of Hedonism. (85)

Both utilitarianism and intuitionism sometimes require self-sacrifice. Indeed, utilitarianism seems more liable to require self-sacrifice than does intuitionism.

> For [Intuitionism] seems to leave a man free to pursue his own happiness under certain definite limits and conditions; whereas Utilitarianism seems to require a more comprehensive and unceasing subordination of self-interest to the common good. (87)

And in the history of ethics, utilitarianism and intuitionism were long combined: in the initial reaction to Thomas Hobbes,

> Utilitarianism appears in friendly alliance with Intuitionism. It was not to supersede but to support the morality of Common Sense, against the dangerous innovations of Hobbes, that Cumberland declared "the common good of all Rationals" to be the end to which moral rules were the means. (86)

The idea that there is an important opposition between intuitionism and utilitarianism appears significantly later in the history of ethics; Sidgwick traces it to Butler's *Dissertation of the Nature of Virtue* appended to his *Analogy of Religion* (1736).[7]

2.6. Sidgwick's Fairness

The most standard way of locating Sidgwick in the history of moral philosophy—as the last of the three classical utilitarians—invites the reader to assume that the aim of the *Methods* is to argue for utilitarianism. A number of his contemporaries shared that assumption. Sidgwick denied it, doing so with particular force in the Preface to the second edition:

> There is, however, one fundamental misunderstanding, on which it seems desirable to say a few words. I find that more than one critic has overlooked or disregarded the account of the plan of my treatise, given in the original preface and in section 5 of the introductory chapter: and has consequently supposed me to be writing as an assailant of two of the methods which I chiefly examine, and a defender of the third. Thus one of my reviewers seems to regard [Book III] (on Intuitionism) as containing merely hostile criticism from the outside: another has constructed an article on the supposition that my principal object is the 'suppression

of egoism': and a third [F. H. Bradley] has gone to the length of a pamphlet under the impression (apparently) that the 'main argument' of my treatise is a demonstration of Universalistic Hedonism. I am concerned to have caused so much misdirection of criticism: and I have carefully altered in this edition the passages which I perceive to have contributed to it. (xii)

Sidgwick's express aim is to provide not an argument for utilitarianism but instead a neutral examination of the three methods. He claims to treat each method fairly and impartially.

I have certainly criticised [intuitionism] unsparingly: but I conceive myself to have exposed with equal unreserve the defects and difficulties of the hedonistic method. (xii)

One question about Sidgwick's fairness is the question whether his conceptual framework allows for an impartial treatment of intuitionism and of egoism. The answer to this question is yes. Sidgwick's conceptual framework is much better adapted for that purpose than are the conceptual frameworks of Moore and of Ross.

Sidgwick's, Moore's, and Ross's conceptual frameworks have something important in common. All three philosophers think there are very few fundamental ethical concepts. Both Sidgwick and Moore think there is just one fundamental ethical concept.[8] Ross thinks that there are only two. This commitment to what Thomas Hurka has called "conceptual minimalism" is shared by many earlier and later philosophers, but rejected by many others.[9]

Though Sidgwick and Moore both think there is just a single fundamental ethical concept, they disagree about what that fundamental ethical concept is. One possibility Sidgwick considers (and, as we have seen, adopts) is to make the fundamental concept the one expressed by "right" or "ought." Another possibility, which he rejects, is to make goodness the fundamental concept. Sidgwick's gives his reasons for making rightness rather than goodness the fundamental concept in Section 2 of I.I. He notes "two different forms in which the fundamental problem of ethics is stated" (2):

> Ethics is sometimes considered as an investigation of the true Moral laws or rational precepts of Conduct; sometimes as an inquiry into the nature of the Ultimate End of reasonable human action—the Good or 'True Good' of man. (3)

The first kind of view is

> the Intuitional view; according to which conduct is held to be right when conformed to certain precepts of duty, intuitively known to be unconditionally binding. (3)

Sidgwick says, in his characteristically nuanced way, that it is hard properly to formulate the intuitional view if we make goodness the fundamental concept. And he does not want to stack the deck against the intuitional view at the start. As he puts it at the end of Section 2:

> As I do not wish to start with any assumption incompatible with [Intuitionism] [. . .] I prefer to consider Ethics as the science or study of what is right or what ought to be. (2)

By contrast Moore insists that the only fundamental ethical concept is goodness. He then goes on to insist that right or duty must be defined in terms of goodness, and that the intuitional view is therefore incoherent.[10] One place this line of thought gets developed is on page 148 of *Principia*:

> Our 'duty,' therefore, can only be defined as that action, which will cause more good to exist in the Universe than any possible alternative [. . .] But if this be recognised [. . .] It is plain that

no moral law is self-evident, as has commonly been held by the Intuitional school of moralists.¹¹

Let me spell out this line of thought a little more: If goodness is the only fundamental concept, then the concept expressed by "ought," "right," or "duty" cannot be a fundamental concept. The concept expressed by "ought," "right," or "duty" must instead be definable in terms of goodness. The obvious way to define "duty" in terms of goodness is the way Moore specifies: to define our duty as what will produce the most good. But then it makes no sense to say, as intuitionists want to say, that there are principles of duty—or absolute moral rules—that are independent of goodness. The definition of duty in terms of goodness makes any such rules impossible.

The line of thought is simpler and more explicit in Moore than it is in Sidgwick. Again, though, what matters for us is the contrast in their attitudes to this line of thought. Sidgwick thinks: making the fundamental concept goodness makes it difficult to formulate one familiar view, intuitionism. That is a reason not to stack the deck at the start of the investigation by making goodness the fundamental concept. Moore agrees that making the fundamental concept goodness makes it difficult—or impossible—to formulate intuitionism. His attitude is: so much the worse for intuitionism.

Moore's insistence in *Principia* that goodness is the only fundamental ethical concept also makes short work of egoism, as we will see later, in Chapter 9. But it is not only Moore's framework that does that. Ross, unlike Moore, has a framework one of whose fundamental concepts is "right" (as you would expect, given that his most famous book is entitled *The Right and the Good*). Still, however, he too dismissed egoism very quickly, in passages like the following:

> We are never conscious of a duty to get pleasure or avoid pain for ourselves, as we are conscious of a duty to give pleasure to or prevent pain for others.¹²

This points to a difference between Sidgwick's concept of rightness and Ross's concept of rightness. This difference can be illuminated by reference to a passage from Allan Gibbard.

> In the history of moral philosophy, there seem to be at least two sharply different conceptions of what morality is. On the broadest of conceptions, morality is simply practical rationality in the fullest sense: to say that an act is morally right is to say that it is rational. Sidgwick is a prime exponent of this broad conception.[13]

Because Sidgwick has this broadest conception of morality, he treats egoism as a moral theory. It is not that Sidgwick is insensitive to the considerations that push Ross to dismiss egoism out of hand: to the idea that egoism cannot be an adequate account of duty because it gives no weight to the interests of others. But these considerations are outweighed by the fact that, nonetheless, egoism seems a coherent and initially plausible account of practical reason, of what it is rational to do. This comes out in passages like the following, from the very beginning of Book III:

> The effort to examine, closely but quite neutrally, the system of Egoistic Hedonism [...] may not improbably have produced on the reader's mind a certain aversion to the principle and method examined, even though (like myself) he may find it difficult not to admit the 'authority' of self-love, or the 'rationality' of seeking one's own individual happiness. (199)

For Sidgwick, because he has the broadest conception of morality according to which morality is ultimately just practical reason, egoism counts as a method of ethics and cannot be summarily dismissed. For others, like Ross, whose conception of morality is different, what Sidgwick elsewhere calls the "sense of the ignobility of egoism" is enough to rule it out at the start. In this way too, Sidgwick's initial framework is fairer than those of his key successors.

This is not the last word on Sidgwick's fairness. As we will see later, in Chapters 4, 6, 7, and 8, there are other reasons to worry that in his later detailed treatment of intuitionism Sidgwick did not entirely overcome the early "antagonism" he reports in the short intellectual autobiography. But his conceptual framework is clearly much better adapted to fairly consider the merits of both egoism and intuitionism than are the conceptual frameworks of his most important successors in the Sidgwick to Ewing school, Moore and Ross.

Notes

1. Parfit 2011a, 166.
2. Most influentially articulated in Scanlon 1998.
3. Parfit 2011a and 2011b.
4. Sidgwick (1879) 2000.
5. Schneewind 1977, 194–195.
6. Ross 1930, Chapter II.
7. In Butler 2017.
8. Strictly speaking this is true only of the Moore of *Principia Ethica*. By the time he wrote *Ethics* (Moore 1912), Moore shared Ross's view that there are two fundamental concepts, right and good. For ease of exposition I will ignore this complication in the text.
9. Hurka 2014a, Chapter 1.
10. Moore had changed his position by the time he wrote *Ethics* (Moore 1912). As Ross explains the change "Professor Moore seems . . . to have passed to the view that productivity of maximum good is not the definition of 'right' but another characteristic which underlies and accounts for the rightness of acts" (Ross 1930: 10).
11. Moore 1903, 148.
12. Ross 1939, 277.
13. Gibbard 1990, 40.

Further Reading

Daurio 1997 is a good place to start in thinking further about Sidgwick's project and about how much difference it makes, and whether it is a good thing, to think in terms of methods of ethics rather than in terms of moral theories.

3
Meaning, Motivation, and Free Will
(*Methods* I.III, I.IV, and I.V)

In Chapters III, IV, and V of Book I, Sidgwick discusses the meaning of moral judgments, motivation, and the importance of free will. He summarizes the conclusions of these three Chapters at the start of Chapter VI:

> The aim of Ethics is to systematize and free from error the apparent cognitions that most men have of the rightness or reasonableness of conduct [. . .] These cognitions are normally accompanied by emotions of various kinds, known as "moral sentiments": but an ethical judgment cannot be explained as affirming merely the existence of such a sentiment: indeed it is an essential characteristic of a moral feeling that it is bound up with an apparent cognition of something more than mere feeling. Such cognitions, again, I have called 'dictates' or 'imperatives'; because, in so far as they relate to conduct on which any one is deliberating, they are accompanied by a certain impulse to do the acts recognised as right, which is liable to conflict with other impulses [. . .] there seems to be no ground for regarding [desires for pleasures and aversions to pains] as the sole, or even the normal, motives of human volitions. Nor, again, is it generally important to determine whether we are always, metaphysically speaking, 'free' to do what we clearly see to be right. (77–78)

In these three chapters Sidgwick is not, as he was in the chapters we just discussed, explaining his own project. He is instead giving the first important articulation of his position on some foundational matters that had divided his predecessors, and so locating himself in relation to them. In the first two of these chapters he sharply distinguishes himself from Mill, who (as Sidgwick understood him) thought moral judgments were an ordinary kind of factual judgment. And Mill famously embraced psychological hedonism, the thesis that the only thing we desire for its own sake is pleasure. Sidgwick argues to the contrary that the fundamental moral concept is quite distinct from factual concepts, and that psychological hedonism is false. In Chapter V, he emphasizes a key distinction between his own view and the views of Kant and his followers. Kant and Kantians think the free will question is central to ethics. Sidgwick argues to the contrary that it has little practical importance.

3.1. *Methods* I.III: Sidgwick's Metaethics

3.1.1. Metaethics Then and Now

The metaethical view Sidgwick argues for in I.III is historically important in distinguishing him from his utilitarian predecessors like Mill. It is historically important too in its influence on his successors. The most famous presentation of a metaethical view like Sidgwick's is G. E. Moore's in *Principia Ethica*. Moore (mistakenly) credits Sidgwick as the only moral philosopher who has fully anticipated his own position.

> "Good," then, is indefinable; and yet, so far as I know, there is only one ethical writer, Prof. Henry Sidgwick, who has clearly recognised and stated this fact.[1]

Sidgwick states the central conclusion Moore is referring to in two different places in I.III. The first is on page 25:

> The fundamental notion represented by the word "ought" or "right" [... is] essentially different from all notions representing facts of physical or psychical experience.

The second is on page 32:

> The notion which [the] terms ["right" and "ought"] have in common is too elementary to admit of any formal definition.

The standard name today for the metaethical view Sidgwick and Moore shared is "non-naturalism." In the late nineteenth and early twentieth century, when Sidgwick wrote the multiple editions of the *Methods* and Moore wrote *Principia Ethica*, there were only two main kinds of metaethical view on the standard menu of options. One was the view that both Sidgwick and Moore attributed to Mill, naturalism. The other was non-naturalism. Naturalists think that in making moral judgments we are making statements that are true or false, and that moral judgments are a kind of ordinary factual judgment. Non-naturalists agree with the first part of this but disagree with the second part: they agree that in making moral judgments we are making statements that are true or false, but think that moral judgments are essentially different from ordinary factual judgments. Both Sidgwick and Moore defend non-naturalism by arguing that the most fundamental moral concepts cannot be defined in terms of "facts [...] of physical or psychical experience."

There has been a huge amount of work in metaethics since the early twentieth century. One thing that philosophers have done is to add to the metaethical menu. Two prominent positions articulated after the *Methods* and *Principia* are non-cognitivism and error theory. Non-cognitivists deny the thing that naturalists and non-naturalists agree on, that in making moral judgments we are making statements that are true or false. They hold instead that we are doing something different: expressing feelings, or expressing desires, or issuing commands (non-cognitivists don't agree among themselves about what the something different is; all these possibilities have been exhaustively explored). Error theorists agree with naturalists and non-naturalists that what we mean to be doing in making moral judgments is making statements that are true or false. But they think that moral judgments are all fundamentally mistaken. Just as an atheist might say that all the statements religious believers make about God are false because there is no God, so an error theorist might say that all the moral judgments we make are false because there are no objective moral truths.

Another thing that philosophers have done since the early twentieth century is to add greatly to the sophistication of metaethical arguments. There are still non-naturalists. Indeed, the position has had a resurgence in recent years, being defended by influential philosophers including Thomas Nagel, Derek Parfit, and T. M. Scanlon.[2] Like Sidgwick and Moore, these contemporary non-naturalists characteristically hold that the fundamental ethical concept or concepts are indefinable. But much else about the ways in which contemporary non-naturalists argue for their positions differs from the ways in which Sidgwick and Moore argue for theirs. That is necessitated both by general changes in the philosophical landscape and by specific features of the contemporary alternatives, in particular sophisticated contemporary versions of naturalism and of non-cognitivism, that contemporary non-naturalists have to argue against.

3.1.2. Motivation and Meaning: The Argument of *Methods* I.III

Though Sidgwick and Moore are both non-naturalists, nothing in *Principia Ethica* has the structure of *Methods* I.III. Unlike Moore, Sidgwick begins not with a question about definition but with a question about motivation. The question is whether reason can motivate. On the one hand, Sidgwick suggests in the first couple of sentences of the chapter, it is widely held that it can.

> In the first chapter I spoke of actions that we judge to be right and what ought to be done as being "reasonable" or "rational," and similarly of ultimate ends as "prescribed by Reason": and I contrasted the motive to action supplied by the recognition of such reasonableness with "non-rational" desires and inclinations. This manner of speaking is employed by writers of different schools, and seems in accordance with the common view and language on the subject. (23)

On the other hand:

> It is widely maintained that, as Hume says, "Reason, meaning the judgment of truth and falsehood, can never of itself be any motive to the Will"; and that the motive to action is in all cases some Non-rational Desire.

The initial focus of Chapter III is on this question about moral motivation. Sidgwick refines the issue on page 24, clarifying the ways in which the Humean view allows for reason to play a subsidiary role in motivation. Then at the top of page 25 he asks whether the Humean view that reason plays only this subsidiary role in motivation is correct. This is not one of those cases where Sidgwick's view is nuanced or unclear. He quite definitely rejects the Humean view:

> I hold that this is not the case[.] (25)

When he returns to the motivational question, on page 34, he characterizes the alternative view which he accepts, the view that reason can motivate, in Kantian terms.

> Further, when I speak of the cognition or judgment that 'X ought to be done' [. . .] as a dictate' or 'precept' of reason to the persons to whom it relates, I imply that in rational beings as such this cognition gives an impulse or motive to action [. . .] I am aware that some persons will be disposed to answer all the preceding argument by a simple denial that they can find in their consciousness any such unconditional or categorical imperative as I have been trying to exhibit. (34–35)

The phrases "dictates of reason" and (particularly) "categorical imperatives" are self-consciously Kantian. It is clear, then, where Sidgwick stands on the motivational issue: The Humean view is wrong. The Kantian view is correct.

This seems quite a different issue from the issue of the definability of moral concepts. Yet Sidgwick treats the two issues as in some important way connected. The initial transition from the question of motivation to the question of definition occurs at the top of page 25:

> The question, then, is whether the [Humean] account [. . .] of the influence of the intellect on desire and volition is not exhaustive [. . .] I hold that this is not the case; that the ordinary moral or prudential judgments which, in the case of all or most minds have some—though often an inadequate—influence on volition, cannot legitimately be interpreted as judgments respecting the present or future existence of human feelings of any facts of the sensible world; the fundamental notion represented by the word "ought" or "right," which such judgments contain expressly or by implication, being essentially different from all notions representing facts of physical or psychical experience. (25)

This passage suggests that Sidgwick will defend the Kantian view about motivation by defending the non-naturalist view that the fundamental moral concept (the one expressed by "ought" or "right") is indefinable. It is far from obvious how the connection here goes. Just why is it that in order to defend the Kantian view about moral motivation one needs to defend the non-naturalist view about definition? This question is discussed in literature on Sidgwick.[3] It is a difficult question, and for our purposes it is best not to pursue it. We should simply note that Sidgwick apparently thinks the way to defend the Kantian view about motivation is to argue that the fundamental moral concept is indefinable.

What is crucial for our purposes is what happens next in Chapter III, from page 25 to page 32. This is where Sidgwick defends the key non-naturalist claim that the fundamental moral concept is indefinable. He proceeds by considering, and giving reasons to reject, a number of possible naturalistic definitions of that fundamental moral concept. The discussion is a bit involved, and Sidgwick considers different variants of the most important kinds of definitions he considers. He considers three basic kinds of such definitions.

The first kind is considered quite briefly on page 26. According to it:

> "Rightness" is properly an attribute of means, not of ends: so that the attribution of it merely implies that the act judged right is the fittest or only fit means to the realisation of some end understood if not expressly stated. (26)

Sidgwick rejects this kind of definition on the grounds that it does not fit with some important uses of "right" and "ought":

> It seems clear (1) that certain kinds of actions [. . .] are commonly held to be right unconditionally, without regard to ulterior results: and (2) that we similarly regard as "right" the adoption of certain ends—such as the common good of society, or general happiness. In either of these cases the interpretation above suggested seems clearly inadmissible. (26)

The second kind of definition defines the fundamental moral concept in terms of feelings or emotions. Sidgwick considers a number of variants, differing as to whose feelings or emotions are referred to: just the speaker's, or those of some group. He begins with the first of these possibilities.

> Here we are met by the suggestion that the judgments or propositions which we commonly call moral [...] really affirm no more than the existence of a specific emotion in the mind of the person who utters them; that when I say 'Truth ought to be spoken' [...] I mean no more than that the idea of truthspeaking excites in my mind a feeling of approbation or satisfaction. (26–27)

The argument Sidgwick offers against this view came to be important in mid-twentieth-century metaethics, when it was offered as an argument in favor of non-cognitivist theories as against the kind of subjectivist view Sidgwick is here considering. The argument is that the subjectivist view gets it wrong about when people disagree.

> It is absurd to say that a mere statement of my approbation of truth-speaking is properly given in the proposition 'Truth ought to be spoken'; otherwise the fact of another man's disapprobation might equally be expressed by saying 'Truth ought not to be spoken'; and thus we should have two coexistent facts stated in two mutually contradictory propositions. (27)

Sidgwick's point is that if I say 'Truth ought to be spoken' and you say 'Truth ought not to be spoken' we are disagreeing with each other; what I say contradicts what you say. But the proposed naturalistic definition makes this disagreement and contradiction disappear. Suppose Sidgwick and I disagree in this way about the morality of truth-speaking. Then according to the proposed naturalistic definition, Sidgwick's statement really means, "Henry Sidgwick approves of truth-speaking," and my statement really means, "David Phillips disapproves of truth-speaking." These two statements do not contradict one another. The proposed naturalistic definition turns two statements that contradict one another into two statements that do not contradict one another. So the proposed naturalistic definition must be wrong.

To appreciate how this argument works, it may help to think about the same kind of argument applied not to definitions within one language but to translations between two different languages. Suppose I start with two statements in English that contradict one another, and ask you to translate them into French. Here is one thing we know about whether your translation is correct: if you translate two statements in English that contradict one another into two statements in French that don't contradict one another, something is wrong with your translation. Sidgwick's point about naturalistic definitions is fundamentally the same point. If your proposed naturalistic definition turns two statements that contradict one another into two statements that do not contradict one another, something is wrong with your proposed naturalistic definition.[4]

The third main kind of naturalistic definition Sidgwick considers defines the fundamental concept not in terms of feelings or emotions but instead in terms of punishments or penalties.

> When we say that a man 'ought' to do anything [. . .] we mean that he is bound under penalties to do it. (29)

As with definitions in terms of feelings of approbation, Sidgwick considers a number of different variants of this kind of view, differing as to the source of the penalties. Again, he gives reasons to reject each of them. At the start of Section 3 he summarizes the results of the discussion:

> It seems then that the notion of 'ought' or 'moral obligation' as used in our common moral judgments, does not merely import (1) that

> there exists in the mind of the person judging a specific emotion [...] nor (2) that certain rules of conduct are supported by penalties which will follow upon their violation [...] What then, it may be asked, does it import? What definition can we give of 'ought,' 'right,' and other terms expressing the same fundamental notion? To this I should answer that the notion these terms have in common is too elementary to admit of any formal definition. (31–32)

Sidgwick thus endorses metaethical non-naturalism. And, as we will see in the next chapter, his non-naturalism underlies a further key difference between Sidgwick and Mill: Sidgwick's endorsement of intuitionism in moral epistemology.

3.2. *Methods* I.IV: Sidgwick's Rejection of Psychological Hedonism

As we saw in the first chapter, in the short intellectual autobiography included by E. E. Constance Jones in the Preface to the sixth edition, Sidgwick says:

> The effect of [Butler's] influence carried me a further step away from Mill: for I was led by it to abandon the doctrine of Psychological Hedonism, and to recognize the existence of 'disinterested' or 'extra-regarding' impulses to action. (xxi)

The details of this further step away from Mill are to be found in Book I Chapter IV.

Sidgwick begins by defining Psychological Hedonism (a term which he coined for a view that had long been discussed by moral philosophers). He characterizes it as:

> The view that volition is always determined by pleasures or pains actual or prospective. (40)

Moore's definition is pithier:

> Pleasure alone is the object of all our desires[5]

Sidgwick also gives a preliminary and provisional definition of pleasure and pain (he says more about how to define pleasure and pain in Book II, which we will turn to in Chapter 5). According to this preliminary definition,

> Pleasure is a kind of feeling which stimulates the will to actions tending to sustain or produce it,- to sustain it, if actually present, and to produce it, if it be represented in idea -; and similarly pain is a kind of feeling which stimulates to actions tending to remove or avert it. (42–43)

In the paragraph beginning in the middle of page 44, Sidgwick notes the difference between Mill's and Butler's views, and summarizes Butler's famous argument against psychological hedonism:

> It is rather curious that one of the best known of English moralists regards the exact opposite of what Mill thinks so obvious, as being not merely a universal fact of our experience, but even a necessary truth. Butler, as is well known, distinguishes self-love, or the impulse towards our own pleasure, from "particular movements towards particular external objects—honour, power, the harm or good of another"; the actions proceeding from which are "no otherwise interested than as every action of every creature must from the nature of the case be; for no one can act but from a desire, or choice, or preference of his own." Such particular passions or appetites are, he goes on to say, "*necessarily presupposed by the very idea* of an interested pursuit; since the very idea of interest or happiness consists in this, that an appetite or affection enjoys its object." We could not pursue pleasure at all, unless we had desires for something else than pleasure; for pleasure consists in

the satisfaction of just these "disinterested" impulses. (44; italics in the original)

It may be helpful to illustrate Butler's famous argument with an example. Some people (like me) are pleased when Arsenal win football matches. Lots of others are indifferent or displeased. What makes me susceptible to getting pleasure from Arsenal winning football matches? The fact that I have a prior, independent desire for something other than pleasure: a desire for Arsenal to win. Butler's argument is that all pleasures are like this. They depend on a prior desire for something other than pleasure. If you didn't have the prior desire for that other thing, you could not get the pleasure. It is thus impossible successfully to be motivated only by desires for pleasure. You can only get pleasure if you desire something other than pleasure.

Sidgwick's view is that Butler's argument is too strong, but that his basic point is nonetheless correct.

> Butler has certainly overstated his case so far as my own experience goes; for many pleasures—especially those of sight, hearing and smell, together with many emotional pleasures, - occur to me without any perceptible relation to previous desires, and it seems quite *conceivable* that our primary desires might be entirely directed towards such pleasures as these. But as a matter of fact, it appears to me that throughout the whole scale of my impulses, sensual, emotional, and intellectual alike, I can distinguish desires of which the object is something other than my own pleasure. (44–45; italics in the original)

Sidgwick, that is, denies that the argument against psychological hedonism has the sort of necessity Butler attributes to it. It would have that kind of necessity only if it were true, as Butler supposes, that all pleasures depend on prior desires for something other than pleasure. Sidgwick thinks Butler is wrong about that. Lots of pleasures don't depend on such prior desires. But still, Sidgwick thinks, the point Butler helps us to see shows us that psychological hedonism is mistaken. For as a matter of fact lots of our pleasures do depend on prior desires for something other than pleasure.

There follows an acute and interesting psychological discussion of various kinds of pleasures and pains. As with the similarly acute and interesting psychological discussion in much of Book II, we will not have space to pursue the details. What matters most for understanding the relation of Sidgwick's position to Mill's and Butler's positions is to be found in the passages we have already discussed.

3.3. *Methods* I.V: Sidgwick on Free Will

The chapter on free will has a different character from the two chapters that precede it. In those two chapters, as we have just seen, Sidgwick defends definite positions on the main issues at stake in the controversy. In I.III he argues that the fundamental ethical concept is indefinable and in favor of a Kantian view of moral motivation. In I.IV he argues with Butler against Mill that psychological hedonism is false. In I.V, Sidgwick does not aim to defend a definite view about the free will issue, in the way that he has defended definite views about moral judgments and motivation and psychological hedonism. He aims instead to argue that the free will question has less importance for moral philosophy than is often supposed. In taking this position he is disagreeing primarily not with Mill and earlier utilitarians but with Kant and his nineteenth-century followers, who thought the free will controversy was of central importance to moral philosophy.

The key question at issue in the free will controversy is whether, when we deliberate, in particular when we deliberate between doing what we think we ought to do and doing something else we are tempted to do, we really have the power to choose either way. Determinists hold that we don't. They hold that our choice in any such case will be fully determined by our character and circumstances. Libertarians hold that we do, that our characters and circumstances do not fully determine our choice.

In Sections 2 and 3 of Chapter V, Sidgwick characterizes the evidence on either side of the controversy. On the one hand, there is "a cumulative argument of great force" (62) on the determinist side. As science has developed, ever more aspects of existence have turned out to be open to deterministic causal explanation. Such explanation already extends to some parts of psychology, for everyone thinks unconscious volitions are deterministically explicable, and the boundary between the conscious and the unconscious is vague.[6] And we explain both other people's actions and our own past actions in ways that presuppose causal determinism.[7] So we should assume that there are deterministic causal explanations of conscious actions, though psychology has not yet advanced to a point at which it can generally supply such explanations.

On the other hand, libertarianism is supported by

> the immediate affirmation of consciousness in the moment of deliberate action [...] When I have a distinct consciousness of choosing between alternatives of conduct, one of which I conceive as right or reasonable, I find it impossible not to think that I can now choose to do what I so conceive [...] however strong may be my inclination to act unreasonably, and however uniformly I may have yielded to such inclinations in the past. (65)

Sidgwick does not say which view is correct. His aim is instead to argue that the issue has less practical importance than is often supposed.

> In this conflict of arguments, it is not surprising that the theoretical question as to the Freedom of the Will is still differently decided by thinkers of repute; and I do not myself wish at present to

pronounce any decision on it. But I think it is possible and useful to show that the ethical importance of deciding it one way or another is liable to be exaggerated; and that any one who will consider the matter soberly and carefully will find this importance to be of a strictly limited kind. (66)

He goes on to say that it is those on the libertarian side who, in his view, are more disposed to exaggerate the importance of the controversy. In arguing for the limited importance of the free will question Sidgwick is arguing against this libertarian line. He is arguing, that is, that the truth of determinism would have relatively little ethical importance.

His argument for this conclusion has two main elements. First, Sidgwick argues (on pages 67–68) that in ordinary cases a conviction that determinism is true will not have a demoralizing effect. He concedes that if we knew not only that determinism was true but also that, in this particular instance, we would necessarily choose not to do what we thought we ought to do, that *would* be demoralizing.

> It seems to me undeniable that this judgment will exclude or weaken the operation of the moral motive in the act contemplated (67)

But, Sidgwick argues, even if we know that determinism is true, in normal cases we will not know that we are determined specifically not to choose to do what we think we ought in this particular instance.

> Ordinarily the legitimate inference from a man's past experience, and from his general knowledge of human nature, would not go beyond a very strong probability that he would choose to do wrong; and a mere probability—however strong—that I shall not will to do right cannot be regarded by me in deliberation

as a reason for not willing; while it certainly supplies a rational ground for willing strongly[.] (67–68)

Second, Sidgwick argues that a conviction as to the truth of determinism will not alter our views as to the value of the ends that we usually take to be ultimate, or as to the means by which to get them. Neither happiness nor excellence lose their value if determinism is true.

> If happiness, whether private or general, be taken as the ultimate end of action on a Libertarian view, the adoption of a Determinist view affords no ground for rejecting it: and if Excellence is in itself admirable and desirable, it surely remains equally so whether any individual's approximation to it is entirely determined by inherited nature and external influences or not[.] (68)

He does, however, concede that the acceptance of determinism will have an important effect on one kind of moral judgment: judgments as to rewards and punishments.

> It must be admitted, I think, that the common retributive view of punishment, and the ordinary notions of "merit," "demerit," and "responsibility," also involve the assumption of Free Will: if the wrong act, and the bad qualities of character manifested in it, are conceived as the necessary effects of causes antecedent or external to the existence of the agent, the moral responsibility—in the ordinary sense—for the mischief caused by them can no longer rest on him. At the same time, the Determinist can give to the terms "ill-desert" and "responsibility" a signification which is not only clear and definite, but, from a utilitarian point of view, the only suitable meaning. In this view, if I affirm that A is responsible for a harmful act, I mean that it is right to punish him for it; primarily, in order that the fear of punishment may prevent him and others from committing similar acts in future. (71–72)

How far Sidgwick succeeds in his express aim of showing the limited importance of free will is questionable. In particular we can wonder about the first argument he gives. Though Sidgwick is right that it would be hard to know in a particular instance whether we were determined to act wrongly, he still concedes the demoralizing general effect of accepting determinism. This might be taken to be enough to show that the question is of fundamental rather than limited ethical importance, even if its practical impact on our attitude to decision-making would be limited in the way he argues it would.

There has been a huge amount of work on free will and moral responsibility in recent years. The line of argument Sidgwick pursues has affinities with the lines of argument pursued by philosophers like Derk Pereboom.[8] Pereboom argues that even if free will is illusory there is still room for an attractive, though revamped, framework for thinking about morality. But he concedes that the revamping will be a substantial one. And, notwithstanding his aim to argue for the limited ethical importance of free will, one reaction to Sidgwick's treatment of the issue is that philosophers like Pereboom are right. There is room for ethics without free will. But it looks substantially different from ethics with free will.

Notes

1. Moore 1903, 17. Sidgwick knew that his claim that the fundamental ethical concept is indefinable was not original. Discussing Richard Price's *Review of the Principal Questions of Morals* published in 1758 (Price 1974), Sidgwick notes, "[Price's] conception of 'right' and 'wrong' as 'single ideas' incapable of definition or analysis—the notions 'right,' 'fit,' 'ought,' 'duty,' 'obligation,' being coincident or identical" (Sidgwick 1886, 224).
2. Nagel 1986, Chapter VIII; Scanlon 1998, Chapter 1; Parfit 2011b, Part Six; Scanlon 2014.
3. Schneewind 1977, Chapter 7; Deigh 1992; Shaver 2003; Shaver 2006; Phillips 2020.

4. Moore also gives this argument in his later book, *Ethics* (Moore 1912, 42–43).
5. Moore 1903, 68.
6. Sidgwick was writing before Sigmund Freud's work became widely known. So when Sidgwick uses the term "unconscious" he does so without any specifically Freudian connotations.
7. Sidgwick was writing before the development of quantum mechanics, at a time when it was generally assumed that all good scientific theories were deterministic.
8. Pereboom 2001.

Further Reading

Fuller treatments of Sidgwick's metaethics are Shaver 2003 and Phillips 2011 Chapter 2. A fuller treatment of Sidgwick on free will is Crisp 2015, Chapter 2.

4
Intuitionism and Goodness
(*Methods* I.VIII and I.IX)

Sidgwick's official agenda in Chapters VIII and IX of Book I is to "remove certain ambiguities as to the general nature" of intuitionism (87). (Book I Chapter VII is supposed to play a corresponding role for egoism.) The discussion in these chapters builds on Book I Chapter III and completes the initial outline of Sidgwick's metaethical position. They are crucial for understanding his own view and his influence on the subsequent history of moral philosophy.

4.1. Intuitionism as a Hybrid Concept: Epistemic and Moral-Theoretic Components

As we noted in Chapter 1, the standard mid-Victorian menu of options in moral philosophy featured just two choices: the empirical utilitarianism of Mill and the intuitive absolutism of Whewell. One of Sidgwick's key contributions was to reject this constrained view of the available options. The position for which he wanted to argue combined Mill's moral theory with Whewell's epistemology: utilitarianism on an intuitional basis. By framing things as he did, Sidgwick set the stage for the Sidgwick to Ewing school. Once Sidgwick had shown that an intuitionist metaethical view could properly be combined with a full range of positions in moral theory, the philosophers who succeeded him could accept the intuitionist metaethics and debate the merits of the different moral theories.

Though Sidgwick made this major advance, he did not properly update the terminology he inherited. His use of the term "intuitionism" is problematic because it still combines two quite distinct ideas, one epistemic and the other moral theoretic.

The epistemic idea is that fundamental moral truths are self-evident or can be grasped by intuition. In explaining this idea it is best to focus on the property of self-evidence rather than on the faculty of intuition. Propositions are self-evident if they can be seen to be true by people who properly understand them. Like most philosophers who think moral intuitions are important, Sidgwick often appeals to mathematical knowledge as a model for moral knowledge. Fundamental moral propositions are supposed to be self-evident in the way $1 + 1 = 2$ is self-evident. To know that $1 + 1 = 2$, you just need to understand the concepts involved. When you do, you can see that it is true. It is not a factual claim for which you need empirical evidence: it would not be sensible to try to show that $1 + 1 = 2$ was true by finding lots of collections of one object plus one object, finding that in each case they made two objects, and concluding on the basis of this evidence that $1 + 1 = 2$. Mathematical claims are established in a very different way than empirical propositions like "there is an oak tree in my back yard." Observation and experience are required to establish empirical truths; they are irrelevant to fundamental mathematical truths. On the epistemic intuitionist view of philosophers like Sidgwick, fundamental moral truths are self-evident in the same way mathematical truths are.

The moral theoretic idea is that the fundamental moral truths are absolute rules which do not take into account the consequences of actions. As we said in Chapter 2, if you want a simple model for this moral theoretic idea, start with the Judeo-Christian Ten Commandments. Subtract those that seem to you to be religious rather than moral. Then imagine a moral theory that says: what morality tells you to do is always to obey those commandments. This simple model is useful only to get a starting idea of what an intuitionist moral theory looks like. Actual such theories are more complex in two important ways. One is that the absolute rules need not be simple. Indeed, philosophers like Whewell (and Sidgwick following him, in Book III of the *Methods*) are concerned to get all the right qualifications and exception clauses into the moral rules. It is in no way a requirement of an absolutist moral theory that its individual rules be simple. Second, the idea that the rules don't take into account the consequences of actions is too strong. As Sidgwick notes, any plausible absolutist theory will include some rules that tell you to take the consequences of actions into account: the obvious examples are rules that tell you to promote the good of others. A theory will be absolutist because it also includes some rules that take no account of consequences.

These days, moral theories like this are standardly called "deontological." And the theories they oppose are standardly called "consequentialist." Sidgwick is central to the development of this contemporary terminology. The term "deontological" (and its relative "deontology") in their current senses were introduced into moral philosophy by C. D. Broad in his *Five Types of Ethical Theory* (1930). He introduced them to clear up the confusion caused by Sidgwick's use of the single term "intuitionist" to cover both the epistemic idea and the moral theoretic idea. Here is the key passage from Broad:

> Sidgwick reduces the fundamental types of ethical theory to three, viz., *Intuitionism, Egoistic Hedonism,* and *Utilitarianism.* The only criticism that I wish to make at this point is that his division does not seem to rest on any very clear principle. The name "Intuitionism" seems to suggest an epistemic principle of classification, and the opposite of it would seem to be "Empiricism." On the other hand, the opposition of Egoistic and Universalistic Hedonism to Intuitionism rests on a quite different basis, viz., on

whether some types of action are *intrinsically* right or wrong or whether the rightness or wrongness of actions always depends on their conduciveness to certain *ends*. This of course is not an epistemic question at all. And this cross-division leads to needless complications in Sidgwick's exposition [. . .] All this seems rather untidy and unsatisfactory. I would therefore propose the following amendments. I would first divide ethical theories into two classes, which I will call respectively *deontological* and *teleological*.

Deontological theories hold that there are ethical propositions of the form: "Such and such a kind of actions would always be right (or wrong) in such and such circumstances, no matter what its consequences might be." [. . .] Teleological theories hold that the rightness or wrongness of an action is always determined by its tendency to produce certain consequences which are intrinsically good or bad [. . .] The principles of division which I have suggested are clear in outline, and they have the advantage of not introducing epistemological considerations.[1]

In this passage Broad coined the term "deontological" in its now-standard philosophical sense as the name for the moral-theoretic component of what Sidgwick called "intuitionism." This leaves "intuitionism," more properly, as the name only for the epistemic component. (To be as careful as possible to avoid confusion, I will often call the epistemic component "epistemic intuitionism.") Broad's understanding of the moral-theoretic distinction has been widely adopted in contemporary moral philosophy, as has his term "deontological."[2] The term he introduced to contrast with "deontological," "teleological," is not nearly so widely used today. It is much more standard to use instead the term "consequentialist," coined later by Elizabeth Anscombe.[3] But though it is Anscombe's term that philosophers tend to use these days as the name for the non-deontological theories, they normally mean by it just what Broad meant by "teleological."

4.2. The Argument for Epistemic Intuitionism

Sidgwick observes in the second sentence of I.VIII:

> There is [...] considerable ambiguity as to the exact antithesis implied by the terms 'intuition,' 'intuitive' ... as currently used in ethical discussion[.] (96)

His aim in the first section of I.VIII is to remove this ambiguity. He first focuses on the opposition between intuitionists and philosophers who think the morality of actions depends on consequences (i.e., using the terminology we just discussed, the contrast between deontologists and consequentialists). He notes that the intuitionist disregard of consequences is not complete: as we just saw, some virtues, like benevolence, require us to consider consequences; and consequences are involved in determining whether acts fall into the classes that intuitionist rules forbid (for example, the class of lies). He then turns to a second antithesis, between intuitionists and hedonists: a hedonist judges all other things as good insofar as they conduce to happiness, whereas intuitionists (in this sense) judge some other things (perfection, art, knowledge) to be good

> immediately, and not by inference from experience of the pleasures they produce[.] (97)

What follows is a passage absolutely crucial to the project of the *Methods*: the passage which contains the argument for epistemic intuitionism. One might expect Sidgwick to do much more to highlight the importance of this passage. His own distinctive position, after all, is "utilitarianism on an intuitional basis"; this is the passage where he gives the general argument that utilitarians have to be epistemic intuitionists. Yet the passage is introduced with little fanfare in the middle of a paragraph. If one consulted the analytical table of contents, one would not know it was there. Here is what he says:

> It should, however, be observed that the current contrast between 'intuitive' or '*a priori*' and 'inductive' or '*a posteriori*' morality commonly involves a certain confusion of thought. For what the 'inductive' moralist professes to know by induction, is commonly not the same thing as what the 'intuitive' moralist professes to know by intuition. In the former case it is the conduciveness to pleasure of certain kinds of action that is methodically ascertained: in the latter case their rightness: there is therefore no proper opposition. If Hedonism claims to give authoritative guidance, this can only be in virtue of the principle that pleasure is the only reasonable ultimate end of human action: and this principle cannot be known by induction from experience. Experience can at most tell us that all men always do seek pleasure as their ultimate end (that it does not support this conclusion I have already tried to show): it cannot tell us that any one ought so to seek it. If this latter proposition is legitimately affirmed in respect either of private or of general happiness, it must either be immediately known to be true—and therefore, we may say, a moral intuition—or be inferred from premises which ultimately include at least one such intuition. (97–98)

The passage begins with the "current contrast" we have talked about. "Intuitive" moralists (like Whewell) claim to know the truth of their absolute rules by intuition; their utilitarian opponents (like Mill) are supposed to proceed solely by induction. Sidgwick then argues that the idea that the utilitarians can proceed solely by induction is mistaken. Induction could establish the factual claim that all men do seek pleasure as their ultimate end (as the argument of Chapter IV shows, it does not in fact establish that conclusion). But that is just a factual claim. Utilitarians or egoists, however, are not ultimately in the business of defending such factual claims. They are ultimately committed to defending the evaluative claim that pleasure is the only reasonable ultimate end of human action. To properly draw such an evaluative conclusion, you need an evaluative premise that is justified. This evaluative premise cannot be justified by factual evidence, so it must be self-evident. So hedonists must either take hedonism itself to be self-evident, or derive it from some other evaluative claim that is self-evident.

The argument of this passage relies on the argument of *Methods* I.III. One of its crucial premises is the non-naturalist claim defended there. If the fundamental ethical concept could be defined wholly in factual terms, then it would be possible to justify an evaluative conclusion wholly on the basis of factual evidence. The other crucial, and independent, premise is a claim about the structure of justification: that justification is linear and has to begin with propositions that provide justification but do not themselves require justification from other propositions. This view about the structure of justification is called "foundationalism." The usual alternative is "coherentism," according to which justification may properly involve sets of propositions which fit together and are mutually supporting.

There are lots of further questions to ask about this argument and about what it reveals about Sidgwick's moral epistemology. One such question is what to make of the argument if one rejects foundationalism. Another related question is about the extent to which Sidgwick himself accepts foundationalism. It is clearly a premise in this crucial argument. But in other ways, as we will see, Sidgwick's later treatment of the possibility of proving moral theories has encouraged some philosophers to see him as partly embracing coherentism. We will discuss these issues more in Chapter 9, by which point we will have covered all the different parts of the *Methods* that are relevant to understanding and assessing Sidgwick's moral epistemology.

4.3. The Three Phases of Intuitionism

Sidgwick goes on in the rest of the chapter to distinguish and discuss three different phases (he also calls them "species" and "varieties") of intuitionism: perceptional, dogmatic, and philosophical. (He really does write "perceptional" not "perceptual.") These varieties of intuitionism agree that some moral claims are self-evident, but they differ as to the particularity or generality of the self-evident claims.

The first phase, perceptional intuitionism, is the view that the self-evident moral judgments are judgments about particular cases:

> judgments or perceptions relating to the rightness or wrongness of particular acts[.] (98)

Unlike dogmatic intuitionism, to which the bulk of Book III is devoted, Sidgwick spends very little time on perceptional intuitionism. The argument against it is given in a single paragraph.

> These particular intuitions do not, to reflective persons, present themselves as quite indubitable and irrefragable: nor do they always find when they have put an ethical question to themselves with all sincerity, that they are conscious of clear immediate insight in respect of it. Again, when a man compares the utterance of his conscience at different times, he often finds it difficult to make them altogether consistent: the same conduct will wear a different moral aspect at one time from that which it wore at another, although our knowledge of its circumstances and conditions is not materially changed. Further, we become aware that the moral perceptions of different minds, to all appearances equally competent to judge, frequently conflict: one condemns what another approves. In this way serious doubts are aroused as to the validity of each man's particular moral judgments. (100)

Though Sidgwick spends vastly less time on perceptional intuitionism than he does on dogmatic intuitionism, the arguments against them have some striking commonalities. As we will see in Chapter 6, when Sidgwick develops his critique of dogmatic intuitionism in *Methods* III.XI he relies crucially on four conditions that supposedly self-evident axioms have to meet (the conditions are articulated and discussed on pages 338 through 342). We will spend time on the details in Chapter 6. For current purposes we can summarize the four conditions like this: (1) The supposed axioms must be clear and precise; (2) They must genuinely seem self-evident; (3) All the self-evident axioms must be consistent with one another; (4) There should be no disagreement between people about them. The argument against perceptional intuitionism seems to involve a version of these very same four conditions, adapted to be applicable to particular moral judgments rather than to general rules. Thus the first sentence of the paragraph quoted above seems to give a version of conditions (1) and (2) adapted to fit particular moral judgments. The second sentence gives a version of condition (3): since the judgments are particular, one cannot require a form of intrapersonal consistency that involves consistency between the different rules an individual endorses; so what is required instead is intrapersonal consistency over time in making a given particular judgment. And the final sentence quoted contains a close relative of the later condition (4), which doesn't require much alteration to be applicable to particular moral judgments. So, though Sidgwick dismisses perceptional intuitionism much more quickly than he dismisses dogmatic intuitionism, he dismisses it for strikingly similar reasons.

Dogmatic intuitionism is the view that what are really self-evident are not particular moral judgments but general rules. It is worth quoting the paragraph containing Sidgwick's introductory characterization of dogmatic intuitionism, the topic of the bulk of Book III:

Here then we have a second Intuitional Method: of which the fundamental assumption is that we can discern certain general rules with really clear and finally valid intuition. It is held that such general rules are implicit in the moral reasoning of ordinary men, who apprehend them adequately for most practical purposes, and are able to enunciate them roughly; but that to state them with proper precision requires a special habit of contemplating clearly and steadily abstract moral notions. It is held that the moralist's function is to perform this process of abstract contemplation, to arrange the results as systematically as possible, and by proper definitions and explanations to remove vagueness and prevent conflict. It is such a system as this which seems to be generally intended when Intuitive or *a priori* morality is mentioned, and which will chiefly occupy us in [Book III]. (101)

Philosophical intuitionism is the view that what is really self-evident is something still more abstract and further removed from particular moral judgments:

A third species or phase of Intuitionism, which [. . .] attempts [. . .] to get one or more principles more absolutely and undeniably true or evident, from which the current rules might be deduced. (102)

This classification scheme is illuminating but also problematic. To see why it is problematic, begin by noticing that it is not the scheme you would most straightforwardly arrive at if you started with the thought with which we began this chapter: that there is a need to distinguish the epistemic from the moral-theoretic component of intuitionism (which is why Broad introduced "deontology" as the name for the moral-theoretic component). A classification scheme drawing on that thought might be expected to give you versions of intuitionism with the same epistemic component but different moral-theoretic components. But this is not the way perceptional, dogmatic, and philosophical intuitionism are supposed to differ. As Sidgwick characterizes them, they differ as to the particularity or generality of the genuinely self-evident claims, not as to moral theory.

That might lead you to expect each variety of intuitionism to be neutral with respect to moral theory. You might expect that you could be either a utilitarian or a deontological perceptional intuitionist, depending on whether you take the self-evident particular moral intuitions to support utilitarianism or deontology. You might expect that you could be either a utilitarian or a deontological dogmatic intuitionist, depending on whether you think the only self-evident moral rule is the utilitarian principle, or whether you think there are multiple self-evident moral rules, none of which is the utilitarian principle. And you might expect that you could be either a utilitarian or a deontological philosophical intuitionist, depending on whether you think the more abstract self-evident principles that justify moral rules justify utilitarian or deontological rules.

But that is not how Sidgwick typically presents things. Though the official definitions of perceptional, dogmatic, and philosophical intuitionism are in terms of levels of generality, not of moral theory, he nonetheless associates the phases of intuitionism with particular positions in moral theory. This is clearest in the case of dogmatic intuitionism: it is evident in I.VIII and elsewhere that dogmatic intuitionism is supposed to be a deontological view. By contrast, as we will see in III.XIII, philosophical intuitionism turns out to support utilitarianism. This running together of questions of the level of generality of the self-evident intuitions with questions of moral theory threatens to have problematic implications. These arise particularly in connection with dogmatic intuitionism. If you combine the association of dogmatic intuitionism with deontology and of philosophical intuitionism with utilitarianism with the idea—suggested by the very names of the phases and present in I.VIII and elsewhere—that philosophical intuitionism is the better view, you see the risk that a bias against deontology is built into the classification scheme. The scheme makes it the default assumption that deontology is not fully justified; that, unlike utilitarianism, it is dogmatic rather than philosophical. It helps obscure the possibility of a fully justified deontological theory: of a deontological form of philosophical intuitionism, of the philosophical intuitionist project justifying deontology.

For our current purposes the main point is not that Sidgwick definitely yields to this bias; that is a question for later chapters. The point is rather about the problematic character of the classification scheme itself. The three phases of intuitionism are officially distinguished by the level of generality of the genuinely self-evident principles in a way that should be neutral with respect to moral theory. But Sidgwick treats them as not neutral. Though this is not the way in which the difference between them is explained, he nonetheless associates the three phases with particular views in moral theory. This would not be so problematic if he associated all the phases with deontology. But he doesn't; he tends to associate dogmatic intuitionism with deontology and philosophical intuitionism with utilitarianism.

Another aspect of Sidgwick's classification scheme is illuminated when you compare it with the most celebrated view about the justification of moral judgments in contemporary moral philosophy, reflective equilibrium theory. Here is T. M. Scanlon's summary:

> In broad outline, the method of reflective equilibrium can be described as follows. One begins by identifying a set of considered judgments, of any level of generality, about the subject in question. These are judgments that seem clearly to be correct and seem so under conditions that are conducive to making good judgments of the relevant kind about this subject matter. If the subject in question is morality, for example, they may be judgments about the rightness or wrongness of particular actions, general moral principles, or judgments about the kind

of considerations that are relevant to determining the rightness of actions [...] The method does not privilege judgments of any particular type—those about particular cases, for example—as having special justificatory standing.

The next step is to formulate general principles that would "account for" these judgments [...] principles such that, had one simply been trying to apply them, rather than trying directly to decide what is the case about the subject at hand, one would have been led to this same set of judgments. If, as is likely, this attempt to come up with such principles is not successful, one must decide how to respond to the divergence between these principles and considered judgments: whether to give up the judgments that the principles fail to account for, to modify the principles, in hopes of achieving a better fit, or to do some combination of these things. One is then to continue in this way, working back and forth between principles and judgments, until one reaches a set of principles and a set of judgments that "account for them." This state is [...] reflective equilibrium.[4]

The key contrast between reflective equilibrium theory and Sidgwick's classification scheme is a matter of what Scanlon calls "privileging judgments of a particular type." As he says, the method of reflective equilibrium does not so privilege any type of judgments. By contrast, Sidgwick's classification scheme gives three options defined in terms of which type of judgment gets privileged. Perceptional intuitionism privileges judgments about the rightness or wrongness of particular actions; dogmatic intuitionism privileges judgments about general moral principles; philosophical intuitionism privileges more abstract judgments about the kinds of considerations that are relevant to determining the rightness of actions. Sidgwick's classification scheme does not allow for the possibility that no type of judgment is privileged.

4.4. The Right and the Good

As we saw in the previous chapter, in *Methods* I.III Sidgwick defends the non-naturalist view that the fundamental ethical concept, the concept expressed by "right" and "ought," is essentially different from all ordinary factual concepts. As we also noted there, the most famous historical expression of a non-naturalist view of this kind is Moore's in *Principia Ethica*.

To understand the importance of *Methods* I.IX, we need to focus on a difference between Sidgwick's and Moore's non-naturalism, and on a distinction between the two formulations of the key thesis of *Methods* I.III. The difference between Sidgwick and Moore is a difference as to which is the fundamental ethical concept, a difference to which Moore pays no attention when he commends Sidgwick for anticipating his own non-naturalist view. For Sidgwick, the fundamental unanalyzable concept is the concept expressed by "ought" or "right"; for Moore it is the concept expressed by "good."[5] So in committing himself in *Methods* I.III to the view that the concept expressed by "ought" or "right" is unanalyzable, Sidgwick has not yet committed himself to agreeing with Moore about the concept expressed by "good."

The distinction between the two formulations of the key thesis is the distinction between non-naturalness and simplicity. The first formulation of the key thesis in I.III is the claim that the fundamental ethical concept is non-natural:

> [T]he fundamental notion represented by the word "ought" or "right" [is . . .] essentially different from all notions representing facts of physical or psychical experience. (25)

The second formulation of the key thesis in I.III is the claim that the fundamental ethical concept is simple:

[T]he notion which [the] terms ['ought' and 'right'] have in common is too elementary to admit of any formal definition. (32)

Non-naturalness and simplicity are distinct and separable properties. There can be simple natural properties. In Chapter I of *Principia*, Moore talks of the property of being yellow, which he thinks is simple but natural. There can be complex non-natural properties. A complex non-natural property is a property which is definable, but definable only in terms of a simple non-natural property. When Moore defines "right" as meaning "maximally productive of good," he is treating rightness as a complex non-natural property: as a property that is definable in terms of other simple properties, one of which (goodness) is non-natural.

Much later critical commentary on *Principia Ethica* (including commentary by Moore himself) notes that he failed to pay consistent attention to this distinction, to be clear whether the thing he really wanted to say about goodness was that it was simple or that it was non-natural.[6] Though he has been much less criticized for it, Sidgwick is vulnerable to a similar charge: that he wasn't clear enough in *Methods* I.III about whether what he really wanted to claim about the fundamental notion represented by "right" and "ought" was that it was simple or that it was non-natural. When we come to *Methods* I.IX, the distinction matters. For, it ultimately turns out, Sidgwick's view about goodness requires the distinction. What he thinks about goodness is that it is non-natural but not simple: that it is a complex, definable, non-natural property.

The argument in Sections 2 and 3 of I.IX proceeds in much the same way as the argument of Sections 1 and 2 of I.III. In both cases Sidgwick considers and argues against naturalistic analyses. The first such naturalistic analysis he considers in I.IX defines goodness as productiveness of pleasure. Sidgwick offers three reasons to reject this analysis. First, when we judge of the good things in life—dinners, wines, poems, pictures, music—that they are good, this goodness is not a matter of all the pleasures they produce, but only of certain kinds of pleasures. We would not

> judge a poem good on account of its moral lessons[.] (107)

Second, even pleasures of the right kind are excited by good things not in people generally but only in people of good taste. Third, if we define goodness as productiveness of pleasure it does not make sense to say, as hedonists clearly want to say, that pleasure or happiness is good. Sidgwick thus clearly rejects the naturalistic analysis of goodness as productiveness of pleasure.

The other kind of naturalistic analysis of goodness Sidgwick considers is in terms of desire. He rejects this analysis too (or so most readers, including me, think). But that he does so is much less clear. Some interpreters have understood him as endorsing the naturalistic analysis of goodness in terms of desire that he gives. And even those who have not so read him have often thought that his account of goodness in terms of desire is a model for those who are inclined to accept such a naturalistic analysis.

He begins with a simple version of the idea, as expressed in a famous line from Hobbes:

> '[W]hatsoever is the object of any man's Desire, that it is which he for his part calleth Good'[.] (109)

But this simple version has a number of problems. Sometimes we desire things we know will be bad for us. We also know that we sometimes find things we wanted much less satisfying than we expected. And our desires are limited by our knowledge of our capacities; we don't desire what we think unattainable. To address these problems, Sidgwick offers the following complex, amended definition of goodness in terms of desire:

If we interpret the notion 'good' in relation to 'desire,' we must identify it not with the actually *desired*, but rather with the *desirable*: - meaning by 'desirable' not necessarily 'what *ought* to be desired' but what would be desired, with strength proportioned to the degree of desirability, if it were judged attainable by voluntary action, supposing the desirer to possess a perfect forecast, emotional as well as intellectual, of the state of attainment or fruition. (110-11)

But it is still possible that it will be on balance bad for us to pursue any particular thing that is in this sense good. The further idea we need at this point is that of our "good on the whole." Sidgwick provides a definition of it too in terms of desire.

A man's future good on the whole is what he would now desire and seek on the whole if all the consequences of all the different lines of conduct open to him were accurately foreseen and adequately realized in imagination at the present point of time. (111-12)

As Sidgwick observes, this is still a naturalistic analysis:

The notion of 'Good' thus attained has an ideal element: it is something that is not always actually desired and aimed at by human beings: but the ideal element is entirely interpretable in terms of *fact*, actual or hypothetical, and does not introduce any judgment of value, fundamentally distinct from judgments relating to existence; - still less any 'dictate of Reason' [.] (112)

As most commentators read him, Sidgwick goes on to reject this naturalistic analysis, and to endorse instead a definition of "good" in terms of "right" or "ought." What he says at this point in I.IX is:

> It seems to me, however, more in accordance with common sense to recognize—as Butler does—that the calm desire for my 'good on the whole' is *authoritative*; and therefore carries with it implicitly a rational dictate to aim at this end, if in any case a conflicting desire urges the will in an opposite direction. (112)

This suggests that there is a definition of "good" in terms of "ought" but does not succinctly state any such definition. In passages elsewhere Sidgwick does suggest a succinct definition. On page 381 he says,

> We may define 'good' as what one ought to aim at.

This definition makes goodness a complex non-natural property: complex because it is definable, non-natural because one of the properties in terms of which it is defined is the simple non-natural property referred to by "ought."

4.5. What Things are Good? (Part 1)

As we saw, one of Sidgwick's criticisms of himself was that his work was poorly organized. The charge seems particularly applicable to his treatment of the question of what things are intrinsically good. The question is discussed in I.I, at the end of I.IX, and in III.XIV. And III.XIV is itself, as we will see in Chapter 8, somewhat opaquely structured.

It is important to notice the provisional conclusions Sidgwick draws at the end of I.IX. In I.I he had already taken as a working assumption for the purposes of enumerating different methods of ethics that

> the only two ends which have a strongly and widely supported claim to be regarded as rational ultimate ends are [...] Happiness and Perfection. (9)

INTUITIONISM AND GOODNESS 77

Sidgwick adds two further ideas in I.IX. First:

> [...] we can find nothing that [possesses the] quality of goodness out of relation to human existence, or at least to some consciousness or feeling.
>
> For example, we commonly judge some inanimate objects, scenes, etc., to be good as possessing beauty, and others to be bad from ugliness: still no one would consider it rational to aim at the production of beauty in external nature, apart from any possible contemplation of it by human beings (113–14)

He generalizes from this to claim that all the "ideal goods" including beauty are only instrumentally good (good as means) rather than intrinsically good (good in themselves).

> It will, I think, be generally held that beauty, knowledge, and other ideal goods [...] are only reasonably to be sought by men in so far as they conduce either (1) to Happiness or (2) to the Perfection or Excellence of human existence. (114)

Moore argues against Sidgwick's views about what things are good. Most of his objections are directed against the arguments developed in III.XIV. But in a famous passage Moore responds to the claim about beauty made in I.IX:

> "'No one,' says Prof. Sidgwick, 'would consider it rational to aim at the production of beauty in external nature, apart from any contemplation of it by human beings.' Well, I may say at once, that I, for one, do consider this rational; and let us see if I cannot get any one to agree with me. Consider what this admission really means. It entitles us to put the following case. Let us imagine one world exceedingly beautiful. Imagine it as beautiful as you can; put into it whatever on this earth you most admire—mountains, rivers, the sea; trees and sunsets, stars and moon. Imagine these

all combined in the most exquisite proportions, so that no one thing jars against another, but each contributes to increase the beauty of the whole. And then imagine the ugliest world you can possibly conceive. Imagine it simply one heap of filth, containing everything that is most disgusting to us, for whatever reason, and the whole, so far as may be, without one redeeming feature. Such a pair of worlds we are entitled to compare: they fall within Prof. Sidgwick's meaning, and the comparison is highly relevant to it. The only thing we are not entitled to imagine is that any human being ever has or ever, by any possibility, *can*, live in either, can ever see and enjoy the beauty of the one or hate the foulness of the other. Well, even so, supposing them quite apart from any possible contemplation by human beings; still, is it irrational to hold that it is better that the beautiful world should exist, than the one which is ugly? Would it not be well, in any case, to do what we could to produce it rather than the other? Certainly I cannot help thinking that it would.[7]

The thought experiment Moore appeals to in this passage is a striking one. But not many—including, later, Moore himself—are persuaded to accept its conclusion. Moore has stronger objections to other aspects of Sidgwick's case for hedonism, as we will see in Chapter 8.

Notes

1. Broad 1930, 206–7. For a fuller history of the terminology, see Louden 1996.
2. As we noted in Chapter 2, most contemporary deontologists are not absolutists. They instead are moderate deontologists who treat deontological rules as principles of *prima facie* duty. While Broad's initial definition of "deontology" in the passage above appears to restrict the term to absolutist views (and so to be inconsistent with the way the term is normally used today), Broad goes on shortly afterwards to "state a form of Intuitionism which is not open to Sidgwick's objections" (218). That form of intuitionism

features Broad's version of the concept of *prima facie* duty. While Broad does not there explicitly apply his new term "deontology" to this moderate form of intuitionism as well as to absolutism, it seems natural to think that he would call moderate as well as absolutist views "deontological." If so, Broad's usage of "deontology" closely tracks contemporary usage.

I say more about the moderate form of intuitionism and its relation to Sidgwick in Chapter 6.

3. Anscombe 1958.
4. Scanlon 2014, 76–77.
5. We discussed some important consequences of this difference in conceptual schemes in section 6 of Chapter 2.
6. See Moore 1993, 1–27, and Frankena 1939.
7. Moore 1903, 83–84.

Further Reading

For a fuller treatment of Sidgwick's argument for epistemic intuitionism, see Phillips 2011, Chapter 3, Sections 1–3. For a fuller treatment of I.IX, see Shaver 1997.

5
The Method of Egoism
(*Methods* I.VII and Book II)

I.VII and Book II are devoted to the method of egoism. As we noted in Chapter 1, though, this doesn't mean that the issues discussed in these chapters are relevant only to egoism. Egoism and utilitarianism have much in common. Both are consequentialist, and both give us the same end: the greatest possible balance of pleasure over pain. (The key difference, of course, is that egoism tells us to maximize our own happiness, while utilitarianism tells us to maximize everyone's happiness.) These chapters contain Sidgwick's most important discussions of the nature and measurability of happiness. They are thus crucial to his treatment of utilitarianism as well as to his treatment of egoism.

5.1. Egoism: Method and Principle

In I.VII, Sidgwick begins by making it clear that the end of egoism as he will understand it is the greatest possible balance of pleasure over pain. As he puts it at the end of the chapter:

> According to [Egoistic Hedonism] the rational agent regards quantity of consequent pleasure and pain for himself as alone important in choosing between alternatives of action; and seeks always the greatest attainable surplus of pleasure over pain—which [. . .] we may designate as his 'greatest happiness.' (95)

He rejects other possible ways of understanding the end of egoism: the idea in Hobbes that the end is (at least in part) self-preservation, and the idea in other philosophers that the end is self-realization.

As we noticed in Chapter 2, Sidgwick is sensitive to the concern that egoism is not really a method of ethics. As he does elsewhere, Sidgwick treats this issue by distinguishing two ideas: the idea that ethical rules have a certain content, and the idea that they have the authority of reason.

> It may be doubted whether this ought to be included among the received "methods of *Ethics*"; since there are strong grounds for holding that a system of morality, satisfactory to the moral consciousness of mankind in general, cannot be constructed on the basis of simple Egoism [. . .] it seems sufficient to point to the wide acceptance of the principle that it is reasonable for a man to act in the manner most conducive to his own happiness. (119)

Sidgwick's line here is that there are two features we use to distinguish the ethical: having the content of a system of morality as ordinarily conceived, and having authority. In the case of egoism, these two features come apart. Egoism may not generate a system of moral rules as ordinarily conceived, but it does appear to have practical authority. In such cases of conflict, practical authority is the more important feature. So we should consider egoism a method of ethics.

Book II is the place in the *Methods* where the distinction between methods and first principles is most prominent. As he explicitly tells us on page 132, Sidgwick will not consider the adequacy of the egoist first principle anywhere in Book II:

> We are not now to consider whether it is reasonable for an individual to take his own happiness as his ultimate end.

In a footnote he points to later discussions, in particular to the discussion in the Concluding Chapter. This postponement of the key question of the rationality of egoism is unfortunate. As we will see in Chapters 7, 9, and 11, Sidgwick's views on the question are hard to track and have occasioned significant disagreement among his interpreters.

For better or worse, though, Book II is concerned only with the egoist method, not with the egoist first principle. Or, perhaps it would be better to say, Book II is concerned with egoist *methods*. As we saw in Chapter 2, it is not obvious that there is a one-to-one correspondence between methods and first principles. It is possible that there may be more than one method by which the aim given by a first principle can be pursued. And indeed this turns out to be the case with egoism. Sidgwick distinguishes three egoist methods in Book II. The first, which is his main focus, is what he calls on page 131, "the empirical-reflective method of Egoistic Hedonism":

> The empirical-reflective method of Egoistic Hedonism will be, to represent beforehand the different series of feelings that our knowledge of physical and psychical causes leads us to expect from the different lines of conduct that lie open to us; judge which series, as thus represented, appears on the whole preferable, taking all probabilities into account; and adopt the corresponding line of conduct. (131)

The second, which is his topic in Chapter IV of Book II, is "objective hedonism." The objective hedonist relies on "the judgments of common sense respecting the sources of happiness" (158), rather than relying on individual calculations and predictions. The third is "deductive hedonism," associated in particular with the work of Sidgwick's now obscure contemporary, Herbert Spencer, which is the topic of Chapter VI. The deductive hedonist is supposed to rely on "scientific investigation of the causes of pleasure and pain" (176), rather than individual calculations and predictions or common sense. Sidgwick argues that neither objective hedonism nor deductive hedonism remedies the defects he finds in the empirical-reflective method of egoistic hedonism. We will focus almost exclusively on his discussion of this first egoistic method.

5.2. What is Happiness?

5.2.1. Higher and Lower Pleasures

Questions about the nature and measurability of happiness had, unsurprisingly, been much discussed in the earlier utilitarian tradition. In Chapter IV of *Principles of Morals and Legislation*, Bentham emphasized two features to be taken into account in measuring pleasures and pains: intensity and duration.[1] John Stuart Mill was famously dissatisfied with Bentham's view. He proposed an amendment according to which pleasures differ also in "quality." Here is some of what he says in making his proposal:

> If I am asked what I mean by difference of quality in pleasures, or what makes one pleasure more valuable than another, merely as a pleasure, except its being greater in amount, there is but one possible answer. Of two pleasures, if there be one to which all or almost all who have experience of both give a decided preference, irrespective of any feeling of moral obligation to prefer it, that is the more desirable pleasure. If one of the two is, by those who are competently acquainted with both, placed so far above the other that they prefer it, even though knowing it to be attended with a greater amount of discontent, and would not resign it for any quantity of the other pleasure which their nature is capable of, we are justified in ascribing to the preferred enjoyment a superiority in quality so far outweighing quantity as to render it, in comparison, of small account.

> Now it is an unquestionable fact that those who are equally acquainted with and equally capable of appreciating and enjoying both do give a most marked preference to the manner of existence which employs their higher faculties. Few human creatures would consent to be changed into any of the lower animals for a promise of the fullest allowance of a beast's pleasures; no intelligent human being would consent to be a fool, no instructed person would be an ignoramus, no person of feeling and conscience would be selfish and base, even though they should be persuaded that the fool, the dunce, or the rascal is better satisfied with his lot than they are with theirs.[2]

On this issue Sidgwick sides with Bentham. He gives a dilemma argument against Mill's proposal at the end of I.VII: either Mill's proposal is nothing new and quality of pleasure is really just a matter of intensity and duration, or Mill is giving up on hedonism by making something in addition to happiness intrinsically good.

> It seems to me that in order to work out consistently the method that takes pleasure as the sole ultimate end of rational conduct, Bentham's proposition must be accepted, and all *qualitative* comparison of pleasures must really resolve itself into quantitative [...] If [...] what we are seeking is pleasure as such, and pleasure alone, we must evidently always prefer the more pleasant pleasure to the less pleasant: no other choice seems reasonable, unless we are aiming at something besides pleasure. And often when we say that one kind of pleasure is better than another—as (*e.g.*) that the pleasures of reciprocated affection are superior in quality to the pleasures of gratified appetite—we mean that they are more pleasant. No doubt we many mean something else: we may mean, for instance, that they are nobler and more elevated, although less pleasant. But then we are clearly introducing a non-hedonistic ground of preference. (94–95)

This dilemma argument against Mill was given by others too, including Moore.[3] A number of contemporary philosophers have suggested a way Mill could avoid the dilemma. They say that the key idea in Mill is the idea of what sometimes gets called "infinite superiority." The pleasures Mill calls "higher pleasures" are infinitely superior to those he calls "lower pleasures": any amount of a higher pleasure, however small, is worth more than any amount of a lower pleasure, however great. This makes Mill's proposal something new that was not part of standard Benthamite utilitarianism. But Mill's proposal, so understood, is still compatible with hedonism.[4]

Sidgwick does not consider this way of interpreting Mill. But he does at the start of II.II consider and reject the idea that the pleasure and pain scale includes infinite superiorities:

> We find it sometimes asserted by persons of enthusiastic and passionate temperament, that there are feelings so exquisitely delightful, that one moment of their rapture is preferable to an eternity of agreeable consciousness of an ordinary kind [. . .] in the case of pain, it has been deliberately maintained by a thoughtful and subtle writer [. . .] that "torture" so extreme as to be "incommensurable with moderate pain" is an actual fact of experience [. . .] This doctrine, however, does not correspond to my own experience: nor does it appear to me to be supported by the common sense of mankind:-at least I do not find, in the practical foresight of persons noted for caution, any recognition of the danger of agony such that, in order to avoid the smallest extra risk of it, the greatest conceivable amount of moderate pain should reasonably be incurred. (123–24, footnote)

What Sidgwick says is persuasive. So even if there is a way for Mill to escape the dilemma argument by appealing to infinite superiorities, his proposal to modify hedonism still does not ultimately seem plausible. Sidgwick has good reason to agree with Bentham on this matter.

5.2.2. Defining Pleasure

II.II contains Sidgwick's most important and extended discussion of the nature of pleasure. He considers three main possible views: that pleasure is a feeling of a distinctive kind, that it can be defined in terms of desire, and that it can be defined in terms of desirability. He endorses the third alternative. As he puts it at the beginning of II.III:

> Let, then, pleasure be defined as a feeling which the sentient individual at the time of feeling it implicitly or explicitly apprehends to be desirable. (131)

In II.II Sidgwick begins with the view that pleasure can be defined in terms of desire. He himself provisionally suggested this view in the discussion of psychological hedonism in I.IV. In II.II he quotes Herbert Spencer's articulation of it, according to which pleasure is:

> A feeling which we seek to bring into consciousness and retain there. (125)

The problem he raises for this view is that the intensity of pleasures is sometimes not proportional to the desires and aversions they arouse. One example he gives is the sensation of being tickled: it is only slightly painful but tends to arouse strong desires for its removal.

Sidgwick then considers the possibility that pleasure is a feeling of a distinctive kind. He rejects it by appeal to what later philosophers sometimes call the "heterogeneity objection": that there is nothing that the diverse set of feelings we call "pleasures" have in common other than some relation to desire.

> Shall we then say that there is a measurable quality of feeling expressed by the word "pleasure," which is independent of its

relation to volition, and strictly undefinable from its simplicity? - like the quality of feeling expressed by "sweet," of which we also are conscious of varying degrees of intensity. This seems to be the view of some writers: but, for my own part, when I reflect on the notion of pleasure, - using the term in the comprehensive sense which I have adopted, to include the most refined and subtle intellectual and emotional gratifications, no less than the coarser and more definite sensual enjoyments, - the only common quality that I can find in the feelings so designated seems to be that relation to desire and volition expressed by the general term "desirable"[.] (127)

What remains is the third view, which he favors, that pleasure is definable in terms of desirability.

> I propose then to define Pleasure—as a feeling which, when experienced by intelligent beings, is at least implicitly apprehended as desirable. (127)

Immediately after giving this definition, Sidgwick notes a problem. In discussing and rejecting Mill's proposed amendment to utilitarianism, Sidgwick talked of the possibility of preferring some pleasures on the grounds that they are higher or more noble even though less pleasant. But the definition of pleasure in terms of desirability might seem to make this kind of preference impossible. It might seem contradictory to say that a pleasure can be thought more desirable though it is less pleasant because to be pleasant just is to be thought desirable.

Sidgwick's solution is to appeal to different grounds of preference for feelings. It is one thing to prefer feelings for themselves. It is another to prefer them because of something else connected to the feelings:

> I should conclude that when one kind of pleasure is judged to be qualitatively superior to another, although less pleasant, it

is not really the feeling itself that is preferred, but something in the mental or physical conditions or relations under which it arises. (128)

An example might help here. To adapt one from Bentham that is often referred to in discussions of higher and lower pleasures, consider someone who prefers reading poetry to playing pushpin though acknowledging that playing pushpin brings her more pleasure. Sidgwick says that such a person's preferences do make sense even given his definition of pleasure. What is going on is something like this: the person prefers reading poetry overall because she values the insight that she thinks reading poetry gives her, but she acknowledges that if all that were at issue was the experience involved she would prefer playing pushpin.

One concern about the *Methods* raised by critics, including Sidgwick's most hostile nineteenth-century critic F. H. Bradley, is that the discussion is rigged in favor of hedonism.[5] This charge does no justice to the complexity of the *Methods* as a whole, but it does introduce an important concern about Sidgwick's definition of pleasure. As we saw in Chapter 4, Sidgwick defines goodness in terms of desirability. If pleasure is also defined in terms of desirability, does it follow automatically from the definitions that pleasure is good? And is that a problem?

Sidgwick addresses this charge in the paragraph that begins at the top of page 129:

> It should be observed that if this definition of pleasure be accepted, and if, as before proposed, 'Ultimate Good' be taken as equivalent to 'what is ultimately desirable,' the fundamental proposition of ethical Hedonism has chiefly a negative significance; for the statement that 'Pleasure is the Ultimate Good' will only mean that nothing is ultimately desirable except desirable feeling, apprehended as desirable by the sentient individual at the time of feeling it. This being so, it may be urged against the definition

that it could not be accepted by a moralist of stoical turn, who while recognising pleasure as a fact refused to recognise it as in any degree ultimately desirable. But I think such a moralist ought to admit an implied judgment that a feeling is *per se* desirable to be inseparably connected with its recognition as pleasure; while holding that sound philosophy shows the illusoriness of such judgments. (129)

Sidgwick's response here substantially concedes the correctness of the charge. He points out that it does not follow from the definitions of pleasure and ultimate goodness that hedonism is true because it does not follow that pleasure is the only thing that is good. But if pleasure is defined as desirable feeling, to think of something as a pleasure is to think of it as good. Someone who denies that pleasure is even one of the things that is good will have to say that the judgment we make in classifying a feeling as a pleasure is mistaken.

And there is a further problem with Sidgwick's view. We don't normally think that only human beings can feel pleasure and pain. We think non-human animals can too. As we will see in Chapter 9, Sidgwick himself follows Bentham and Mill in specifying that utilitarianism requires us to consider animal as well as human pleasures and pains in deciding how to act. But Sidgwick's view about the nature of pleasure seems to make it impossible for most non-human animals and, indeed, for human infants to feel pleasure and pain. It seems to imply that only beings that have the concept of goodness or desirability are capable of feeling pleasure and pain. Since human infants and most non-human animals don't have the cognitive sophistication required to have that concept, on his view it seems that they are not capable of feeling pleasure and pain.

Thus, while Sidgwick considers a nice range of views and arguments about the nature of pleasure and pain, there are significant reasons to be dissatisfied with the position he ends up endorsing.

5.3. Problems in Measuring Happiness

At the end of II.III Sidgwick identifies

> the fundamental assumption of [. . .] Quantitative Hedonism [. . .] that all pleasures and pains, estimated merely as feelings, have for the sentient individual cognisable degrees of desirability, positive or negative[.] (129)

In II.III he turns to objections. Those which he identifies as "more serious" (140) are objections that bring this fundamental assumption into question:

> Objections [. . .] against the possibility of performing, with definite and trustworthy results, the comprehensive and methodical comparison of pleasures and pains which the adoption of the Hedonistic standard involves[.] (140)

We do habitually compare pleasures and pains, but

> it may still be maintained (1) that this comparison as ordinarily made is both occasional and very rough, and that it can never be extended as systematic Hedonism requires, nor applied, with any accuracy, to all possible states however differing in quality; and (2) that as commonly practiced it is liable to illusion, of which we can never measure the precise amount, while we are continually forced to recognise its existence. (140)

Sidgwick basically concedes that these objections are correct. We cannot in fact make the comparisons with precision in most cases. As he puts it:

> When I reflect on my pleasures and pains, and endeavour to compare them in respect of intensity, it is only to a very limited extent

that I can obtain clear and definite results from such comparisons, even taking each separately in its simplest form:-whether the comparison is made at the moment of experiencing one of the pleasures, or between two states of consciousness recalled in imagination. This is true even when I compare feelings of the same kind: and the vagueness and uncertainty increases, in proportion as the feelings differ in kind. (142–43)

These difficulties are compounded by the problem that judgments about the intensity of pleasures are not stable over time. Our current state affects our judgments as to the relative value of different pleasures.

[I]n danger we value repose, overlooking its *ennui*, while the tedium of security makes us imagine the mingled excitement of past danger as almost purely pleasurable. (145)

He concludes at the end of II.III:

The foregoing considerations must, I think, seriously reduce our confidence in what I have called the empirical-reflective method of Egoistic Hedonism. I do not conclude that we should reject it altogether: I am conscious that, in spite of all the difficulties that have been urged, I continue to make comparisons of pleasures and pains with practical reliance on their results. But I conclude that it would be at least highly desirable, with a view to the systematic direction of conduct, to control and supplement the results of such comparisons by the assistance of some other method. (150)

The other methods Sidgwick considers are objective and deductive hedonism. But they do not provide the assistance needed to remove the imprecision and uncertainty in the empirical-reflective method. That imprecision and uncertainty remains.

5.4. Happiness and Duty

In Book II Chapter V, Sidgwick asks whether it is always in your own individual interest to do what morality tells you to do: whether happiness and duty coincide. At this stage he sets aside any appeal to the idea that there is an all-powerful deity who will make it always in your interest to do the right thing. He asks instead whether happiness and duty can be shown to coincide on the basis of ordinary non-religious experience. And he concludes that they cannot.

This is the chapter in Book II that has the most importance for the overall conclusions of the *Methods*. Sidgwick draws explicitly on it later, in the Concluding Chapter, in articulating the dualism of practical reason, the idea that there is a contradiction or unresolvable conflict between utilitarianism and egoism. The immediate topic of II.V is not, however, the relationship between utilitarianism and egoism. It is instead the relationship between egoism and intuitionism. This focus makes the chapter unusual. Sidgwick often focuses on conflicts between two of the three methods. Almost always, though, his main focus is on the conflict between utilitarianism and egoism or on the conflict between utilitarianism and intuitionism, not on the conflict between egoism and intuitionism. Because the chapter comes where it does, before Sidgwick's systematic examination of intuitionism in Book III, he relies in II.V on a pretheoretical understanding of intuitionistic morality rather than on the results of that systematic examination. But there is no suggestion that this limitation affects the chapter's conclusion, that it would make any difference to the question whether happiness and duty coincide if we substituted the fully worked out account of duty generated by Book III for the provisional account employed in II.V.

The key terminology in the chapter, the terminology of "sanctions," derives from Bentham.

> It will be convenient to adopt with some modification the terminology of Bentham; and to regard the pleasures consequent on

conformity to moral rules, and the pains consequent on their violation, as the 'sanctions' of these rules. (164)

Sidgwick distinguishes three kinds of sanctions:

> These 'sanctions' we may classify as External and Internal. The former class will include both 'Legal Sanctions,' or penalties inflicted by the authority, direct or indirect, of the sovereign; and 'Social Sanctions,' which are either the pleasures that may be expected from the approval and goodwill of our fellowmen generally, and the services that they will be prompted to render both by this goodwill and by their appreciation of the usefulness of good conduct, or the annoyance and losses that are to be feared from their distrust and dislike. The internal sanctions of duty [. . .] will lie in the pleasurable emotion attending virtuous action, or in the absence of remorse, or will result more indirectly from some effect on the mental constitution of the agent produced by the maintenance of virtuous dispositions and habits. (164)

In the discussion that follows, Sidgwick argues that while it is usually in our interest to do our duty, these sanctions do not, individually or together, suffice to make it always in our individual interest to do as duty requires. The concluding paragraph of the chapter nicely summarizes that discussion:

> Although the performance of duties towards others and the exercise of social virtue seem to be *generally* the best means to the attainment of the individual's happiness, and it is easy to exhibit this coincidence between Virtue and Happiness rhetorically and popularly; still, when we carefully analyse and estimate the consequences of Virtue to the virtuous agent, it appears improbable that this coincidence is complete and universal. We may conceive the coincidence becoming perfect in a Utopia where men were as much in accord on moral as they are now on mathematical

questions, where Law was in perfect harmony with Moral Opinion, and all offences were discovered and duly punished: or we may conceive the same result attained by intensifying the moral sentiments of all members of the community, without any external changes (which indeed then would be unnecessary). But just in proportion as existing societies and existing men fall short of this ideal, rules of conduct based on the principles of Egoistic Hedonism seem likely to diverge from those which most men are accustomed to recognise as prescribed by Duty and Virtue. (175)

5.5. Egoism: Conclusions from Book II

As we noted at the start of this chapter, Sidgwick deliberately sets aside the question of the correctness of the egoistic first principle, and focuses in Book II only on egoistic methods. A central message of Book II is that the main method of egoism—the empirical-reflective method—will not in practice give precise results. In principle it promises such precision. Each possible action open to us will have a certain range of consequences; and those will include the consequences for our own pleasures and pains, which, according to egoism, are the only consequences that matter in deciding what we should do. If we knew all the consequences and could measure pleasures and pains precisely, egoism would give a verdict on every case.

But, even setting aside the immense difficulties in knowing the future, we cannot in practice rank pleasures and pains with the precision required. That each pleasure and pain has a numerically precise degree of pleasurableness or painfulness remains an assumption that we make rather than a conclusion we can justify. So in many actual cases we will not be able to tell which course of action egoism tells us to take.

What is interesting for the overall structure of the *Methods* is Sidgwick's response to this problem. He does not take it to constitute a reason to reject egoism. Its main method admittedly does not in practice give precise results, but that is not a decisive reason to reject either the method or the associated first principle. The question of the fairness of Sidgwick's treatment of intuitionism as against egoism again arises. For, as we will see in the next chapter, Sidgwick does not in the same way separate the dogmatic intuitionist's method from the dogmatic intuitionist's first principles. And the failure of the dogmatic intuitionist's method to give precise results in every case does seem for him to constitute a decisive reason to reject the method of dogmatic intuitionism in a way that the failure of the egoistic method to give precise results in every case does not seem to constitute a decisive reason to reject the method of egoism.

Notes

1. Bentham (1789) 2003.
2. Mill (1861) 2003, 100–01.
3. Moore 1903, 78–79.
4. For this interpretation of Mill on higher and lower pleasures, see Riley 2003.
5. Bradley 1877.

Further Reading

For a fuller and sympathetic discussion of Sidgwick's views about happiness (or pleasure), see Shaver 2016. For a much more critical treatment, see Hurka 2014a, 194–98.

6
The Critique of Common-Sense Morality (*Methods* III.I–III.XI)

In the short intellectual autobiography, Sidgwick tells us that the model for the first eleven chapters of Book III was Aristotle.[1]

> What he gave us [in the *Nicomachean Ethics*] was the Common-Sense Morality of Greece, reduced to consistency by careful comparison: given not as something external to him but as what "we"—he and others—think, ascertained by reflection [. . .]
>
> Might I not imitate this: do the same for *our* morality here and now, in the same manner of impartial reflection on common opinion?
>
> Indeed *ought* I not to do this before deciding on the question whether I had or had not a system of moral intuitions? At any rate the result would be useful, whatever conclusion I came to.
>
> So this was the part of my book first written [Book III, Chapters I–XI], and a certain imitation of Aristotle's manner was very marked in it at first, and though I have tried to remove it when it seemed to me affected or pedantic, it still remains to some extent. (xxi–xxii)

As he also tells us there, his conclusions about common sense morality are basically negative. It is not a system of self-evident moral principles. Strictly speaking, one principle which may be an element of common-sense morality, a principle of justice, is a genuine, self-evident axiom. But no other element of common-sense morality has this status. By contrast, as we will see in the next chapter, Sidgwick argues in III.XIII that there are genuine, self-evident axioms which support utilitarianism.

There is much of enduring philosophical interest in these chapters of Book III. Anyone concerned with the topics discussed there—including wisdom, benevolence, justice, and veracity—will learn much from consulting the relevant parts of the *Methods*. But, given the aims of this Guide and the limitations of available space, I will not be able to discuss all these chapters in detail. What I will do instead is to focus on the overall character of Sidgwick's argument, tracking the specifics of his treatment of just one element of the common-sense morality he discusses: promissory obligation.

6.1. Dogmatic Intuitionism, or Common-Sense Morality

Sidgwick gives a helpful initial characterization of the theory that is his main topic in Book III:

> We have the power of seeing clearly that certain kinds of actions are right and reasonable in themselves, apart from their consequences—or rather with a merely partial consideration of consequences, from which other consequences admitted to be possibly good or bad are definitely excluded. (200)

In the case of promissory obligation, for example, the view would be that the principle

> Promises ought to be kept

is self-evident. This principle involves consideration of the consequences of actions only to the extent that such consideration is required to identify acts as instances of keeping promises. Good or bad consequences beyond these are excluded.

The philosopher who had most influentially advocated this kind of view in the generation before Sidgwick was William Whewell. Sidgwick has two alternative names for the view—"dogmatic intuitionism" and "common-sense morality" (or "the morality of common sense"). Neither name is unproblematic. As we saw in Chapter 4, the problem with the name "dogmatic intuitionism" is that when Sidgwick is distinguishing the three phases (or "versions" or "varieties") of intuitionism, he does so officially by reference to the particularity or generality of the genuinely self-evident intuitions, rather than by reference to views in moral theory. The problem with the name "common-sense morality" is that associating this particular moral theory with common sense may seem to imply that there is no basis in common sense for the competing moral theories, egoism and utilitarianism. But this is not Sidgwick's view. At the end of I.I, he writes:

> The truth seems to be that most of the practical principles that have been seriously put forward are more or less satisfactory to the common sense of mankind so long as they have the field to themselves. They all find a response in our nature: their fundamental assumptions are all such as we disposed to accept, and such as we find to govern to a certain extent our habitual conduct. When I am asked "Do you not consider it ultimately reasonable to seek pleasure and avoid pain for yourself?" "Have you not a moral sense?" "Do you not intuitively pronounce some actions to be right and others wrong?" "Do you not acknowledge the general happiness to be a paramount end?" I answer 'yes' to all these questions. My difficulty begins when I have to choose between the different principles or inferences drawn from them. (14)

As this passage makes clear, the common sense of mankind is disposed to accept egoist and utilitarian principles as well as deontological principles. To avoid confusion on this point we might distinguish broad and narrow senses of the term "common-sense morality." In the broad sense, common-sense morality includes the egoistic and utilitarian principles common sense is disposed to accept as well as the deontological principles common sense is disposed to accept. In the narrow sense (the sense employed in Sidgwick's use of the term "common-sense morality" in Book III), common-sense morality includes only the deontological principles common sense is disposed to accept.

6.2. The Project of III.II–III.X

Sidgwick explains the project of III.II–III.X in an important passage at the end of III.I that is worth quoting at length:

> When, however, we try to apply these currently accepted principles, we find that the notions composing them are often deficient in clearness and precision. For instance, we should all agree in recognising Justice and Veracity as important virtues; and we shall probably all accept the general maxims, that 'we ought to give every man his own' and that 'we ought to speak the truth': but when we ask (1) whether primogeniture is just, or the disendowment of corporations, or the determination of the value of services by competition, or (2) whether and how far false statements may be allowed in speeches of advocates, or in religious ceremonials, or when made to enemies or robbers, or in defense of lawful secrets, we do not find that these or any other current maxims enable us to give clear and unhesitating decisions. And yet such particular questions are, after all, those to which we naturally expect answers from the moralist. For we study Ethics, as Aristotle says, for the sake of Practice: and in practice we are concerned with particulars.
>
> Hence it seems that if the formulae of Intuitive Morality are really to serve as scientific axioms, and to be available in clear and cogent demonstrations, they must first be raised—by an effort of reflection which ordinary persons will not make—to a higher degree of precision than attaches to them in the common thought

and discourse of mankind in general. We have, in fact, to take up the attempt that Socrates initiated, and endeavour to define satisfactorily the general notions of duty and virtue which we all in common use for awarding approbation or disapprobation to conduct. This is the task upon which we shall be engaged in the nine chapters that follow. I must beg the reader to bear in mind that throughout these chapters I am not trying to prove or disprove Intuitionism, but merely by reflection on the common morality which I and my reader share, and to which appeal is so often made in moral disputes, to obtain as explicit, exact, and coherent a statement as possible of its fundamental rules. (215–16)

This passage, like others, suggests that the key aim in III.II–III.X is to make the principles of common-sense morality clear and precise (or exact). And it suggests a particular way of understanding what would be required to make the principles clear and precise: they would have to answer all particular questions we might ask, they would have to generate a verdict about every case. As we will see, the insistence on clarity and precision understood in this way is a key element of Sidgwick's critique of common-sense morality. In reflecting on that critique we will need to ask both whether it is reasonable to require moral principles to be clear and precise in this way, and whether Sidgwick imposes the same clarity and precision requirement on egoist and utilitarian principles as he does on intuitionist principles.

6.3. The Four Conditions

The key chapter in which Sidgwick's critique of common-sense morality is articulated is III.XI. He begins by explaining the project on which he has been engaged in III.II–III.X, in much the same way as in the passage just quoted from I.I. He then turns to the critique:

I now wish to subject the results of this survey to a final examination, in order to decide whether these general formulae possess the characteristics by which self-evident truths are distinguished from mere opinions.

There seem to be four conditions, the complete fulfilment of which would establish a significant proposition, apparently self-evident, in the highest degree of certainty attainable: and which must be approximately realized by the premises of our reasoning in any inquiry, if that reasoning is to lead us cogently to trustworthy conclusions. (338)

There is much to unpack even in these two opening sentences of the critique. The procedure Sidgwick envisages involves testing apparently self-evident principles. The fact that these principles seem self-evident does not establish their self-evidence (or even their truth). Something more is required; they have to satisfy the four conditions. Moreover when the conditions are applied, these sentences suggest, the answer will not be all or nothing: that the principles are either genuinely self-evident or not self-evident at all. Rather, it will yield something, certainty, which comes in degrees. Some principles will, the suggestion seems to be, turn out to be more certain than others. How certain they are will be determined by how fully they satisfy the four conditions.

Sidgwick then goes on to introduce and discuss the four conditions.[2] In the case of conditions 1 and 3, the first sentence of what he says in introducing the condition gives a helpful formulation of that condition. That is not true of conditions 2 and 4.

Condition 1 is the clarity and precision condition:

1. The terms of the proposition must be clear and precise. The rival originators of modern Methodology, Descartes and Bacon, vie with each other in the stress that they lay on this point: and the latter's warning against the "notiones male terminatae" of ordinary thought is peculiarly needed in ethical discussion. In fact

my chief business in the preceding survey has been to free the common terms of Ethics, as far as possible, from objection on this score. (338–39)

Here the first sentence does indeed constitute a helpful formulation of the condition. And Sidgwick emphasizes what we would anticipate given the earlier characterization of his project in III.II–III.X: that his main aim in the lengthy discussion there has been to get the principles of common-sense morality to satisfy this clarity and precision condition.

In introducing condition 2, Sidgwick writes:

> 2. The self-evidence of the proposition must be ascertained by careful reflection. It is needful to insist on this, because most persons are liable to confound intuitions, on the one hand with mere impressions and impulses, which to careful observation do not present themselves as claiming to be dictates of Reason; and on the other hand, with mere opinions, to which the familiarity that comes from frequent hearing and repetition often gives a false appearance of self-evidence which attentive reflection disperses. (339)

The key idea here is that there is more than one reason why we might be inclined immediately to judge that a proposition is true. We might do so because it is a proposition, like $1 + 1 = 2$, of which it seems to us if we understand it that it has to be true. But we also might immediately judge that a proposition is true for other reasons: because, for instance, everyone we know accepts it. Condition 2 requires us to filter out propositions that we immediately assent to for these other reasons, leaving only propositions that we immediately assent to for the same reason we immediately assent to $1 + 1 = 2$: that it seems to us if we understand them that they have to be true. A slightly paradoxical-sounding but helpful way to formulate condition 2 is to say that it requires the genuine appearance of self-evidence.

Condition 3 is more straightforward. The first sentence of what Sidgwick says in introducing it contains a helpful formulation:

> 3. The propositions accepted as self-evident must be mutually consistent. Here, again, it is obvious that any collision between two intuitions is a proof that there is error in one of the other, or in both. (341)

We can say that this condition requires "intrapersonal consistency"—consistency between the propositions that a person takes to be self-evident.

Condition 4 is concerned not with intrapersonal but with interpersonal consistency. Here is some of what Sidgwick says in introducing it:

> 4. Since it is implied in the very notion of Truth that it is essentially the same for all minds, the denial by another of a proposition that I have affirmed has a tendency to impair my confidence in its validity [. . .] It will be easily seen that the absence of such disagreement must remain an indispensable negative condition of the certainty of our beliefs. For if I find any of my judgments, intuitive or inferential, in direct conflict with a judgment of some other mind, there must be error somewhere: and if I have no more reason to suspect error in the other mind than in my own, reflective comparison between the two judgments necessarily reduces me temporarily to a state of neutrality. And though the total result in my mind is not exactly suspense of judgment, but an alternation and conflict between positive affirmation by one act of thought and the neutrality that is the result of another, it is obviously something very different from scientific certitude. (341–42)

The latter part of this passage is often quoted or cited today in philosophical literature on what has become a significant topic in epistemology: peer disagreement. The key question in that literature is what to make of a situation where someone just as well qualified to judge as you, an "epistemic peer," disagrees with you. We can adopt this contemporary terminology in naming Sidgwick's condition 4, and say that what it requires is "absence of peer disagreement."

The four conditions (or "criteria") are introduced in the *Methods* with striking abruptness. You might well want to ask: why does Sidgwick think just these four conditions are the conditions apparent axioms have to meet? Nothing in the *Methods* fully and directly addresses this question. But you can learn significantly more about Sidgwick's views on these topics from his articles in general epistemology, which are collected in *Essays on Ethics and Method*, edited by Marcus Singer.[3] In those articles Sidgwick considers criteria of knowledge put forward both by empiricists and by rationalists. He argues that there is no infallible criterion. Instead, the best we can do is to substitute for infallible criteria what he calls "methods of verification" in the "humbler task of excluding error."[4] The criteria he supports, which closely resemble conditions 1 through 4 in the *Methods*, are justified on the basis of past experience in correcting error (not only or primarily in ethics but in all fields of knowledge). They are, that is:

> based on the experience of the ways in which the human mind has actually been convinced of error, and been led to discard it.[5]

6.4. The Argument That the Principles of Common-Sense Morality Do Not in General Satisfy the Four Conditions

Immediately after introducing the four conditions, Sidgwick explains why the principles of common-sense morality do not in

THE CRITIQUE OF COMMON-SENSE MORALITY 105

general satisfy them. Again, the relevant passage is worth quoting at length:

> Now if the account given of the Morality of Common Sense in the preceding chapters be in the main correct, it is clear that, generally speaking, its maxims do not fulfil the conditions just laid down. So long as they are left in the state of somewhat vague generalities, as we meet them in ordinary discourse, we are disposed to yield them unquestioning assent, and it may be fairly claimed that the assent is approximately universal—in the sense that any expression of dissent is eccentric and paradoxical. But as soon as we attempt to give them the definiteness which science requires, we find that we cannot do this without abandoning the universality of acceptance. We find, in some cases, that alternatives present themselves, between which it is necessary that we should decide; but between which we cannot pretend that Common Sense does decide, and which often seem equally or nearly equally plausible. In other cases the moral notion seems to resist all efforts to obtain from it a definite rule: in others it is found to comprehend elements which we have no means of reducing to a common standard, except by the application of the Utilitarian—or some similar—method. Even where we seem to be able to educe from Common Sense a more or less clear reply to the questions raised in the process of definition, the principle that results is qualified in so complicated a way that its self-evidence becomes dubious or vanishes altogether. And thus in each case what at first seemed like an intuition turns out to be either the mere expression of a vague impulse, needing regulation and limitation which it cannot itself supply, but which must be drawn from some other source: or a current opinion, the reasonableness of which has still to be shown by a reference to some other principle. (342–43)

The general strategy of argument against common-sense morality sketched here depends crucially on the application of condition 1, the clarity and precision condition. As Sidgwick indicates at the beginning of the paragraph, the maxims of common-sense morality may appear to satisfy the other three conditions when "left in the state of somewhat vague generalities." But condition 1 requires that they not be left in that state, that instead they be given "the definiteness that science requires." Once they are required in this way to meet condition 1, the rest of the paragraph suggests, they can no longer be regarded as independent principles that satisfy all the other three conditions. Either they no longer command universal acceptance (or, as we formulated the condition, are no longer immune to peer disagreement) and so fail to satisfy condition 4. Or they are no longer in the right way independent, needing instead to be supplemented by an appeal to utilitarian considerations. Or they become so complicated that they no longer seem self-evident, and so fail to satisfy condition 2.

In the rest of the chapter Sidgwick again reviews the different elements of common-sense morality discussed in III.II through III.X, now with a view to demonstrating in each case that the general argument against common-sense morality applies: that common-sense morality does not consist of intuitive truths, of genuinely self-evident principles. To see how this works in one specific instance, we will focus on the example of promissory obligation. We will draw both on the discussion earlier in Book III, in III.VI, and on the discussion in III.XI.

There are two reasons to choose promissory obligation as the particular example on which to focus. One is that Sidgwick himself suggests that it is the most apparently compelling example of a self-evident common-sense axiom.

> [The duty of fulfilling express promises and distinct understandings] certainly seems to surpass in simplicity, certainty, and definiteness the moral rules that we have hitherto

discussed. Here, then, if anywhere, we seem likely to find one of those ethical axioms of which we are in search. (353)

The other reason is that promissory obligation is the go-to example that Sidgwick's most important deontological opponent in the later British intuitionist tradition, W. D. Ross, employs in arguing against consequentialism.

Sidgwick grants, as we would expect, that the principle

Promises ought to be kept

seems self-evident. He goes on, again as we would expect, to ask about a number of kinds of problem cases. Some such problem cases involve the situation under which the promise was made. There are cases both of promises elicited by force or fraud, and of promises to do something immoral. Sidgwick thinks common sense is clear that promises to do something immoral are not binding. He also thinks common sense holds that promises clearly elicited by force or fraud are not binding. But there are harder cases of the same kind.

> A promise may be made in consequence of [...] a fraudulent statement, and yet made quite unconditionally. Even so, if it were clearly understood that it would not have been made but for the false statement, probably most persons would regard it as not binding. But the false statement may be only one consideration among others, and it may be of any degree of weight; and it seems doubtful whether we should feel justified in breaking a promise, because a single fraudulent statement had been a part of the inducement to make it: still more if there has been no explicit assertion, but only a suggestion of what is false: or no falsehood at all, stated or suggested, but only a concealment of material circumstances. (306)

Other problem cases involve changes in the circumstances between the time at which the promise was made and the time at which it is to be kept. Granting that a binding promise was originally made, the question is whether the obligation still holds in these new circumstances. One kind of such problem case is a situation where the promisee dies between the time at which the promise is made and the time at which it is to be kept. Others involve changes the promiser perceives in the effects of keeping the promise. What if the change of circumstances means that keeping the promise is much more burdensome to the promiser than either the promiser or the promisee originally envisaged? What if the promiser now thinks that keeping the promise will harm the promisee, though the promisee does not agree?

At the end of III.VI, Sidgwick concludes:

> To sum up the results of the discussion: it appears that a clear *consensus* can only be claimed for the principle that a promise, express or tacit, is binding, if a number of conditions are fulfilled: viz. if the promiser has a clear belief as to the sense in which it was understood by the promisee, and if the latter is still in a position to grant release from it, but unwilling to do so, if it was not obtained by force or fraud, if we do not believe that its fulfilment will be harmful to the promisee, or will inflict a disproportionate sacrifice on the promiser, and if circumstances have not materially changed since it was made. If any of these conditions fails, the *consensus* seems to become evanescent, and the common moral perceptions of thoughtful persons fall into obscurity and disagreement. (310–11)

In drawing on this discussion in III.XI, Sidgwick notes in the same way that in cases where all these conditions are fulfilled there is a clear consensus that a promise has been made and is binding. And he emphasizes again that there are a range of other problem cases where there is no such consensus as to whether a promise has been made and as to how binding it remains.

The case is different with the other qualifications which we had to discuss. When once the question of introducing these has been raised, we see that Common Sense is clearly divided as to the answer. If we ask, (*e.g.*) how far our promise is binding if it was made in consequence of false statements, on which, however, it was not understood to be conditional; of if important circumstances were concealed, or we were in any way led to believe that the consequences of keeping the promise would be different from what they turn out to be; or if circumstances have materially altered since it was given, and we find that the results of fulfilling it will be different from what we foresaw when we promised; or even if it be only our knowledge of the consequences which has altered, and we now see that fulfilment will entail on us a sacrifice out of proportion to the benefit received by the promisee; or perhaps see that it will even be injurious to him though he may not think so—different conscientious persons would answer these and other questions (both generally and in particular cases) in different ways: and though we could perhaps obtain a decided majority for some of these qualifications and against others, there would not in any case be a clear *consensus* either way [. . .] It should be added, that some of these qualifications themselves suggest a reference to the more comprehensive principle of Utilitarianism, as one to which this particular rule is naturally subordinate. (353–54)

6.5. Responses to the Argument

The best way to assess the effectiveness of Sidgwick's critique of common-sense morality is to consider possible responses. We will consider two: defending absolutist deontology and moving to moderate deontology.

6.5.1. Defending Absolutist Deontology: Donagan

Most philosophers who have written about Sidgwick's argument think at least that he succeeds in showing that the Whewellian view he targets is untenable. But there is one important exception: the late-twentieth-century philosopher Alan Donagan. Donagan claimed that the Whewellian view survived Sidgwick's critique.

> [The intuitionist moralists'] formulations, definitions, and explanations for the most part varied in such ways as to admit of being taken for approximations, in different degrees, to the true system they were seeking; and to encourage them in the hope that by persevering they might find it.
>
> Sidgwick's demonstrations in [Book III, Chapters II–XI], that the deliverances of the ordinary moral consciousness are too imprecise and unclear to constitute precepts of an acceptable moral system, therefore fully accord with intuitionism. And his further demonstrations that the various formulations, definitions, and explanations of intuitionist morality are too controversial for them to claim that the system they are seeking has yet been found also accord with it. The intuitionists did not claim that all the precepts of any system then existing fully satisfied the four conditions Sidgwick laid down, but only that many of them approximated to doing so. And they might fairly have objected to Sidgwick's fourth condition as prejudicially rigorous: Even were the ideal intuitionist system to be discovered, it might be expected that some informed eccentrics would be found to dissent from parts of it.
>
> Sidgwick's elaborate campaign against intuitionism was therefore misdirected. It gained its objectives; but they were not defended, and the intuitionists were left unmolested in the positions they did defend. To dislodge them, Sidgwick had to

show, not that their method had not yet led to the complete success they looked for, but that it could not.[6]

Donagan's line in this passage is that Whewellian intuitionism should be understood as an ongoing philosophical program rather than as a project that has already been definitively completed. When Whewellian intuitionism is understood that way, he suggests, and when we relax condition 4 by not requiring agreement from some informed eccentrics, Sidgwick's critique will not seem decisive. The program of developing Whewellian intuitionism, of determining the correct view about all the problem cases Sidgwick appeals to, is still tractable. (Donagan himself tried to advance this program in a book called *The Theory of Morality*.[7]) And Donagan goes on to argue that Whewell had provided convincing solutions to some of the difficulties Sidgwick raises for the dogmatic intuitionist treatment of promissory obligation, those involving promises made partly on the basis of false beliefs.[8]

6.5.2. Moderate Deontology: Ross and Broad

Donagan defends a Whewellian view against Sidgwick's critique. A different deontological response was much more influential: to cease to treat deontological principles as absolute, adopting instead what these days is often called "moderate deontology." The philosopher most responsible for the development of moderate deontology was W. D. Ross.[9]

Ross's key innovation was to treat deontological principles as principles not of duty proper but of *prima facie* duty. In introducing this key concept, he says:

> I suggest "*prima facie* duty" [...] as a way of referring to the characteristic (quite distinct from that of being a duty proper) which

an act has, in virtue of being of a certain kind (e.g., the keeping of a promise), of being an act that would be a duty proper if it were not at the same time of another kind which is morally significant. Whether an act is a duty proper depends on *all* the morally significant kinds it is an instance of.[10]

Ross's main explicit motivation for introducing the concept is to avoid a standard problem for absolutist deontology that Sidgwick does not emphasize: the problem that absolute duties might conflict with one another (so, for example, that you might find yourself in a situation where the only way not to break a promise was to tell a lie). Ross explains how thinking of deontological principles as principles of *prima facie* duty rather than as principles of duty proper solves this problem in a passage from his later book, *Foundations of Ethics*.

> It is the overlooking of the distinction [. . .] between actual obligatoriness and the tendency to be obligatory, that leads to the apparent problem of conflict of duties, and it is by drawing the distinction that we solve the problem. For while an act may well be *prima facie* obligatory in respect of one character and *prima facie* forbidden in virtue of another, it becomes obligatory or forbidden only in virtue of the totality of its ethically relevant characteristics. We are perfectly familiar with this way of thinking when we are face to face with actual problems of conduct, but in theories of ethics responsibilities have often been overstated as being absolute obligations admitting of no exception, and the unreal problem of conflict of duties has thus been supposed to exist.[11]

Ross did not have Sidgwick particularly in mind when he introduced the concept of *prima facie* duty in *The Right and the Good*. Strikingly, though, in the very same year in which *The*

THE CRITIQUE OF COMMON-SENSE MORALITY 113

Right and the Good was published, the concept was independently introduced by C. D. Broad in *Five Types of Ethical Theory*. And Broad did have Sidgwick particularly in mind. He explicitly introduced the concept to develop a form of deontology that avoids Sidgwick's critique of dogmatic intuitionism.

> I think that anyone who reads the relevant chapters in Sidgwick will agree that the extreme form of Intuitionism which he ascribes to common-sense cannot be maintained. And he is no doubt right in thinking that common-sense wants to hold something like this, and retreats from it only at the point of the bayonet. Sidgwick's conclusion is that we are forced to a mainly teleological view [...] This does not seem to me to be certain: and I propose as briefly as possible [...] to state a form of Intuitionism which is not open to Sidgwick's objections and is not flagrantly in conflict with reflective-common sense.[12]

The key to this new form of intuitionism is Broad's version of the concept of *prima facie* duty (though Broad, unsurprisingly, doesn't use Ross's name for the concept).

> It seems quite clear that the Intuitionist will have to moderate his claims very greatly. He will be confined to statements about *tendencies* to be right and *tendencies* to be wrong. He can say that a lie has a very strong tendency to be wrong, and that it will be wrong unless telling the truth will have very great disutility or unless the situation be of a certain special kind in which it is a matter of honour to shield a third person.[13] (italics in the original)

It is worth thinking more about how the move from absolutist deontology to moderate deontology helps the deontologist respond to criticisms. One criticism, the one on which Ross focuses in introducing the concept of *prima facie* duty, is the criticism that conflicts of duty render absolutist deontology incoherent. This criticism is in the background in Sidgwick's critique of dogmatic intuitionism but he does not much emphasize it.[14] To respond to this criticism, the key is simply the idea of *prima facie* duty itself: the idea that two deontological principles can both apply to a situation, and point in opposite directions, without generating any contradiction.

The other criticism, the criticism which, as we have seen, Sidgwick emphasizes much more, is that the deontologist cannot provide principles which simultaneously satisfy conditions 1, 2, and 4.

To see how the move to moderate deontology helps the deontologist respond to this second criticism, we need to think more both about condition 1, the clarity and precision condition, and about the character of moderate deontology. As Sidgwick applies condition 1 to absolutist deontology, the absolutist has to answer for every problem case the question: is there a valid promise? If there is a valid promise, then it has to be kept. The principle about promising must, all on its own, settle the moral status of every case in which it applies.

No such condition can reasonably be applied to moderate deontology. The moderate deontologist may have, like the absolutist, to answer for every problem case the question: is there a valid promise? But the moderate deontologist's principle about promising cannot be required, all on its own, to settle the moral status of every case in which it applies. As Ross says, "whether an act is a duty proper depends on *all* the morally significant kinds it is an instance of"; an act's moral status will not be settled simply by its falling into the class of promises. So if there is a version of condition 1 that can reasonably be applied to moderate deontology, it will have to be different from the version of condition 1 Sidgwick applies to absolutist deontology.

Moreover, as we will see in more detail in Chapter 10, Ross does not think that all promises are equally obligatory. He thinks instead that different promises have different amounts of moral weight. It can seem problematic for the absolutist that there can be promises given on the basis of false beliefs, where the false beliefs can have varying degrees of importance, because the absolutist is committed to thinking either that there is a promise which has to be kept or that there is no promissory obligation at all. The moderate deontologist, by contrast, can allow the weight of promissory obligation to vary. Indeed, the moderate deontologist can allow the weight of promissory obligation to vary systematically with the kinds of considerations to which Sidgwick points in sketching his ranges of problem cases.

What all this means is that it is one thing to argue, as Sidgwick does, that the absolutist deontologist cannot provide a principle about promissory obligation that satisfies conditions 1, 2, and 4. It is a quite different and harder thing to argue that the moderate deontologist cannot provide a principle about promissory obligation that satisfies an appropriately modified version of condition 1, together with conditions 2 and 4. And, because he regrettably doesn't have the idea of moderate deontology, Sidgwick himself gives no such argument.

6.6. Dogmatic Intuitionism and Sidgwick's Fairness

We just considered responses to Sidgwick's argument that focused on the effectiveness of his critique of common-sense morality, and on whether it is possible to develop forms of deontology that are not vulnerable to his critique. Another kind of question about his critique is a question about his fairness: about whether he subjects the other two methods of ethics, egoism and utilitarianism, to the same level of critical scrutiny as intuitionism.

One concern about fairness is about Sidgwick's treatment of dogmatic intuitionism in contrast to his treatment of egoism. It arises when we compare his treatment of and conclusions about egoism, which we discussed in the previous chapter, with his treatment of and conclusions about dogmatic intuitionism. As we saw, in Book II Sidgwick sharply separates questions of the workability of the egoist method (or, strictly, as we saw, *methods*) from the question of the correctness of the egoist first principle. And he does not reject egoism even though he acknowledges that difficulties in measuring pain and pleasure mean that in a range of situations the main egoist method will not give a clear answer as to what we ought to do. By contrast, it might be said, in Book III Sidgwick is much harder on common-sense morality. He does not separate the question of the workability of the common-sense moralist's method from the question of the correctness of the common-sense moralist's first principles. And he does reject common-sense morality on the ground that difficult problem cases mean that in a range of situations common-sense morality does not give a clear answer to what we ought to do.

One way to defend Sidgwick from this charge of unfairness would be to argue that the reason egoism fails to give clear answers is different from the reason common-sense morality fails to give clear answers. If we allow the egoist the controversial assumption that each pleasure or pain always has a precise degree of pleasurability or painfulness, then it can be argued that the reason egoism doesn't give precise guidance is that we lack knowledge of consequences and of these precise degrees of pleasurability and painfulness. But such factual information is in principle available. And with the addition of that information, egoism would give a clear verdict about every case. By contrast, it can be argued, the reason common-sense morality fails to give a clear verdict on every case is different. The

THE CRITIQUE OF COMMON-SENSE MORALITY 117

theory itself lacks the resources to settle some questions about what we ought to do even if we combine it with full factual information.

Still, it is hard to see why this difference justifies Sidgwick in being harder on the intuitionist method than on the egoist method. Though the reason the egoist method fails to give verdicts in a significant range of cases may be different from the reason the intuitionist method fails to give verdicts in a significant range of cases, as methods the two seem equally problematic. Neither supplies a procedure which will in practice tell us how to act in every case. If we set aside the question of the justifiability of their first principles—as Sidgwick does for egoism in Book II—the dogmatic intuitionist method looks no more problematic than the egoist method.

A different question about Sidgwick's fairness arises when we contrast his treatment of the supposed first principles of the common-sense moralist with his treatment of his own favored philosophical intuitions. As we will see in the next chapter, when he introduces those intuitions, he says of them that they are

> of too abstract a nature, and too universal in their scope, to enable us to ascertain by immediate application of them what we ought to do in any particular case[.] (379)

When we reflect on the importance of condition 1, the clarity and precision condition, in Sidgwick's critique of the supposed intuitions of the common-sense moralist, an obvious concern arises. Isn't Sidgwick here exempting his own favored philosophical intuitions from the condition that plays a central role in his critique of the supposed intuitions of the common-sense moralist, the clarity and precision condition? And isn't this unfair? We will encounter this concern again in the next chapter.

Notes

1. That Sidgwick took the *Nichomachean Ethics* as in this respect a model does not mean that he was uncritical of it. He remarks at one point: "On the whole, there is probably no treatise so masterly as Aristotle's *Ethics*, and containing so much close and valid thought, that yet leaves on the reader's mind so strong an impression of dispersive and incomplete work" (Sidgwick 1886, 70).
2. Sidgwick gives Roman numerals for the four conditions. To try to avoid any confusion between references to the conditions and references to chapters of the Methods, I have used Arabic numerals for the four conditions.
3. Sidgwick 2000.
4. Sidgwick (1905) 2000, 166.
5. Sidgwick (1905) 2000, 170.
6. Donagan (1977a) 1992, 129.
7. Donagan 1977b.
8. Donagan (1977a) 1992, 132–34.
9. Richard Price articulated a form of moderate deontology in his 1758 book, *A Review of the Principal Questions of Morals* (Price 1974). But his version was not much noticed by later philosophers. As he says in the preface to *The Right and the Good*, Ross was directly influenced by Prichard 1912. But Ross developed moderate deontology much more clearly than Prichard did.
10. Ross 1930, 19–20.
11. Ross 1939, 86.
12. Broad 1930, 217–18.
13. Broad 1930, 222.
14. The third condition sets Sidgwick up to make the incoherence objection. He notes the way that the objection has been in the background of his critique but not its main focus at the end of III.XI: "It is therefore scarcely needful to proceed to a systematic examination of the manner in which Common Sense provides for the coordination of these principles. In fact, this question seems to have been already discussed as far as profitable: for the attempt to define each principle singly has inevitably led us to consider their mutual relations: and it was in the cases where two moral principles came into collision that we most clearly saw the vagueness and inconsistency with which the boundaries of each are determined by Common Sense" (360).

Further Reading

For more on the fairness and effectiveness of Sidgwick's critique of deontology, see Donagan 1977a; Phillips 2011, Chapter 4; and Hurka 2014b. For a defense of Sidgwick against charges of unfairness, see Lazari-Radek and Singer 2014, Chapter 5, Section 5. For a treatment of Sidgwick on virtue and virtues in Book III, see Crisp 2015, Chapters 5 and 6.

7
Philosophical Intuitionism
(*Methods* III.XIII)

In III.XI, as we saw in Chapter 6, Sidgwick argues that the principles put forward by common-sense moralists are not genuinely self-evident. By contrast, in III.XIII he argues that there are some genuinely self-evident ethical axioms. And he argues that these axioms support utilitarianism. III.XIII is the most important chapter in the *Methods*. As we have seen, Sidgwick sometimes characterized his distinctive view as "utilitarianism on an intuitional basis." III.XIII is the chapter in which the intuitional basis of utilitarianism is articulated.

The chapter is dense and presents significant interpretive difficulties. It is unfortunately not as clear as one would like it to be either just what the axioms say or just how they are related to utilitarianism. Discussing the chapter will therefore require us to address tricky issues both of interpretation and of philosophical substance.

7.1. Scylla and Charybdis

At the beginning of Section 3 Sidgwick writes,

> Can we then, between this Scylla and Charybdis of ethical inquiry, avoiding on the one hand doctrines that merely bring us back to common opinion with all its imperfections, and on the other hand doctrines that lead us round in a circle, find any way of obtaining self-evident moral principles of real significance? (379)

In Mediterranean mythology, Scylla and Charybdis are dangers that sailors face: a monster on one side of a narrow strait, a whirlpool on the other. The metaphor is used here to point to twin dangers facing those seeking genuine ethical intuitions, genuinely self-evident ethical principles. One danger is that they will provide principles which have real content but are not self-evident. The other is that they will provide principles which are self-evident, but only because they lack real content and are mere tautologies or the products of uninformative circular reasoning.

As we saw in the previous chapter, Sidgwick thinks the advocates of common-sense morality succumb to the first danger. They provide principles that have genuine content. But these principles are not self-evident. They do not satisfy the four conditions.

In Section 2, as he does elsewhere, Sidgwick suggests that Greek philosophers and those influenced by them systematically succumb to the second danger. By way of illustration, here is some of what he says about the supposed axiom, "It is right to act rationally":

> Here a word of caution seems required [. . .] against a certain class of sham-axioms, which are very apt to offer themselves to the mind that is earnestly seeking for a philosophical synthesis of practical rules, and to delude the unwary with a tempting aspect of clear self-evidence. These are principles which appear certain and self-evident because they are substantially tautological: because, when examined, they are found to affirm no more than that it is right to do that which is—in a certain department of life, under certain circumstances and conditions—right to be done [. . .] If we are told that [the dictate of Wisdom is]
> (1) It is right to act rationally
> [. . .] we do not at first feel that we are not obtaining valuable information. But when we find [. . .] that "acting rationally" is merely another phrase for "doing what we see to be right" [. . .] the tautology of our "principles" is obvious. (374–75)

The challenge Sidgwick faces in III.XIII is to avoid these twin dangers: to discover "self-evident moral principles of real significance."

7.2. Justice

Sidgwick thinks he can avoid the twin dangers. In introducing the philosophical intuitions, he writes:

> There are certain absolute practical principles, the truth of which, when they are explicitly stated, is manifest; but they are of too abstract a nature, and too universal in their scope, to enable us to ascertain by immediate application of them what we ought to do in any particular case; particular duties have still to be determined by some other method. (379)

The first part of this sentence says that the principles are self-evident. The second part, as we saw at the end of Chapter 6, raises the question whether Sidgwick is exempting his favored principles from the clarity and precision condition that was central to his critique of common-sense morality.

The obvious source of names for the philosophical intuitions is the paragraph beginning at the bottom of page 382, immediately following Sidgwick's articulations of them:

> I have tried to show how in the principles of Justice, Prudence, and Rational Benevolence as commonly recognised there is at least a self-evident element, immediately cognisable by abstract intuition. (382)

The intuitions are articulated in this order. And there is reason to believe that the order is not arbitrary—that Sidgwick thinks seeing that there is a self-evident principle of justice helps us see that there is a self-evident principle of prudence, and that seeing that there is a self-evident principle of prudence helps us see that there is a self-evident principle of rational benevolence. Given the importance of the claims in these passages to the overall project of the *Methods*, the passages in which Sidgwick articulates his philosophical intuitions are surprisingly brief. They will all be worth quoting in full.

In the main paragraph on the principle of justice, Sidgwick writes,

> One such principle was given in chap. i sec.3 of this Book; where I pointed out that whatever action any of us judges to be right for himself, he implicitly judges to be right for all similar persons in similar circumstances. Or, as we may otherwise put it, 'if a kind of conduct that is right (or wrong) for me is not right (or wrong) for some one else, it must be on the ground of some difference between the two cases, other than the fact that I and he are different persons.' A corresponding proposition may be stated with equal truth in respect of what ought to be done *to*—not *by*—different individuals. These principles have been most widely recognised, not in their most abstract and universal form, but in their special application to the situation of two (or more) individuals similarly related to one another: as so applied, they appear in what is popularly known as the Golden Rule, 'Do to others as you would have them do to you.' This formula is obviously unprecise in statement; for one might wish for another's co-operation in sin, and be willing to reciprocate it. Nor is it even true to say that we ought to do to others only what we think it right for them to do to us; for no one will deny that there may be differences in the circumstances—and even in the natures—of two individuals, A and B, which would make it wrong for A to treat B in the way in which it is right for B to treat A. In short, the self-evident principle strictly stated must take some such negative form as this; 'it cannot be right for A to treat B in a manner in which it would be

wrong for B to treat A, merely on the ground that they are two different individuals, and without there being any difference between the natures or the circumstances of the two which can be stated as a reasonable ground for difference of treatment.' Such a principle manifestly does not give complete guidance—indeed its effect, strictly speaking, is merely to throw a definite *onus probandi* [burden of proof] on the man who applies to another a treatment of which he would complain if applied to himself; but Common Sense has amply recognised the practical importance of the maxim: and its truth, so far as it goes, appears to me self-evident. (379–80)

This passage contains the official, precise formulation of the principle of justice, which we can label (J).

(J) It cannot be right for A to treat B in a manner in which it would be wrong for B to treat A, merely on the ground that they are two different individuals, and without there being any difference between the natures or the circumstances of the two which can be stated as a reasonable ground for difference of treatment. (380)

The earlier passage Sidgwick here refers back to, in III.I, tells us other things about (J). First, it can be obtained

by merely reflecting on the general notion of rightness as commonly conceived. (208)

Second, it reflects an important difference between our conceptions of ethical and of physical objectivity.

In the variety of coexistent physical facts we find an accidental or arbitrary element in which we have to acquiesce [. . .] If we ask, for example, why any portion of space contains more matter than any similar adjacent portion, physical science can only answer by stating (along with certain laws of change) some antecedent position of the parts of matter which needs explanation no less than the present [...] But within the range of our convictions of right and wrong, it will be generally agreed that we cannot admit a similar unexplained variation. We cannot judge an action to be right for A and wrong for B, unless we can find in the natures or circumstances of the two some difference which we can regard as a reasonable ground for difference in their duties. (209)

We can employ the language Sidgwick uses here to say that the principle of justice has two elements. First, there is the idea that there cannot be unexplained ethical variation: that if certain facts make an action right for me, the same facts would make an identical action right for anyone else. Second, there is a limit on what kind of fact can make actions right or ground rightness: mere differences as to who the people involved are, the mere fact that they are two different individuals, is not the kind of fact that can ground a difference in rightness.

We have had occasion to notice the principle of justice at earlier points in connection both with Sidgwick's verdict about common-sense morality and with his view of Kant's ethics. It matters to how we frame Sidgwick's verdict about common-sense morality because, if the principle of justice is one element of common-sense morality, then it is not strictly speaking true that Sidgwick thinks no principle of common-sense morality is self-evident. For the principle of justice is then a part of common-sense morality and it is self-evident. There is no deep philosophical question as to whether the principle of justice is a part of common-sense morality. But the shallower terminological question is still tricky. In Chapter 6 we distinguished broader and narrower conceptions of common-sense morality. On the broader conception, common-sense morality includes all the principles—egoist, utilitarian, and deontological—that common sense is disposed to accept. On the narrower conception, common-sense morality includes only the deontological principles common sense is disposed to accept. But even this clarification doesn't really settle the question of where to put the principle of justice. For it is neither distinctively deontological nor distinctively egoist or utilitarian. Deontologists, egoists, and utilitarians can all accept it; in itself it commits us to none of the three views.

Sidgwick thinks that the principle of justice is the right way to capture the truth that is less precisely captured by the familiar golden rule. He also thinks that the principle of justice is the important element of truth in Kant's first and most famous formulation—the universal law formulation—of the test for the rightness of actions, the categorical imperative. Sidgwick's view about Kant is that he has here identified a genuine intuition but exaggerated the amount of guidance it can give. As we saw in Chapter 1, Sidgwick makes this point informally in the short intellectual autobiography. He makes it more fully and carefully in III.I.

> If [. . .] I judge any action to be right for myself, I implicitly judge it to be right for any other person whose nature and circumstances do not differ from my own in some important respects [. . .] Indeed this test of the rightness of our volitions is so generally effective that Kant seems to have held that all particular rules of duty can be deduced from the one fundamental rule "Act as if the maxim of thy action were to become by thy will a universal law of nature." But this appears to me an error analogous to that of supposing that Formal Logic supplies a complete criterion of truth. I should agree that a volition which does not stand this test is to be condemned; but I hold that a volition which does stand it may after all be wrong. (209–10)

Given the project of III.XIII, the key philosophical question about the principle of justice (as about all the other philosophical intuitions) is: Does it avoid Scylla and Charybdis? Is it both self-evident and non-tautological?

My own inclination is to agree with Sidgwick that it is. But, when we recall his treatment of common-sense morality in III.XI, that answer again raises the question of his fairness. There is surprisingly little explicit reference to the four conditions in III.XIII. But, given the use of the conditions in III.XI, in saying that the principle of justice is self-evident Sidgwick is implicitly committed to saying that it satisfies the four conditions. The obvious worry is (again) about condition 1, the clarity and precision condition. Is it fair to say that the axiom of justice satisfies condition 1 even though it "manifestly does not give complete guidance," while requiring the putative axioms of the common-sense moralist to give a verdict about every problem case in order for them to satisfy that same condition?

7.3. Prudence

In articulating the principle of prudence, Sidgwick writes:

> The principle just discussed, which seems to be more or less clearly implied in the common notion of 'fairness' or 'equity', is obtained by considering the similarity of the individuals that make up a Logical Whole or Genus. There are others, no less important, which emerge in the consideration of the similar parts of a Mathematical or Quantitative Whole. Such a Whole is presented in the common notion of the Good—or, as is sometimes said, 'good on the whole'—of any individual human being. The proposition 'that one ought to aim at one's own good' is sometimes given as the maxim of Rational Self-Love or Prudence: but as so stated it does not clearly avoid tautology; since we may define 'good' as 'what one ought to aim at.' If, however, we say 'one's good on the whole,' the addition suggests a principle which, when explicitly stated, is, at any rate, not tautological. I have already referred to this principle as that 'of impartial concern for all parts of our conscious life'—we might concisely express it by saying 'that Hereafter *as such* is to be regarded neither less nor more than Now.' It is not, of course, meant that the good of the present may not reasonably be preferred to that of the future on account of its greater certainty: or again, that a week ten

years hence may not be more important to us than a week now, through an increase in our means or capacities of happiness. All that the principle affirms is that the mere difference of priority and posteriority in time is not a reasonable ground for having more regard to the consciousness of one moment than to that of another. The form in which it practically presents itself to most men is 'that a smaller present good is not to be preferred to a greater future good'(allowing for difference of certainty): since Prudence is generally exercised in restraining a present desire (the object or satisfaction of which we commonly regard as *pro tanto* 'a good'), on account of the remoter consequences of satisfying it. The commonest view of the principle would no doubt be that the present *pleasure* or *happiness* is reasonably to be foregone with the view of obtaining greater pleasure or happiness hereafter: but the principle need not be restricted to a hedonistic application; it is equally applicable to any other interpretation of 'one's own good,' in which good is conceived as a mathematical whole, of which the integrant parts are realized in different parts or moments of a lifetime. And therefore it is perhaps better to distinguish it here from the principle 'that Pleasure is the sole Ultimate Good,' which does not seem to have any logical connexion with it. (380–81)

There is much to unpack in this dense paragraph. The most important question about it is: just what *is* the principle of prudence? Exactly what does the principle of prudence say? This is a much trickier question to answer than is the question of what the principle of justice says. There are two different candidates in the paragraph to be the official, canonical formulation of the principle. And one of these candidates is itself ambiguous. So there are actually three possible interpretations of the principle.

The first candidate to be the canonical formulation of the principle is suggested by, though not explicitly stated in, the third and fourth sentences of the paragraph:

One ought to aim at one's own good on the whole.

The other candidate is variously stated further down in the paragraph. It is the idea that, as it is sometime put, pure time preference is irrational. We can employ the succinct statement,

> Hereafter *as such* is to be regarded neither less nor more than Now

to express this other candidate to be the canonical formulation of the principle.

To see that this means that there are indeed three different possible interpretations of the principle, begin with:

> Hereafter *as such* is to be regarded neither less nor more than Now.

As just noted, one standard way to describe what this sentence says is to say that it rules out pure time preference. The idea here is that it would be irrational to favor a present good over a future good of the same size merely because it is in the present not the future. It would not be irrational to prefer a present good over a future good of the same size on the grounds that you are less likely to be around to enjoy the good in the future. Nor would it be irrational to prefer a present good over a future good of the same size on the grounds that your capacity to enjoy the good will decay, so you will get more out of it in the present than the future. But if there are no reasons like these involving probabilities or changes in your capacities—if you prefer a present good over a future good of the same size merely because it is present—then you are being irrational.

> To see that this idea is different from the idea that
> One ought to aim at one's good on the whole

just notice that the principle that rules out pure time preference says nothing whatsoever about a requirement to aim at one's own good. It could be accepted by someone who had the extreme altruistic view that one should not aim at all at one's own good; that one should aim only at the good of other people. Such a person could still think it was self-evident that, in pursuing the good of other people, it was irrational to aim for smaller present goods for other people rather than larger future goods for other people merely on the ground that the present goods were present.

The interpretive problems do not end there. There is the further question of the meaning of the other formulation:

> One ought to aim at one's good on the whole.

To see that there are two different ways to interpret this principle, recall Ross's distinction between *prima facie* duty and duty proper. As we saw in Chapter 6, Ross reframes deontological principles. He understands them not, as the common-sense moralist does, as absolute principles. Instead, he understands them as principles of *prima facie* duty. So a deontological principle about promising would not say, "It is always right to keep a promise"; it would say instead, "There is a *prima facie* duty to keep a promise."

On one, weaker, interpretation,
One ought to aim at one's good on the whole

means:

> There is a *prima facie* duty to aim at one's good on the whole.

On the other, stronger, interpretation,

> One ought to aim at one's good on the whole

means:

> There is an absolute duty to aim at one's good on the whole.

These two possible interpretations of the maxim of prudence differ from each other in just the same way the two possible interpretations of deontological principles differ from one another. On the stronger interpretation of deontological principles, a deontological principle about promising would say that you always have to keep promises. On the weaker, *prima facie* duty interpretation, a deontological principle about promising would say that there is always a reason to keep your promises. But that reason might in some cases be outweighed by other considerations, so in those cases you should on balance not keep your promise. Similarly, on the stronger interpretation, the principle of prudence says you always have to aim at your own good. On the weaker interpretation, the principle of prudence says that there is a reason to aim at your own good. But that reason might get outweighed by other considerations, so on balance in certain cases you ought not to aim at your own good.

Having distinguished these three possible interpretations of the principle of prudence, we can now ask of each possible interpretation of the principle whether, so interpreted, the principle avoids Scylla and Charybdis—whether it is both genuinely self-evident and non-tautological.

Begin with the interpretation on which the principle of prudence simply rules out pure time preference. So interpreted, the principle of prudence resembles the principle of justice. And, like the principle of justice, it seems to me a good candidate to be both self-evident and non-tautological.

Now consider the two different interpretations of:
One ought to aim at one's good on the whole.

On the first, weaker, interpretation, this principle also looks self-evident. The key idea here is expressed by Sidgwick early in the paragraph about prudence: the idea that to be good just is to be that at which we ought to aim. If so, to say of something that it is my own good is to say that it is something at which there is *some* reason to aim. By the same token, however, the worry Sidgwick expresses early in the paragraph arises: the principle does not so obviously avoid tautology if it is self-evident just because of the definition of goodness, just because to be good is to be something at which one ought to aim.

> On the stronger interpretation,
> One ought to aim at one's good on the whole

says that there is an absolute duty to aim at one's own good. On this stronger interpretation, the principle is less likely to be a tautology. But it also seems unlikely either to be self-evident or indeed to be true. That something is one's good on the whole provides *some* reason to aim at it. But there will be lots of other things that are good, and there will be reasons to aim at these as well. And it is very likely to be the case that sometimes what best promotes one's own good will not be what best promotes these other goods or what best promotes the overall good. It is not at all self-evident that in such cases one ought still to aim at one's own good on the whole rather than aiming at what best promotes other goods or what best promotes the overall good.

These interpretive questions matter immediately for understanding this key passage in III.XIII. They also matter more broadly for understanding Sidgwick's views on egoism and on the dualism of the practical reason. Though he does not focus on it as much as he does on the connection between the maxim of benevolence and utilitarianism, Sidgwick does suggest in III.XIII that there is a connection between the principle of prudence and egoism.

> The axiom of Prudence, as I have given it, is a self-evident principle, implied in Rational Egoism. (386)

Moreover, given that Sidgwick thinks there is a rationally intractable standoff between utilitarianism and egoism, you might expect there to be a fundamental egoist intuition in III.XIII that conflicts with or contradicts utilitarianism.

To address the connection between the principle of prudence and egoism, we need again to remember the three different possible interpretations of the principle. First, consider the interpretation according to which the principle of prudence merely says:

> Hereafter *as such* is to be regarded neither less nor more than Now.

On this interpretation, the principle simply expresses the irrationality of pure time preference. It seems then to have no special connection to egoism. Egoists will endorse it. But so, as we saw earlier, will extreme altruists. And so will utilitarians. Interpreted in this way, the principle has no special connection to egoism, and it doesn't conflict with utilitarianism.

Second, consider the possibility that the principle of prudence is:

> There is a *prima facie* duty to aim at one's good on the whole.

This principle does have a closer connection to egoism. It does not by itself get you to egoism, for there may be other independent, non-egoist principles of duty too. And these independent principles may outweigh the *prima facie* duty to aim at one's own good on the whole. But, if this is the principle of prudence, there is a strategy of argument that would get you from the principle to rational egoism. The strategy would be to argue that there are no other genuine principles either of *prima facie* duty or of duty proper. If so, our only duty would be to aim at our own good on the whole, and egoism would be correct.

Despite this connection to egoism, the principle that there is a *prima facie* duty to aim at one's good on the whole is in itself compatible with utilitarianism. Utilitarians think that anyone's good is something at which we have a reason to aim. They thus can unproblematically accept the principle of prudence understood in this way as a principle of *prima facie* duty.

Third, consider the possibility that the principle of prudence is:

There is a duty proper to aim at one's good on the whole.

This principle has a still closer connection to egoism. If it is true, we always have to act as egoism requires. There is still a further short step from here to egoism. Egoism is the view that this is the only principle of duty. Just endorsing the principle as one true principle of duty does not automatically mean it is the only principle of duty. Still, there is a very limited range of coherent possible views that include this principle and other principles. For if any of the other principles ever require us to do something other than aim at our own good on the whole, there are likely to be situations where the two principles require different actions. If so, any theory that says both principles are true will be self-contradictory. In a way that will return to when we discuss the dualism of practical reason in Chapter 11, this means that the principle of prudence understood as a principle of duty proper is not readily compatible with utilitarianism. It will be compatible with utilitarianism only if utilitarianism and egoism always turn out to require the same actions.

The issues we have been pursuing in this section about how to understand the principle of prudence are important in their own right. But they will also help in the next sections. Though, as we will see, the parallels are not exact, Sidgwick clearly thinks of the discussion of prudence as a model for the discussion of rational benevolence. So the thinking we have done about how to interpret the principle of prudence and about how it is related to egoism will help us in thinking about how to interpret the maxim of benevolence and about how it is related to utilitarianism.

7.4. Rational Benevolence

In articulating the principle of rational benevolence, Sidgwick writes:

> So far we have only been considering the 'Good on the Whole' of a single individual: but just as this notion is constructed by comparison and integration of the different 'goods' that succeed one another in the series of our conscious states, so we have formed the notion of Universal Good by comparison and integration of the goods of all individual human—or sentient—existences. And here again, just as in the former case, by considering the relation of the integrant parts to the whole and to each other, I obtain the self-evident principle that the good of any one individual is of no more importance, from the point of view (if I may say so) of the Universe, than the good of any other; unless, that is, there are special grounds for believing that more good is likely to be realised in the one case than in the other. And it is evident to me that as a rational being I am bound to aim at good generally—so far as it is attainable by my efforts—not merely at a particular part of it.
> From these two rational intuitions we may deduce, as a necessary inference, the maxim of Benevolence in an abstract form: viz, that each one is morally bound to regard the good of any other individual at least as much as his own, except in so far as he judges it to be less, when impartially viewed, or less certainly knowable or attainable by him. (382)

Though, as the first sentence makes clear, the discussion of the principle of prudence is supposed to be a model for the discussion of the principle of rational benevolence, there are some obvious apparent differences between the two discussions. First, unlike in the discussion of the principle of prudence, there is no question about the canonical formulation of the principle of benevolence, which we can label (B):

(B) Each one is morally bound to regard the good of any other individual at least as much as his own, except in so far as he judges it to be less, when impartially viewed, or less certainly knowable or attainable by him.

Second, unlike the principle of prudence, the principle of benevolence is not presented as itself immediately self-evident. Instead it is presented as following from two prior principles, which are immediately self-evident and which we can label (U) and (R):

(U) The good of any one individual is of no more importance, from the point of view (if I may say so) of the Universe, than the good of any other.

(R) As a rational being I am bound to aim at good generally—so far as it is attainable by my efforts—not merely at a particular part of it.

Third, a new element is introduced by the qualification in (U), "from the point of view [. . .] of the Universe" (one of Sidgwick's most famous phrases). The presence of the qualifier in (U) raises obvious questions about (U), and so about (B) which is supposed to be derived from it. I am not the universe. So even if there is a requirement on the universe to be impartial, why does that mean there is a requirement on me to be impartial?

Despite these differences, the discussion of the principle of prudence is still a useful model. To draw on the model, it is helpful to notice an alternative way of formulating the maxim of benevolence. This alternative formulation involves the concept of universal good. Sidgwick refers to "the notion of Universal Good" in the first sentence on page 382. And in Section 4 he finds the maxim of benevolence in Samuel Clarke, expressed as:

A rational agent is bound to aim at universal good. (385)

When the maxim is expressed this way, it is clear that there are two possible interpretations of it, just as there are two possible interpretations of the principle of prudence when it is expressed by:

> One ought to aim at one's good on the whole.

On the weaker interpretation, the maxim of benevolence says that there is a *prima facie* duty to aim at universal good. On the stronger interpretation, the maxim of benevolence says that there is an absolute duty to aim at universal good.

We can then ask of the maxim of benevolence, as we asked of the principles of justice and prudence: Does it avoid Scylla and Charybdis? Is it both self-evident and non-tautological?

Begin with the weaker interpretation, on which the maxim of benevolence is a principle of *prima* facie duty. It does seem self-evident. If to be good is to be that at which we ought to aim, it is difficult to see how there is not a *prima facie* duty to aim at universal good. As with prudence, whether, so explained, the principle avoids tautology is a harder question.

On the stronger interpretation, the principle is less likely to be a tautology. But it is also less likely either to be self-evident or indeed to be true. There is surely strong reason to aim at universal good. But there may still be conflicting reasons. One kind of potentially conflicting reason is a partial reason. It may be that what best promotes universal good will produce much less good for me than some other outcome. In such cases, one view is that I ought to aim at what is best for me, not at what is universally best. Another kind of potentially conflicting reason is a deontological reason. It may be that aiming at universal good means violating a deontological principle (either an absolute deontological principle or a deontological principle of *prima* facie duty). In such cases one view is that I ought not to violate the deontological principle. So it is not at all self-evident that there is an absolute duty to aim at universal good: that I have a duty proper to aim at universal good even where doing so is much less good for me or where doing so means violating deontological principles. On this interpretation, then, the maxim of benevolence is very clearly non-tautological. But it is a poor candidate to be self-evident. It is very hard to see how it would satisfy the fourth condition, absence of peer disagreement.

This question of how to understand the maxim of benevolence—which of these two possible interpretations is correct—is the most important interpretive question about Sidgwick's discussion of rational benevolence. There are lots of additional interpretive questions. Whichever way you interpret the maxim of benevolence, there is the question how the maxim of benevolence (B) is derived from (U) and (R). And, of course, there is then the question what (U) and (R) themselves mean. Given the way Sidgwick presents things, we should expect that both (U) and (R) need to avoid Scylla and Charybdis—that they both need to be self-evident and non-tautological, and that they need to mean different things. So one job for a complete interpretation is to try to assign different meanings to (U) and (R) so that both are, indeed, self-evident and non-tautological. And there is then the further question of what becomes of the qualifier "from the point of view of the universe"? If that qualifier attaches to one of the premises, shouldn't it also attach to the conclusion? There is also the possibility, once you have answered all these questions, of trying to read back the structure of the discussion of rational benevolence into the discussion of prudence. If you did that, you would try to find a way to say that, in the case of prudence as in the case of rational benevolence, the principle is properly to be understood as a deduction from two prior propositions analogous to (U) and (R).

Fortunately, for our purposes there is no need to try to pursue these further very difficult questions.

7.5. Sidgwick's Axioms and Utilitarianism

As we have seen, Sidgwick characterized his own view as "utilitarianism on an intuitional basis." Book III Chapter XIII is where he sets out the genuine philosophical intuitions. So you would expect him, in this chapter, to say that the genuine intuitions support utilitarianism. And indeed he does say that, in two passages:

> I find that I arrive, in my search for really clear and certain ethical intuitions, at the fundamental principle of Utilitarianism. (387)

> Utilitarianism is thus presented as the final form into which Intuitionism tends to pass, when the demand for really self-evident first principles is rigorously pressed. (388)

The principle that supports utilitarianism is the maxim of benevolence. The key interpretive question is just how that support goes. Here again, the central issue is how to understand the maxim of benevolence. Is it a principle of *prima facie* duty or a principle of duty proper?

Interpreting Sidgwick on this matter is not straightforward. One way to approach the interpretive issue is to appeal to a principle of charity in interpretation. If we take this approach we ask: which understanding of the maxim of benevolence gives Sidgwick the better view? If understanding the maxim as a principle of *prima facie* duty gives Sidgwick a better view than he has if we understand it as a principle of duty proper, we should understand the maxim as a principle of *prima facie* duty.

There is a good case to be made that understanding the maxim of benevolence as a principle of *prima facie* duty gives Sidgwick the better view. For if the maxim of benevolence is interpreted as a principle of *prima facie* duty, it is a good candidate to be self-evident. And there is a clear connection between it and utilitarianism, though the connection is indirect. It is indirect because a *prima facie* duty to aim at universal good can be outweighed by competing partial or deontological duties. So, to get from the maxim of benevolence understood as a principle of *prima facie* duty to utilitarianism, you need to argue not just that the maxim of benevolence so understood is self-evident. You need also to argue that no competing principles are self-evident. The claim that the maxim of benevolence is self-evident does not do that further argumentative work for you.

If, on the other hand, the maxim of benevolence is interpreted as a principle of duty proper it is a much less good candidate to be self-evident. There is, it is true, a clear and more direct connection between it and utilitarianism. Utilitarianism is the view that it is the only principle of duty. Just endorsing the maxim of benevolence as one true principle of duty does not automatically mean it is the only principle of duty. But there is a very limited range of coherent possible views that include this principle and other principles. For if any of the other principles ever require us to do something other than aim at universal good there are likely to be situations where the two principles require different actions. If so, any theory that says both principles are true will be self-contradictory.

On balance, though, interpreting the maxim of benevolence as a principle of *prima facie* duty clearly seems to give Sidgwick the better philosophical view. The maxim of benevolence is then a good candidate to be self-evident; and there is still a plausible, though indirect, route from the maxim to the truth of consequentialism and utilitarianism. Thus the charitable interpretation of Sidgwick has it that the maxim of benevolence is a principle of *prima facie* duty rather than a principle of duty proper.

But there is also reason to worry that this interpretation of Sidgwick is too charitable: that it takes us too far away from what is in the text. It would be much easier to justify being charitable in this way if Sidgwick had the concept of *prima facie* duty and made elsewhere the distinction between principles of *prima facie* duty and principles of duty proper. But he does not. As we saw in Chapter 6, when he is considering deontological views he only ever conceives of them as involving principles of duty proper— he has the idea of absolutist deontology but not the idea of moderate deontology. And there is nowhere else in the text where Sidgwick employs Ross's concept of *prima facie* duty. So, it might be argued, the *prima facie* duty interpretation of the maxim of benevolence is too charitable to count as a straightforward interpretation of Sidgwick: it is more plausible as a specification of what he *ought* to have thought than as a specification of what he *did* think.

7.6. Sidgwick and Ross on What Is Really Self-Evident

Sidgwick and Ross are often thought to be the most important of the British intuitionists. It is illuminating to explore the contrasts in their views about what principles are really self-evident. After articulating his self-evident axioms, Sidgwick writes:

> I have tried to show how in the principles of Justice, Prudence, and Rational Benevolence as commonly recognised there is at least a self-evident element, immediately cognisable by abstract intuition; depending in each case on the relation which individuals and their particular ends bear as parts to their wholes, and to other parts of these wholes. I regard the apprehension, with more or less distinctness, of these abstract truths, as the permanent basis of the common conviction that the fundamental precepts of morality are essentially reasonable. No doubt these principles are often placed side by side with other precepts to which custom and general consent have given a merely illusory air of self-evidence: but the distinction between the two kinds of maxims appears to me to become manifest by merely reflecting on them. I know by direct reflection that the propositions, 'I ought to speak the truth,' 'I ought to keep my promises,'—however true they may be—are not self-evident to me; they present themselves as propositions requiring rational justification of some kind. On the other hand, the propositions, 'I ought not to prefer a present lesser good to a future greater good,' and 'I ought not to prefer my own lesser good to the greater good of another,' do present themselves as self-evident; as much (*e.g.*) as the mathematical axiom that 'if equals be added to equals the wholes are equal.' (382–83)

In a passage whose target (as usual in Ross's work) is Moore, not Sidgwick, Ross writes:

> If we are told, for instance, that we should give up our view that there is a special obligatoriness attaching to the keeping of promises

because it is self-evident that the only duty is to produce as much good as possible, we have to ask ourselves whether we really, when we reflect, *are* convinced that this is self-evident, and whether we really *can* get rid of our view that promise-keeping has a bindingness independent of productiveness of maximum good. In my own experience I find that I cannot, in spite of a very genuine attempt to do so; and I venture to think that most people will find the same, and that just because they cannot lose the sense of special obligation, they cannot accept as self-evident, or even as true, the theory that would require them to do so. In fact, it seems, on reflection, self-evident that a promise, simply as such, is something that *prima facie* ought to be kept, and it does *not*, on reflection, seem self-evident that production of maximum good is the only thing that makes an act obligatory.[1]

At first sight Sidgwick and Ross seem here to be in fundamental disagreement. Sidgwick claims consequentialist principles are self-evident and deontological principles are not self-evident. Ross claims consequentialist principles are not self-evident and deontological principles are self-evident.

But this way of putting it overlooks important differences between the principles they consider. Focus first on the consequentialist principles. The consequentialist principle whose self-evidence Ross denies—which he gets from Moore, not from Sidgwick—is "the only duty is to produce as much good as possible." This is a principle even stronger than the maxim of benevolence understood as a principle of duty proper. It is the view that that principle is the only true principle of duty. As we just saw, the charitable interpretation is that Sidgwick affirms only the maxim of benevolence understood as a principle of *prima facie* duty. Not only is this principle not the consequentialist principle whose truth Ross explicitly denies in the passage above. It is a principle Ross himself accepts. As he writes elsewhere in the same chapter:

> It seems self-evident that if there are things that are intrinsically good, it is a *prima facie* duty to bring them into existence rather

than not to do so, and to bring as much of them into existence as possible.[2]

Now focus on the deontological principles. The deontological principles whose self-evidence Sidgwick denies are not the deontological principles whose self-evidence Ross affirms. Sidgwick does not, unfortunately, have the idea that deontological principles might be understood as principles of *prima facie* duty. What he rejects are deontological principles of duty proper. But Ross too rejects deontological principles of duty proper. The deontological principles Ross affirms are deontological principles of *prima facie* duty. The example he gives in the paragraph of a deontological claim that is self-evident is "a promise, simply as such, is something that *prima facie* ought to be kept."

The disagreement between Sidgwick and Ross about what is really self-evident is thus less fundamental than it initially appears to be. If we interpret Sidgwick charitably, the key consequentialist axiom he accepts is the maxim of benevolence understood as a principle of *prima facie* duty. Ross agrees that this principle is self-evident. And Sidgwick and Ross agree that absolutist deontological principles are not self-evident. The remaining room for disagreement is about deontological principles understood, as Ross understands them, as principles of *prima facie* duty. Though Sidgwick regrettably does not consider the possibility of framing deontology in Ross's way, he would be likely to reject deontological principles of *prima facie* duty. As we saw in the previous chapter, he would need a new strategy of argument against such principles. For, as we saw, Rossian deontological principles are not vulnerable to the argument Sidgwick gives in III.XI against the absolutist deontological principles of the common-sense moralist.

As he tells us at more than one point in the chapter, nowhere in III.XIII does Sidgwick consider the truth of hedonism. The most the argument given or sketched in III.XIII could establish is consequentialism, the view that the right action is the one that produces the greatest amount of good. The question whether hedonism is true—whether happiness is the only thing that is intrinsically good—is explicitly reserved for the next chapter, III.XIV, to which we now turn.

Notes

1. Ross 1930, 39–40.
2. Ross 1930, 24.

Further Reading

The importance of III.XIII means that it is discussed by almost everyone who writes on Sidgwick. Two good pieces of literature with which to start are Schneewind 1977, Chapter 10, and Skelton 2008.

8
Hedonism (*Methods* III.XIV)

As we just saw, in III.XIII Sidgwick argues that intuitionism supports one crucial element of utilitarianism: the idea that each person ought to aim at universal good. But Sidgwick explicitly does not there consider another crucial element of utilitarianism: hedonism, the idea that pleasure is the sole intrinsic good.

Sidgwick argues for hedonism in III.XIV. In doing so he draws on two claims that, as we have seen, he made in earlier chapters. One is the claim, made in I.I, that the only candidates to be the sole intrinsic good are happiness and virtue. The other is the claim, made in I.IX, that "nothing [. . .] appears to possess goodness out of relation to human existence, or at least to some consciousness or feeling" (113).

III.XIV has a complex and potentially confusing structure because Sidgwick argues successively against two different alternatives to hedonism.[1] In the first two sections of the chapter, he argues against a monistic alternative according to which virtue is the sole intrinsic good. In the latter half of the chapter, he argues against a pluralistic alternative according to which pleasure is one of the things that are intrinsically good but not the only good thing. According to this pluralist alternative, other states of consciousness—cognition of truth, contemplation of beauty, free or virtuous action—are also intrinsically good.

8.1. Virtue as the Sole Good

Sidgwick begins with the monistic alternative to hedonism suggested by his provisional assumption that the only two candidates to be the sole intrinsic good are happiness and virtue—that virtue is the sole intrinsic good. He considers and argues against three main versions of this idea.

The first version says what is intrinsically good are particular virtues. The most straightforward way to develop this idea is to treat these particular virtues—as Sidgwick did in Book III—as a matter of following absolute moral rules. But then he can draw on the arguments of III.XI and III.XIII, and claim that there are no valid such absolute rules that can be articulated independently of specifying what is intrinsically good.

> If the conclusions of the preceding chapters are to be trusted, it would seem that the practical determination of Right Conduct depends on the determination of Ultimate Good. For we have seen (a) that most of the commonly received maxims of duty—even those which at first sight appear absolute and independent—are found when closely examined to contain an implicit subordination to the more general principles of Prudence and Benevolence: and (b) that no principles except these, and the formal principle of Justice or Equity can be admitted as at once intuitively clear and certain; while, again, these principles themselves, so far as they are self-evident, may be stated as precepts to seek (1) one's good on the whole, repressing all seductive impulses prompting to undue preference for particular goods, and (2) others' good no less than one's own, repressing any undue preference for one individual over another [. . . So . . .] to say that 'General Good' consists solely in general Virtue—if we mean by Virtue conformity to such prescriptions and prohibitions as make up the main part of the morality of Common Sense—would obviously involve us in a logical circle; since we have seen that the exact determination of these prescriptions and prohibitions must depend on the definition of General Good. (391-92)

He then, interestingly, considers a second version of the idea that the good is a matter of particular virtues where the particular virtues are not understood in terms of following definite absolute rules.

> Nor, I conceive, can this argument be evaded by adopting the view of what I have called 'Aesthetic Intuitionism' and regarding Virtues as excellences of conduct clearly discernible by trained insight, although their nature does not admit of being stated in definite formulae. (392)[2]

Here too, Sidgwick claims, the particular virtues cannot be specified without making judgments about what is good, so the attempt to identify virtue as the sole good again generates a vicious circle.

> Our notions of special virtues do not really become more independent by becoming more indefinite: they still contain, though perhaps more latently, the same reference to 'Good' [. . .] as an ultimate standard. This appears clearly when we consider any virtue in relation to the cognate vice [. . .] into which it tends to pass over when pushed to an extreme, or exhibited under inappropriate conditions. For example, Common Sense may seem to regard Liberality, Frugality, Courage, Placability, as intrinsically desirable: but when we consider their relation respectively to Profusion, Meanness, Foolhardiness, Weakness, we find that Common Sense draws the line in each case not by immediate intuition, but by reference [. . .] to the general notion of 'Good'. (392)

In Section 2, Sidgwick considers a third variant of the idea that virtue is the sole good. This variant understands virtue not as a matter of the different particular virtues, but instead as a matter of a single virtuous disposition, the disposition to do what we think to be right. Sidgwick thinks this variant avoids the circularity arguments he has thus far developed. But he still thinks it a view that common sense on reflection clearly rejects.

> I admit that if subjective rightness or goodness of Will is affirmed to be the Ultimate Good, the affirmation does not exactly involve the logical difficulty I have been urging. None the less it is fundamentally opposed to Common Sense; since the very notion of subjective rightness or goodness of will implies an objective standard, which it directs us to seek, but does not profess to supply. It would be a palpable and violent paradox to set before the right-seeking mind no end except this right-seeking itself, and to affirm this to be the sole Ultimate Good, denying that any effects of right volition can be in themselves good, except the subjective rightness of future volitions, whether of self or of others. (394)

When we try to do the right thing, we think we can succeed or fail; we don't think merely making the effort guarantees success.

8.2. Sidgwick, Virtue, and Virtue Ethics

The arguments we have just been considering from the first two sections of III.XIV are arguments that virtue cannot be central to ethics in one way—by being the sole intrinsic good in a consequentialist theory.

The arguments we considered in Chapter 6 are arguments that virtue cannot be central to ethics in a different way. In Book III, Chapters I through XI, Sidgwick discusses virtues and absolute moral rules together. We focused in particular on his discussion of promissory obligation. That discussion is simultaneously a discussion of an absolute moral rule requiring that promises be kept and of a corresponding virtue, good faith. And the same is true in other cases: there is a discussion of an absolute rule requiring truth-telling that is simultaneously a discussion of the corresponding virtue of veracity. The bulk of the discussion in Book III is in this way both a discussion of deontology and a discussion of virtues understood in a deontological way as dispositions to follow such absolute rules.

Neither of these ways of making virtue central to ethics would amount to what is today called virtue ethics. Though Sidgwick has much of philosophical interest to say about virtue in general and about specific virtues, and though he is much influenced by Aristotle, he does not really have the contemporary idea of virtue ethics. Philosophers in the past fifty or sixty years who have argued for virtue ethics have often seen it as a third way in moral theory.[3] They have taken earlier philosophers, most often Aristotle, to supply the model for an alternative approach to moral theory that is neither consequentialist nor deontological. Sidgwick does not consider virtue ethics so conceived. His discussions of virtue always place virtue either in a consequentialist or a deontological framework. They do not involve thinking of the notion of virtue as supplying an alternative to these consequentialist and deontological frameworks.[4]

8.3. Sidgwick on Hedonism and Pluralism

In Section 4 of III.XIV Sidgwick articulates a pluralistic alternative to hedonism. The pluralistic alternative allows that happiness is one of the things that is intrinsically good, but has it that other things are intrinsically good too.

Happiness or pleasure is explained in the way we would expect given the discussion in Book II (which we talked about in Chapter 5). It is a matter of desirable feelings. The route to the pluralist alternative begins with the observation that there is more to consciousness than feelings.

> It may be urged that our conscious experience includes besides Feelings, Cognitions and Volitions, and that the desirability of these must be taken into account. (398)

To employ more familiar contemporary philosophical terminology, we might call cognitions "beliefs" and volitions "desires."

Sidgwick then argues that cognitions and volitions (or beliefs and desires) are not valuable in the way that feelings are. The mere experience of having them is neutral in respect of value.

> I think, however, that when we reflect on a cognition as a transient fact of an individual's psychical experience [...] it is seen to be an element of consciousness quite neutral in respect of desirability: and the same may be said of Volitions. (398)

If we value cognitions and volitions, it is something else about them that we value: not the experience of having them but their correctness. Sidgwick explains the idea on page 399 with the example of knowledge:

> A man may prefer the mental state of apprehending truth to the state of half-reliance on generally accredited fictions, while recognising that the former state may be more painful than the latter, and independently of any effect which he expects either state to have upon his subsequent consciousness. Here, on my view, the real object of preference is not the consciousness of knowing truth, considered merely as consciousness—the element of pleasure or satisfaction in this being more than outweighed by the concomitant pain—but the relation between the mind and something else, which, as the very notion of 'truth' implies, is whatever it is independently of our cognition of it, and which I therefore call objective. (399)

Similarly, if the volitions or volitions and cognitions involved in virtue and in contemplation of beauty are valuable, that is not because of the nature of the experience of having them, but because of their objective correctness.

> The preference of conformity to Virtue, or contemplation of Beauty, to a state of consciousness recognised as more pleasant seems to depend on a belief that one's conception of Virtue or Beauty corresponds to an ideal to some extent objective and valid for all minds. (400)

Sidgwick thus arrives at the pluralistic alternative to hedonism:

> We may regard cognition of Truth, contemplation of Beauty, Free or Virtuous action, as in some measure preferable alternatives to Pleasure or Happiness—even though we admit that Happiness must be included as a part of Ultimate Good. (400)

In Section 5 Sidgwick argues against this pluralistic view and in favor of hedonism. The argument has two main elements. The first is contained in the first paragraph of Section 5, which is worth quoting in full:

> I think, however, that this view ought not to commend itself to the sober judgment of reflective persons. In order to show this, I must ask the reader to use the same twofold procedure that I before requested him to employ in considering the absolute and independent validity of common moral precepts. I appeal first to his intuitive judgment after due consideration when fairly placed before it: and secondly to a comprehensive comparison of the ordinary judgments of mankind. As regards the first argument, to me at least it seems on reflection clear that these objective relations of the conscious subject, when distinguished from the

consciousness accompanying and resulting from them, are not ultimately and intrinsically desirable; any more than material objects are, when considered apart from any relation to conscious experience. Admitting that we have actual experience of such preferences as have just been described, of which the ultimate object is something that is not merely consciousness: it still seems to me that when (to use Butler's phrase) we "sit down in a cool hour," we can only justify to ourselves the importance we attach to any of these objects by considering its conduciveness, in one way or another, to the happiness of sentient beings. (400–401)

In the first part of this paragraph, Sidgwick refers back to the four conditions employed in III.XI in arguing against the common-sense moralist. In describing the procedure as "twofold," Sidgwick here presents the four conditions as coming in two pairs. The first pair consists of conditions 1 and 2, the clarity and precision and genuine appearance of self-evidence conditions. The second pair consists of 3 and 4, the intrapersonal and interpersonal consistency conditions. Sidgwick then says that the pluralist intuition that these "objective relations of the conscious subject" are intrinsically valuable does not satisfy condition 2. When considered in isolation, the fact that a belief is true or that a motivation is virtuous is not intrinsically valuable, any more than material objects considered in isolation are intrinsically valuable.

He then turns to conditions 3 and 4, emphasizing condition 4. He admits that condition 4 presents a difficulty: that it is hard to claim that there is no peer disagreement as to whether the objective relations of the conscious subject are intrinsically valuable.

The second argument, that refers to the common sense of mankind, obviously cannot be made completely cogent; since, as above stated, several cultivated persons do habitually judge that knowledge, art, etc.—not to speak of Virtue—are ends independently of the pleasure derived from them. (401)

But he proposes to minimize the importance of this apparent disagreement in two ways. First, he argues (on pages 401–2) that

> [t]hese elements of "ideal good" [...] seem to obtain the commendation of Common Sense, roughly in proportion to the degree of [their] productiveness [of pleasure]. (401)

Second, he offers on pages 402 through 406 four reasons why common sense might not want to say that pleasure was the sole intrinsic good even if this was in fact common sense's considered view. They are: (I) That saying that pleasure is the only intrinsic good misleadingly suggests that only coarse physical pleasures are valuable, rather than that the full range of pleasures, including refined mental pleasures, are valuable; (II) That saying that pleasure is the only intrinsic good misleadingly suggests that we will be happiest if our only conscious aim is our own pleasure; (III) That saying that pleasure is the only intrinsic good misleadingly suggests the egoist view that only our own pleasure counts rather than the more attractive and more plausible utilitarian view that everyone's pleasure counts equally; (IV) That in the pursuit of general happiness, just as in the pursuit of individual happiness, it will often be better to aim at something else; and (as in II) saying that pleasure is the only intrinsic good misleadingly suggests that we will produce the most general happiness if that is always our conscious aim.

At the end of Section 5 Sidgwick appeals to a further consideration: that pluralistic views are not properly coherent and systematic.

> If, however, [Hedonism] be rejected, it remains to consider whether we can frame any other coherent account of Ultimate Good. If we are not to systematise human activities by taking Universal Happiness as their common end, on what other principles are we to systematise them? (406)

This appeal to a requirement for coherence and system seems liable to be question-begging: to guarantee that some monistic view like hedonism must be correct and that pluralist views must be wrong. Both Moore (who was a pluralist about the good) and Ross (who was a pluralist about both the right and the good) reject this kind of appeal as illegitimate. Moore writes:

> To search for 'unity' and 'system,' at the expense of truth, is not, I take it, the proper business of philosophy, however universally it may have been the practice of philosophers.[5]

Ross concurs:

> Loyalty to the facts is worth more than a symmetrical architectonic or a hastily reached simplicity.[6]

8.4. Moore and Ross on Hedonism and Pluralism

Sidgwick's two most important successors in the British intuitionist tradition, Moore and Ross, both reject hedonism. Characteristically, in doing so Moore responds directly to Sidgwick. Also characteristically, Ross does not. Nonetheless, the pluralistic view Ross defends is strikingly similar to the pluralistic view Sidgwick rejects.

Moore responds in particular to the first element of Sidgwick's argument against pluralism. As we just saw, Sidgwick argues that on their own the "objective relations of the conscious subject" involved in true belief, virtuous action, and the contemplation of genuinely beautiful objects have no intrinsic value. He infers (anyway as Moore sees it) that all the value in complex states involving both pleasure and these objective relations comes from the pleasure. In making this inference, Moore thinks Sidgwick makes the mistake of failing to notice what Moore calls the principle of "organic unities" or "organic relations."

This principle says that the intrinsic value of a whole is not necessarily equal to the sum of the intrinsic values of its parts. For instance, the value of the whole consisting of the admiring contemplation of a genuinely beautiful object might be greater than the sum of the individual values of the admiring contemplation on its own and of the beautiful object on its own. Moore applies this idea to criticize the argument we just saw Sidgwick giving in the first paragraph of Section 5 of III.XIV.

> From the fact that no value resides in one part of a whole, considered by itself, we cannot infer that all the value belonging to the whole does reside in the other half, considered by itself [. . .] Prof Sidgwick's argument [. . .] depends on the neglect of that principle [. . .] I [. . .] call the principle of 'organic relations'. The argument is calculated to mislead, because it supposes that, if we see a whole state to be valuable, and also see that one element of that state has no value *by itself*, then the other element, *by itself*, must have all the value that belongs to the whole state. The fact is, on the contrary, that, since the whole may be organic, the other element need have no value whatever, and that even if it have some, the value of the whole may be very much greater.[7]

Thus, as Moore sees it, Sidgwick makes a mistake in inferring that hedonism is true simply because the objective relations involved in knowledge, virtue, and aesthetic contemplation have no intrinsic value on their own. The whole might have a value that comes neither from the objective relations on their own nor from the conscious experiences on their own.

In the light of the importance Moore thinks the principle of organic unities has, it is unsurprising that his own pluralistic alternative to hedonism emphasizes the importance of goods that are highly complex organic unities. Moore's own positive view is thus not specially like the pluralistic view Sidgwick considers and rejects in III.XIV. Ross, unlike Moore, does not respond directly to Sidgwick. Nonetheless Ross defends a version of pluralism that is strikingly similar to the one Sidgwick considers and rejects. Ross thinks that there are four things that are intrinsically valuable: virtue, happiness, knowledge, and a complex good, desert or deservingness, which is a matter of the virtuous being happy and the vicious miserable rather than the reverse. Three things are on both Sidgwick's and Ross's lists: pleasure, knowledge, and virtue. The lists differ only in that the further items on Sidgwick's list are free action and enjoyment of beauty, while the further item on Ross's list is desert.

Ross characteristically appeals to intuitions about quite abstractly described possible worlds to defend his pluralist view. In arguing, against hedonism, that virtue is also valuable, he writes:

> The first thing for which I would claim that it is intrinsically good is virtuous disposition and action, i.e. action, or disposition to act, from any one of certain motives, of which at all event the most notable are the desire to do one's duty, the desire to bring into being something that is good, and the desire to give pleasure and to save pain to others. It seems clear that we regard all such actions and dispositions as having value in themselves apart from any consequence. And if any one is inclined to doubt this and to think that, say, pleasure alone is intrinsically good, it seems to me enough to ask the question whether, of two states of the universe holding equal amounts of pleasure, we should really think no better of one in which the actions of all the persons in it were thoroughly virtuous than of one in which they were highly vicious.[8]

We saw in the previous chapter that the apparent starkness of the conflict between Sidgwick and Ross as to the intuitiveness of consequentialist and deontological principles is significantly reduced when we focus carefully on the exact consequentialist and deontological principles they consider. It turns out that the deontological principles Ross endorses are not the deontological principles Sidgwick rejects, and that the consequentialist principle Sidgwick endorses is not the consequentialist principle Ross rejects. Nothing similar seems true about their conflicting views about hedonism and pluralism. Sidgwick is perhaps more tentative in arguing in favor of hedonism than Ross is in arguing against it. But their intuitions about the matter nonetheless really do starkly conflict.

8.5. Is Hedonism a Philosophical Intuition?

It is worth asking what status and level of certainty Sidgwick takes his argument for hedonism to have. In doing so we should separate the argument against the monistic alternative to hedonism in the first two sections of III.XIV from the argument against the pluralistic alternative in Sections 4 and 5. Sidgwick seems to take the arguments against the monistic alternative to be decisive and not to need to rely on anything like the candidate intuitions considered in III.XI and in III.XIII. But, as we saw, in giving his argument against the pluralist alternative he does explicitly appeal to intuitions, and indeed to the four conditions articulated in III.XI.

One view about this matter would be that all the genuine philosophical intuitions are to be found in III.XIII. So the fact that Sidgwick does not defend hedonism in III.XIII shows that he does not think it is a philosophical intuition. It must instead have some different and lower status. An opposing view would be that Sidgwick explicitly appeals to the four conditions in III.XIV, and that that shows that he thinks hedonism is a philosophical intuition with exactly the same status and level of certainty as the philosophical intuitions discussed in III.XIII.

But there is also an intermediate possibility that seems to me attractive. To see the availability of this intermediate possibility, we need to remember what Sidgwick says in introducing the four conditions in III.XI:

> There seem to be four conditions, the complete fulfilment of which would establish a significant proposition, apparently self-evident, in the highest degree of certainty attainable: and which must be approximately realised by the premises of our reasoning in any inquiry, if that reasoning is to lead us cogently to trustworthy conclusions. (338)

As we noted, this sentence suggests the possibility that candidate self-evident propositions may fulfill the four conditions to different degrees, and that if they fulfill the conditions less fully they will be less certain. The interpretive suggestion would then be that this is what Sidgwick thinks about hedonism as contrasted with the philosophical intuitions in III.XIII. Hedonism fulfills the conditions, but does so less fully than do the philosophical intuitions in III.XIII. Like them, it is a philosophical intuition. But it fulfills the conditions less completely, and so has a lower level of certainty.

However exactly we answer the question about the status and level of certainty of the intuitional argument for hedonism, the argument for hedonism is an essential part of the intuitional argument for utilitarianism. Chapter XIV (and Book III) end with an endorsement of this argument.

> I am finally led to the conclusion (which at the close of the last chapter seemed to be premature) that the Intuitional method rigorously applied yields as its final result the doctrine of pure Universalistic Hedonism—which it is convenient to denote by the single word, Utilitarianism. (406–7)

Nothing about this passage suggests that the intuitional argument for utilitarianism is anything other than a success. But, as we will see in the next chapter, when Sidgwick returns to the argument in IV.II, things sound very different.

Notes

1. The convoluted structure of III.XIV is a product in part of the chapter's history. In early editions of the *Methods* Sidgwick argued in III.XIV only against the monistic alternative to hedonism. As he notes in the Preface to the fourth edition (xiv–xv), the arguments against pluralistic alternatives to hedonism were added in response to "objections ably urged by Mr. Rashdall." Though it is reasonably clear that Sidgwick argues against the monistic alternative in Sections 1 and 2 of III.XIV, and against a pluralistic alternative in Sections 4 and 5 of III.XIV, that still leaves the question what exactly is going on in Section 3. Thomas Hurka plausibly suggests (Hurka 2014a, 216–18) that Section 3 is supposed in effect to consist of arguments against Rashdall's version of pluralism which are to some extent independent of the arguments against pluralism offered in Sections 4 and 5; and that these are bad arguments because Sidgwick doesn't properly appreciate Rashdall's view. In order to simplify what is already complicated enough and to focus on the stronger parts of Sidgwick's case for hedonism, I will not say more about Section 3.
2. In characterizing aesthetic intuitionism in III.II, Sidgwick says of it:

   the attempt to state an explicit maxim, by applying which we may be sure of producing virtuous acts of any kind, must fail: we can only give a general account of the virtue—a description, not a definition—and leave it to trained insight to find in any particular circumstances the act that will best realise it. (228)

   The idea of aesthetic intuitionism is interesting for at least two reasons. One is that the question arises how aesthetic intuitionism is related to the three "phases" (or "versions" or "varieties") of intuitionism—perceptional, dogmatic, and philosophical—that Sidgwick distinguishes in I.VIII and that we discussed in Chapter 4. It is tempting to identify aesthetic intuitionism with perceptional intuitionism. But if they were straightforwardly the same Sidgwick would not need a new name for the idea introduced in III.II. So the question then arises how to distinguish perceptional intuitionism from aesthetic intuitionism. One answer is that aesthetic intuitionism is a variant of perceptional intuitionism. A perceptional intuitionist could believe that the really self-evident moral judgments are judgments about particular cases and still think that the truth in these particular judgments could be captured in general rules. An aesthetic intuitionist would then be, by contrast, a perceptional intuitionist who denied that such general rules can be framed.

The other reason the idea of aesthetic intuitionism is interesting is that the question arises whether it is vulnerable to the argument against dogmatic intuitionism developed in III.XI. The key issue is about the clarity and precision condition. Aesthetic intuitionism by definition does not give formulae that generate definite verdicts about every case. So either it immediately thereby fails to satisfy the clarity and precision condition, or there is an alternative way to understand that condition. If the latter, that alternative understanding of the clarity and precision condition could be applied to dogmatic intuitionism too.

3. Anscombe 1958; Foot 1978; MacIntyre 1981.
4. Interestingly, one contemporary of Sidgwick's whom he discusses at length—Jacques Martineau—has sometimes been taken by recent philosophers to be a source for virtue ethics. Sidgwick discusses Martineau in the *Lectures on the Ethics of T. H. Green, Mr. Herbert Spencer and J. Martineau* (Sidgwick 1902) and in *Methods* III.XII. As the beginning of III.XII makes clear, Sidgwick regards Martineau as offering not a wholly new kind of theory but instead a variant of deontology (or intuitionism), a variant no more successful than the Whewellian variant on which Sidgwick focuses in the bulk of Book III. As he says:

> It does not therefore follow that comparison of motives is not the final and most perfect form of the moral judgment. It might approve itself as such by the systematic clearness and mutual consistency of the results to which it led, when pursued by different thinkers independently: and by its freedom from the puzzles and difficulties to which other developments of the Intuitional Method seem to be exposed.
>
> It appears, however, on examination that, on the one hand, many (if not all) of the difficulties which have emerged in the preceding discussion of the commonly received principles of conduct are reproduced in a different form when we try to arrange Motives in order of excellence: and on the other hand, such a construction presents difficulties peculiar to itself (364–65).

5. Moore 1903, 222.

6. Ross 1930, 23.
7. Moore 1903, 92–93.
8. Ross 1930, 134.

Further Reading

For more on Sidgwick and hedonism, see Hurka 2014a, Chapter 9, and Crisp 2015, Chapter 3.

9

Utilitarianism: Meaning and Proof (*Methods* IV.I and IV.II)

There is much to discuss in the first two chapters of Book IV. In IV.I Sidgwick makes distinctions and notices issues of enduring significance for the utilitarian tradition. IV.II, meanwhile, is the only rival to III.XIII for the title of most important chapter in the *Methods*. While, on balance, III.XIII is more important overall, IV.II contains the densest concentration of important material.

9.1. The Meaning of Utilitarianism

Sidgwick begins IV.I with a precise characterization of utilitarianism, together with the suggestion that "Universalistic Hedonism" might be a better name.

> By Utilitarianism is here meant the ethical theory, that the conduct which, under any given circumstances, is objectively right, is that which will produce the greatest amount of happiness on the whole; that is, taking into account all whose happiness is affected by the conduct. It would tend to clearness if we might call this principle, and the method based upon it, by some such name as 'Universalistic Hedonism'. (411)

After emphasizing that utilitarianism is distinct from egoism and has no necessary connection with any psychological theory about the origin of the moral sentiments, he makes a distinction of considerable importance for later developments of utilitarianism.

> The doctrine that Universal Happiness is the ultimate *standard* must not be understood to imply that Universal Benevolence is the only right or always best *motive* of action. For, as we have before observed, it is not necessary that the end which gives the criterion of rightness should always be the end at which we consciously aim: and if experience shows that the general happiness will be more satisfactorily attained if men frequently act from other motives than pure universal philanthropy, it is obvious that these other motives are reasonably to be preferred on Utilitarian principles. (413)

The language Sidgwick uses to make this distinction has been widely adopted. The paragraph suggests two terminological options: the distinction between utilitarianism as a *standard* and universal benevolence as a *motive*; and the distinction between utilitarianism as a *criterion of rightness* and utilitarianism as a *decision procedure*. The most immediate application of these distinctions is that they allow the utilitarian to respond to a popular objection. The objection has it that utilitarianism is an untenable view because the attempt always to act on utilitarian principles has worse results in terms of producing general happiness than would acting on some other principles. The response is that utilitarians are committed to the view that utilitarianism is the standard (or the criterion of rightness); they are not committed to the view that universal benevolence is the best or only motive (or that utilitarianism should always be the decision procedure). If some other motive or decision procedure has better results, that is the motive or decision procedure that utilitarianism tells us to cultivate or to employ.

Sidgwick then turns to the question of the scope of utilitarianism, "who the 'all' are, whose happiness is to be taken into account" (p. 414). He follows both Bentham and Mill in not limiting the scope of utilitarianism to humans, but taking it to extend instead to all sentient beings. The discussions of this issue in Bentham, Mill and Sidgwick are relatively brief. But later utilitarian writers have devoted much more attention to these implications of the utilitarian view. Peter Singer, the most prominent philosopher in the modern animal-rights movement, draws explicitly on Bentham and Sidgwick in developing his utilitarian argument that the interests of non-human animals must be given the same consideration as the like interests of human beings.[1]

Sidgwick also notices a second point about the scope of utilitarianism: utilitarianism does not suggest that the only beings whose interests count are those who currently exist. Instead:

> It seems [...] clear that the time at which a man exists cannot affect the value of his happiness from a universal point of view; and that the interests of posterity must concern a Utilitarian as much as those of his contemporaries, except in so far as the effect of his actions on posterity—and even the existence of human beings to be affected—must necessarily be more uncertain. (414)

The issues Sidgwick draws attention to have been explored in much further detail in recent years in population ethics. The seminal text in the field is Part 4 of Derek Parfit's *Reasons and Persons*.[2] Sidgwick does not here highlight one source of perplexities that has received much consideration in that literature: that our actions today may not only influence the happiness of future beings, but also determine which future beings exist in otherwise quite similar scenarios. (Following Parfit, this problem is called "the non-identity problem.") He does, however, notice, at least in outline, the line of thought that leads to what Parfit called "the repugnant conclusion": that there may be a greater overall amount of happiness with a vast number of beings each of whose lives is barely worth living than with a much smaller number each of whose lives is much richer and happier:

If we foresee as possible that an increase in numbers will be accompanied by a decrease in average happiness [. . .] a point arises which has not only not been formally noticed, but which seems to have been substantially overlooked by many Utilitarians. For if we take Utilitarianism to prescribe, as the ultimate end of action, happiness on the whole, and not any individual's happiness, unless considered as an element of the whole, it would follow that, if the additional population enjoy on the whole positive happiness, we ought to weigh the amount of happiness gained by the extra number against the amount lost by the remainder. So that, strictly conceived, the point up to which, on Utilitarian principles, population ought to be encouraged to increase, is not that at which average happiness is the greatest possible [. . .] but that at which the product formed by multiplying the number of persons living into the amount of average happiness reaches its maximum. (415–16)

Finally, he turns to the question how to distribute happiness if two options produce the same overall amount. He argues that the more equal distribution is the better distribution, and that this is one implication of the principle of justice discussed in III.XIII (which we talked about in Chapter 7).

It becomes practically important to ask whether any mode of distributing a given quantum of happiness is better than any other. Now the Utilitarian formula seems to supply no answer to this question: at least we have to supplement the principle of seeking the greatest happiness on the whole by some principle of Just or Right distribution of this happiness. The principle which most Utilitarians have either tacitly or explicitly adopted is that of pure equality—as given in Bentham's formula, "everybody to count for one, and nobody for more than one." And this principle seems the only one which does not need a special justification; for, as we saw, it must be reasonable to treat any one man in the same way as any other, if there be no reason apparent for treating him differently. (416–17)

9.2. Egoism and the Humean Theory of Personal Identity

The density of IV.II is immediately apparent. The first paragraph is the least important part of the chapter for the overall argument of the *Methods*. But it is still extraordinarily rich in philosophical ideas.

> From the point of view, indeed, of abstract philosophy, I do not see why the Egoistic principle should pass unchallenged any more than the Universalistic. I do not see why the axiom of Prudence should not be questioned, when it conflicts with present inclination, on a ground similar to that on which Egoists refuse to admit the axiom of Rational Benevolence. If the Utilitarian has to answer the question, 'Why should I sacrifice my own happiness for the greater happiness of another?' it must surely be admissible to ask the Egoist, 'Why should I sacrifice a present pleasure for a greater one in the future? Why should I concern myself about my own future feelings any more than about the feelings of other persons?' It undoubtedly seems to Common Sense paradoxical to ask for a reason why one should seek one's own happiness on the whole; but I do not see how the demand can be repudiated as absurd by those who adopt the views of the extreme empirical school of psychologists, although those views are commonly supposed to have a close affinity with Egoistic Hedonism. Grant that the Ego is merely a system of coherent phenomena, that the permanent identical 'I' is not a fact but a fiction, as Hume and his followers maintain; why, then, should one part of the series of feelings into which the Ego is resolved be concerned with another

part of the same series, any more than with any other series? (418–419)

One line of thought here, emphasized in the first part of the paragraph, is that there is an important analogy between temporal and personal neutrality. Egoism is temporally neutral—it rejects the preference for present pleasures over future pleasures just because they are present. Utilitarianism is personally neutral—it rejects the preference for a person's own pleasures over other people's pleasures simply because they are his or her own. One way to draw on the analogy is to argue that if we favor temporally neutral egoism over a temporally relative alternative, we should also favor personally neutral utilitarianism over personally relative egoism. This line of thought is clearly part of what is going on in III.XIII. It was explored much more fully later in Thomas Nagel's *The Possibility of Altruism*, and in Part 2 of Parfit's *Reasons and Persons*.[3] One way in which Parfit puts the line of thought is to portray egoism as an unstable middle position that faces the classic strategic danger of war on two fronts. It must fight, on the one side, against a fully relative position and, on the other, against fully neutral utilitarianism.

In the second part of the paragraph a further line of thought is introduced: that there is a connection between egoism and a particular view of personal identity. To understand this line of thought, we need first to be clear about the view Sidgwick is referring to when he talks about "the extreme empirical school of psychologists" and "Hume and his followers." In the *Treatise of Human Nature* Hume famously denied the view (associated with Descartes) that a person is a persisting mental entity.[4] He argued instead that each of us is really just a "bundle of perceptions" and that our identity over time is just a matter of various connections over time between a series of such bundles. Sidgwick suggests that the Humean view can be used to challenge the rationality of egoism. As he puts it at the end of the paragraph, if we accept the Humean view:

> Why [...] should one part of the series of feelings into which the Ego is resolved be concerned with another part of the same series, any more than with any other series? (419)

This line of thought has been explored in much further detail by more recent philosophers. The classic treatment is Part 3 of *Reasons and Persons*. Parfit there explores in various ways the idea that the rationality of egoism can be undermined by defending a Humean view of personal identity.[5]

9.3. Proof, "Proof," and Sanctions

In the next paragraph Sidgwick characterizes the problems facing anyone asked to prove what is supposed to be an ethical first principle.

> A utilitarian who claims to supersede [intuitional or egoist rules] by a higher principle is naturally challenged, by Intuitionists no less than by Egoists, to demonstrate the legitimacy of his claim. To this challenge some Utilitarians would reply that it is impossible to "prove" a first principle; and this of course is true, if by proof we mean a process which exhibits the principle in question as an inference from premises upon which it remains dependent for its certainty; for these premises, and not the inference drawn from them, would then be the real first principles. Nay, if Utilitarianism is to be *proved* to a man who already holds some other moral principles,—whether he be an Intuitional moralist, who regards as final the principles of Truth, Justice, Obedience to authority, Purity, etc., or an Egoist who regards his own interest as the ultimately reasonable end of his conduct,—it would seem that the process must be one which establishes a conclusion actually *superior* in validity to the premises from which it starts. For the Utilitarian prescriptions of duty are *prima facie* in conflict,

at certain points and under certain circumstances, both with rules which the Intuitionist regards as self-evident, and with the dictates of Rational Egoism; so that Utilitarianism, if accepted at all, must be accepted as overruling Intuitionism and Egoism. At the same time, if the other principles are not throughout taken as valid, the so-called proof does not seem to be addressed to the Intuitionist or Egoist at all. How shall we deal with this dilemma? How is such a process—clearly different from ordinary proof—possible or conceivable? (419–20)

There is much to unpack in this paragraph. One important starting idea is shared with Mill: that it is in the nature of first principles that they cannot be proved. As Mill puts it:

> Questions of ultimate ends do not admit of proof in the ordinary acceptation of the term. To be incapable of proof by reasoning is common to all first principles, to the first premises of our knowledge, as well as to those of our conduct.[6]

As we saw in Chapter 2, the impossibility of proving first principles is a direct result of the picture of the structure of our knowledge that the term "first principle" evokes. The idea is that proving anything (else) involves deducing it from a first principle. So it is in the nature of first principles that they themselves cannot be the subject of what Sidgwick calls "ordinary proof" and Mill calls "proof in the ordinary acceptation of the term."

But, as Mill and Sidgwick both recognize, this cannot be the end of the story. Proponents of competing ethical views disagree about what the first principles are. They have to have something to say to try to persuade their opponents. As Mill puts it, in a passage Sidgwick quotes elsewhere, they must be able to present

> considerations capable of determining the intellect either to give or to withhold its assent from the doctrine.[7]

In a way that basically tracks Mill's and Sidgwick's usage, we can call such considerations "proof" (in scare quotes). A "proof" has to be something different from an ordinary proof. It cannot be a matter of deriving the thing to be proved from a first principle. But a "proof" should nonetheless be some kind of rationally compelling argument.

Mill tries to give such an argument in the fourth chapter of *Utilitarianism*. Sidgwick, like Moore, does not think that Mill's argument succeeds.[8] Sidgwick does not look to Mill to supply the right model for a "proof." He develops his own model instead in response to a dilemma he presents as facing the attempt to argue against proponents of competing first principles. Either, on the one hand, you accept your opponent's view that what he or she puts forward as first principles really are first principles. But then there is nothing you can do to persuade the opponent that he or she is wrong. Or, on the other hand, you do not accept that what your opponent takes to be first principles really are first principles. But then you are not addressing your opponent at all, because you are rejecting his or her views.

At the end of the paragraph, Sidgwick provides his solution. He sketches, that is, a kind of argument designed to avoid this dilemma.

> Perhaps we may say that what is needed is a line of argument which on the one hand allows the validity, to a certain extent, of the maxims already accepted, and on the other hand shows them not to be absolutely valid, but needing to be controlled and completed by some more comprehensive principle. (420)

As we may provisionally summarize it, this kind of argument has a positive half and a negative half. The positive half involves saying that there is something right about the opponent's principles, even though they are not strictly speaking first principles; the negative half involves saying that they are not the real first principles and that instead your own favored principles are the real first principles.

The general picture here is already complicated enough. We have distinguished ordinary proof from "proof." We have seen that Mill and Sidgwick differ as to the best way to give a "proof," with Sidgwick thinking that the attempt to do so faces a dilemma. And we have seen Sidgwick's initial sketch of a model for a "proof" designed to avoid this dilemma. But there is a further distinction we need to make to complete the picture of the possible things the proponent of one ethical view can say to the proponent of another competing ethical view: the distinction between "proof" and sanctions. As we saw in Chapter 5, sanctions are incentives—carrots and sticks. One possibility is that the proponent of one ethical theory—for instance, utilitarianism—will be unable to offer an effective "proof" to persuade the proponent of a competing theory—for instance egoism—to accept her view. In that case, all that is left is the possibility of appealing to sanctions. This is a matter not of getting the egoist to accept the truth of utilitarianism and so to act as utilitarianism requires for that reason, but rather of persuading the egoist that it is in her own interest to follow utilitarian rules even though she cannot be persuaded that they are correct. The appeal to sanctions is clearly less satisfactory than a successful "proof." Appealing to sanctions is a fallback if "proof" fails.

9.4. The "Proof" of Utilitarianism Versus Egoism

Sidgwick now characterizes the intuitional argument for utilitarianism given in Book III as constituting "proofs" in the sense he has just explained. After reading Book III it is hard to read these passages in IV.II without feeling a measure of intellectual disorientation. What seemed in Book III to be a single successful argument for utilitarianism is now said to be not one argument but two, addressed to two different opponents. And now we are told also that one of these arguments doesn't work.

> Such a line of argument, addressed to egoism, was given in chap. xiii. of the foregoing book. It should be observed that the applicability of this argument depends on the manner in which the Egoistic first principle is formulated. If the Egoist strictly confines himself to stating his conviction that he ought to take his own happiness or pleasure as his ultimate end, there seems no opening for any line of reasoning to lead him to Universalistic Hedonism as a first principle; it cannot be proved that the difference between his own happiness and another's happiness is not *for him* all-important. In this case all that the Utilitarian can do is to effect as far as possible a reconciliation between the two principles, by expounding to the Egoist the *sanctions* of rules deduced from the Universalistic principle,—i.e. by pointing out the pleasures and pains that may be expected to accrue to the Egoist himself from the observation and violation respectively of such rules. It is obvious that such an exposition has no tendency to make him accept the greatest happiness of the greatest number as his ultimate end; but only as a means to the end of his own happiness. It is therefore totally different from a *proof* (as above explained) of Universalistic Hedonism. When, however, the Egoist puts forward, implicitly or explicitly, the proposition that his happiness or pleasure is Good, not only *for him* but from the point of view of the Universe [. . .] it then becomes relevant to point out to him that *his* happiness cannot be a more important part of Good, taken universally, than the equal happiness of any other person. And thus, starting with his own principle, he may be brought to accept Universal happiness or pleasure as that which is absolutely and without qualification Good or Desirable: as an end, therefore, to which the action of a reasonable agent as such ought to be directed. (420–21)

As we may summarize: there are two ways in which the egoistic principle may be formulated. The sensible egoist will formulate it by saying that his happiness is good for him. There is no room for a "proof" addressed to an egoist who formulates his principle this way. The advocate of utilitarianism can only fall back, in arguing against this sort of egoist, on an appeal to sanctions. By contrast, the less sensible egoist will formulate the egoistic principle so it says that his happiness is good (absolutely). But then there *is* room for a "proof." For then we can point out to the egoist that if his happiness is good (absolutely), so is anybody else's.

This passage from the *Methods* was famously criticized by Moore. Here is some of what he says:

> What, then, is meant by 'my own good'? In what sense can a thing be good *for me*? It is obvious, if we reflect, that the only thing which can belong to me, which can be *mine*, is something which is good, and not the fact that it is good. When I talk of anything I get as 'my own good,' I must mean either that the thing I get is good or that my possessing it is good [. . .] The only reason I can have for aiming at 'my own good" is that it is *good absolutely* that I should *have* something, which, if I have it, others cannot have. But if it is *good absolutely* that I should have it, then everyone else has as much reason for aiming at *my* having it, as I have myself [. . .] Yet Prof. Sidgwick holds that Egoism is rational; and it will be useful briefly to consider the reasons which he gives for this absurd conclusion [. . .] he says 'It cannot be proved that the difference between his own happiness and another's happiness is not *for him* all-important' [. . .] What does Prof. Sidgwick mean by the phrases 'the ultimate rational end for himself,' and '*for him* all-important'? He does not attempt to define them; and it is largely the use of such undefined phrases which causes absurdities to be committed in philosophy.[9]

It is hard not to think that Sidgwick is in the right here: that, notwithstanding the "sense of the ignobility of egoism" that Sidgwick shares with Moore, Moore's view that there is no coherent way to express the egoist position cannot be correct. As the later philosopher J. L. Mackie puts it:

> G. E. Moore's criticism of egoism [. . .] turns upon the allegation that there is a confusion in the conception of "my own good" [. . .] Moore is simply asserting that any being good that can constitute a reason for anyone's aiming at something must be "absolute" [. . .] But he has nothing to support this assertion except his extraordinarily limited views about the possible forms of meaningful linguistic constructions. Quoting [Sidgwick] he asks: "What does Prof. Sidgwick mean by the phrases 'the ultimate rational end for himself' and '*for him* all-important'? He does not attempt to define them; and it is largely the use of such undefined phrases which causes absurdities to be committed in philosophy." This, from the man who is best remembered as the defender of the view that 'good' is indefinable! What effrontery! Or rather, what naivety, for Moore clearly thinks that an undefined one-place predicate 'good' can be straightforwardly meaningful, but a two-place predicate 'good for' or 'all-important for' cannot.[10]

But even if his dismissal of egoism looks like bull-headed dogmatism, Moore knew his Sidgwick. It is hard also to avoid giving Sidgwick some share of the blame for his quite confusing treatment of the first principle and self-evidence of egoism. As we saw, he explicitly does not consider the question of the correctness of the egoist's first principle at all in Book II. Then, in III.XIII, he associates egoism with the principle of prudence. But, as we saw in Chapter 7, there are three different candidates to be the principle of prudence in III.XIII: "hereafter as such is to be regarded neither less nor more than now," "there is a *prima facie* duty to aim at one's good on the whole," and "there is a duty proper to aim at one's good on the whole." Now, in IV.II, we get the first introduction of the distinction between (absolute) goodness and goodness-for. To try to make the discussions in III.XIII and IV.II consistent, one obvious question to ask is: is one of the possible interpretations of the principle of prudence in III.XIII equivalent to the egoistic principle in IV.II formulated in terms of goodness-for? The best candidate would be "there is a duty proper to aim at one's good on the whole." But, in any case, Sidgwick could surely have done a much clearer job of making the discussions in III.XIII and IV.II consistent. If the principle of prudence is best formulated in terms of goodness-for, it should have been so formulated in III.XIII.

And this isn't even the end of the complications in Sidgwick's treatment of the first principle and self-evidence of egoism. As we will see in Chapter 11, Sidgwick in the Concluding Chapter presents something further as supplying the self-evident basis of egoism. And, if we are to trust what he said about this new material when he first introduced it in an article before incorporating it into the Concluding Chapter of the late editions of the *Methods*, nothing presented in earlier editions of the *Methods* or at earlier points in the *Methods* is the self-evident basis of egoism.

More recent philosophers have taken up the question of the coherence of egoism on which Sidgwick and Moore disagreed. The agenda for these more recent discussions was set by Thomas Nagel and Derek Parfit. They introduced new terminology, distinguishing agent-neutral reasons from agent-relative reasons. As Nagel explains the distinction:

> If a reason can be given a general form which does not include an essential reference to the person who has it, it is an *agent-neutral* reason [. . .] If on the other hand the general form of a reason does include an essential reference to the person who has it, it is an *agent-relative* reason.[11]

Using this terminology, Sidgwick's goodness-for is agent-relative; absolute goodness is agent-neutral. Egoistic reasons are agent-relative; in denying the coherence of egoism, Moore is claiming that the only genuine reasons are agent-neutral.

In his first book *The Possibility of Altruism*[12] Nagel tried to give a better argument than Moore himself provided for the Moorean position. In later work including *The View from Nowhere*[13] Nagel changed his mind, arguing instead for a pluralistic view according to which there are both agent-neutral and agent-relative reasons. The agent-relative reasons on which Nagel there focuses most—deontological reasons and reasons to pursue our own projects—are different from the agent-relative reasons that it is easiest to find Sidgwick endorsing, which we might call "egoistic agent-relative reasons." But while Nagel's later pluralism does not have a specially Sidgwickian flavor, Parfit's work on the same issues consistently does. As we will see in Chapter 11, Parfit endorses a version of the dualism of practical reason which he understands not as a fundamental contradiction but instead as the idea that there are both genuine agent-neutral reasons and genuine egoistic agent-relative reasons.

9.5. The "Proof" of Utilitarianism Versus Intuitionism

Sidgwick goes on to say that the argument given in III.XIII was not only an unsuccessful "proof" of utilitarianism addressed to the egoist; it was also a successful "proof" of utilitarianism addressed to the intuitionist.

> This, it will be remembered, is the reasoning that I used in chap. xiii. of the preceding book in exhibiting the principle of Rational Benevolence as one of the few Intuitions which stand the test of rigorous criticism. It should be observed, however, that as addressed to the Intuitionist, this reasoning only shows the Utilitarian first principle to be *one* moral axiom: it does not

prove that it is *sole* or *supreme*. The premises with which the Intuitionist starts commonly include other formulae held as independent and self-evident. Utilitarianism has therefore to exhibit itself in the twofold relation above described, at once negative and positive, to these formulae. The Utilitarian must, in the first place, endeavour to show to the Intuitionist that the principles of Truth, Justice, etc. have only a dependent and subordinate validity: arguing either that the principle is really only affirmed by Common Sense as a general rule admitting of exceptions and qualifications as in the case of Truth, and that we require some further principle for systematising these exceptions and qualifications; or that the fundamental notion is vague and needs further determination, as in the case of Justice; and further, that the different rules are liable to conflict with each other, and that we require some higher principle to decide the issue thus raised; and again, that the rules are differently formulated by different persons, and that these differences admit of no Intuitional solution, while they show the vagueness and ambiguity of the common moral notions to which the Intuitionist appeals.

This part of the argument I have perhaps sufficiently developed in the preceding book. It remains to supplement this line of reasoning by developing the positive relation that exists between Utilitarianism and the Morality of Common Sense: by showing how Utilitarianism sustains the general validity of the current moral judgments, and thus supplements the defects which reflection finds in the intuitive recognition of their stringency; and at the same time afford a principle of synthesis, and a method for binding the unconnected and occasionally conflicting principles of common moral reasoning into a complete and harmonious system. If systematic reflection upon the morality of Common Sense thus exhibits the Utilitarian principle as that to which Common Sense naturally appeals for that further development of its system which this same reflection shows to be necessary, the proof of Utilitarianism sees as complete as it can be made. (421–22)

The first paragraph of this passage presents the argument of III. XI and III.XIII as the negative half of a "proof" of utilitarianism addressed to the intuitionist. None of the maxims of common-sense morality are genuine axioms, as demonstrated in III.XI. The only genuine axioms are the axioms that support utilitarianism, presented in III.XIII.

The second paragraph gives the initial sketch of the other, positive, half of the "proof" of utilitarianism addressed to the intuitionist. Utilitarianism shows that the maxims of the common-sense moralist are generally correct though they are not intuitions. And it provides a way of resolving the troublesome issues common-sense morality cannot resolve and of systematizing common-sense morality. This positive half of the argument is developed in much further detail in IV.III, to which we turn in the next chapter.

9.6. Overview Discussion: Sidgwick's Metaethics and Moral Epistemology

We have now reviewed all the key parts of the *Methods* relevant to understanding Sidgwick's metaethics and moral epistemology. We are thus in a position to give an overview of the secondary literature on those topics.

The most immediate question about Sidgwick's metaethics is where to locate his metaethical view. As we saw in Chapter 3, there were really only two options on the recognized metaethical menu in Sidgwick's own time, naturalism and non-naturalism. Naturalists and non-naturalists agree that moral claims are intended to state truths and that some of them are true. They disagree as to the nature of truths in question. Naturalists think they are ordinary scientific truths; non-naturalists think they belong in a quite different, distinctive category. As we also saw in Chapter 3, subsequent philosophers have added more options to the metaethical menu. Non-cognitivists deny that moral claims are intended to state truths. They say they have some other function—to express feelings, or to express desires, or to give commands. Error theorists agree that moral claims are intended to state truths, but think that none of them are true.

Most readers of Sidgwick have taken him to be a non-naturalist. They include Moore and Broad,[14] who saw themselves as part of the same, then-prominent, non-naturalist tradition; Schneewind, writing in 1977 when non-naturalism was a neglected and widely caricatured view;[15] and most recent interpreters including Crisp, Hurka, Irwin, de Lazari-Radek and Singer, and Parfit,[16] writing more recently when non-naturalism is once again a widely discussed position with very influential defenders (including Parfit himself). The interesting partial exception is Robert Shaver. In his article, "Sidgwick's Minimal Metaethics," Shaver does not deny that Sidgwick was a non-naturalist.[17] But he nonetheless makes some quite provocative claims about how minimal Sidgwick's non-naturalist metaethics are. Among other things, he suggests that Sidgwick's metaethics are so minimal that they are compatible with non-cognitivism and with recent forms of moral naturalism, and he downplays the importance of non-naturalism in the overall argument of the *Methods*, denying that Sidgwick infers epistemic intuitionism from non-naturalism. I reply to these provocative arguments in Chapters 2 and 3 of *Sidgwickian Ethics*.[18]

The other issue raised by the structure of the argument of *Methods* I.III is about the connection between the key non-naturalist claim that the fundamental concept expressed by "ought" and "right" cannot be naturalistically defined and the motivational claim that there is such a thing as conflict between reason and desire. This interesting but difficult issue is discussed by Schneewind, by John Deigh, by Shaver, and by myself.[19]

On the whole, though, there has been relatively little disagreement in the secondary literature about Sidgwick's metaethics. The same could not be said about his moral epistemology: together with the dualism of practical reason (to which we will turn in Chapter 11), the moral epistemology has been the most discussed topic in the secondary literature on Sidgwick, and one on which there has been very significant disagreement.

There are two interlocking general reasons for this disagreement. First, there is the complexity of the *Methods*. There are a number of different elements in Sidgwick's moral epistemology. There is the crucial initial material on intuitionism and its three phases in I.VIII; the introduction of the four conditions and their application in III.XI; the articulation of the self-evident axioms in III.XIII; and, as we just saw, the introduction of the notion of "proof" and the discussions of "proofs" of utilitarianism versus common-sense morality and versus egoism in IV.II.

Second, some of these elements of Sidgwick seem to suggest one familiar approach in epistemology and other elements seem to suggest the alternative approach. The usual names for the two approaches are "foundationalism" and "coherentism." As the distinction is standardly explained, the foundationalist thinks that all non-foundational beliefs have to be justified by deriving them from foundational beliefs. The foundational beliefs do not themselves require justification. One standard explanation why the foundational beliefs do not require justification is that they are self-evident. By contrast, the coherentist denies that there are any beliefs that play this special justificatory role. The coherentist thinks that the only way to justify any belief is to show that it coheres—fits properly together with—other beliefs.

In one way or another most interpreters acknowledge that there are aspects of the *Methods* that seem foundationalist and other aspects that seem more coherentist. On the one hand, the commitment to epistemic intuitionism in Book I, the consistent talk of first principles and of axioms, and the search for self-evident intuitions in III.XIII seem foundationalist. On the other hand, the four conditions in III.XI and the discussions of "proof" in IV.II can seem more coherentist. A further question is whether all of this is consistent, or whether there is tension or inconsistency between the aspects of Sidgwick's moral epistemology that suggest foundationalism and the aspects that suggest coherentism.

Further complicating things, interpreters do not always frame the question in terms of foundationalism and coherentism. They often instead contrast intuitionism with reflective equilibrium (a concept introduced in Chapter 4). It might be supposed that "intuitionism" is just another name for foundationalism and "reflective equilibrium" just another name for coherentism. But things are not that simple. As Sarah McGrath observes in her recent book *Moral Knowledge*:

> Some view the method [of reflective equilibrium] as a kind of coherentist account of justification [...] while others view it as a species of foundationalism [...] Some view the method as a rival to moral intuitionism [...] while others think that the two are perfectly compatible or even complementary.[20]

Add to this the fact that those who have argued for reading Sidgwick as an intuitionist or as a proponent of reflective equilibrium often have an agenda in the broader debate in moral epistemology—they want to attribute a certain position to Sidgwick, which they also think is the correct position in moral epistemology—and it is not at all surprising that there has been a complex ongoing debate.

That debate really began with the publication in 1971 of John Rawls's enormously influential *A Theory of Justice*.[21] In the introductory chapter Rawls indicates that he takes Sidgwick to employ his own favored methodology of reflective equilibrium. In a note he says:

Sidgwick thought of the history of moral philosophy as a series of attempts to state "in full breadth and clearness those primary intuitions of Reason, by the scientific application of which the common moral thought of mankind may be at once systematized and corrected." (*The Methods of Ethics*, p. 373 f.) He takes for granted that philosophical reflection will lead to revisions in our considered judgments, and although there are elements of epistemological intuitionism in his doctrine, these are not given much weight when unsupported by systematic considerations. For an account of Sidgwick's methodology, see J. B. Schneewind, "First Principles and Common Sense Morality in Sidgwick's Ethics," *Archiv fur Geschichte der Philosophie* [. . .] 1963. (Rawls 1971, 51, note)

Rawls did not develop the suggestion about Sidgwick at any more length than this. But in the article Rawls referred to, and at greater length and more famously in *Sidgwick's Ethics and Victorian Moral Philosophy*,[22] Schneewind presented an account of Sidgwick's method that basically develops Rawls's suggestion. Schneewind relies heavily on Sidgwick's characterization of "proof" in IV.II. As he puts it:

> The structure of the argument is outlined in [Book IV, Chapter II]. Although the outline comes after Book III [. . .] we can and indeed we must use his statement as the guide to our interpretation of the relevant parts of that book.[23]

He develops from Sidgwick's characterization of the "proof" of utilitarianism versus intuitionism an account of a complex overall strategy of argument featuring what Schneewind labels "the dependence argument" and "the systematization argument."

The crucial early response to Rawls and to Schneewind was given by Peter Singer in his paper, "Sidgwick and Reflective Equilibrium."[24] Singer both denied that Sidgwick employed the method of reflective equilibrium and independently rejected the method. Some of what he says by way of criticism is clearly dated—naturally enough in a paper published nearly fifty years ago.[25] But Singer also articulates ideas that run through later, more foundationalist critiques of Schneewind's and Rawls's readings of Sidgwick. He denies that the right way to read the moral epistemology is to give central importance, as Schneewind does, to the conception of "proof" articulated in IV.II and in particular to the "proof" of utilitarianism against the common-sense moralist. He suggests that this "proof" is merely an *ad hominem* argument against one particular opponent. And he suggests that there is an intuitionist argument in Book III that is separate from and more important than the *ad hominem* "proofs" sketched in IV.II.

Later authors further develop these competing positions. A nice contrasting pair of papers both appeared in the *Journal of the History of Philosophy*: Stephen Sverdlik's "Sidgwick's Methodology" (1985), which defends a more coherentist interpretation of Sidgwick, and Anthony Skelton's "Henry Sidgwick's Moral Epistemology" (2010), which defends a more foundationalist interpretation.[26]

Another question is how serious the tension is between the apparently foundationalist and the apparently coherentist elements in Sidgwick. In "Common Sense and First Principles in Sidgwick's *Methods*," David Brink emphasizes the tension and argues that the more foundationalist elements are mistaken and that what is valuable in Sidgwick is his coherentist side.[27] In *Rational Egoism*, Robert Shaver also focuses on the tension but argues that Sidgwick has a consistent overall view. And Shaver emphasizes the way in which the third and fourth conditions from III.XI provide support for a more coherentist reading.[28]

Along with this goes the question exactly how to understand the apparently foundationalist and apparently coherentist elements that are in tension. In Chapter 3 of *Sidgwickian Ethics*,[29] I draw on Sidgwick's 1879 article "The Establishment of Ethical First Principles"[30] to try to answer this question: to supply categories with which to understand what I call "the puzzle in Sidgwick's moral epistemology." In that article Sidgwick describes two "quite different" kinds of argument by which a proponent of one putative ethical first principle might try to persuade a proponent of a competing putative ethical first principle. One kind of argument involves

> [establishing] some general criteria for distinguishing true first principles (whether ethical or non-ethical) from false ones; and [. . .] then [constructing] a strictly logical deduction by which, applying [the] general criteria to the special case of ethics, we establish the true first principles of this [. . .] subject.[31]

I label this kind of argument "criterial argument"; I claim that it is what we find in Book III of the *Methods* and in Sidgwick's independent articles in general epistemology. In the other kind of argument:

> I may begin by regarding some limited and qualified statement as self-evident, without seeing the truth of the simpler and wider proposition of which the former affirms a part; and yet, when I have been led to accept the latter, I may reasonably regard this as the real first principle, and not the former, of which the limitations and qualifications may then appear accidental and arbitrary.[32]

I label this kind of argument "bipartite argument"; I claim it is the kind of argument Sidgwick describes in giving his account of "proof" in IV.II. The puzzle in Sidgwick's moral epistemology is then the puzzle as to why Sidgwick considers only bipartite arguments in IV.II, given that he elsewhere articulates a conception of criterial argument which he sharply distinguishes from the conception of bipartite argument, and given that he apparently develops a criterial argument for utilitarianism in Book III.

Notes

1. Singer 1975; Singer 2011, Chapter 3.
2. Parfit 1984.
3. Nagel 1970; Parfit 1984.
4. Hume 1888.
5. One question is whether these two lines of thought are really separable: whether the argument that egoism is an unstable middle position can be made independently of any claim about personal identity, or whether, instead, the only cogent way to attack the rationality of egoism is to rely on a Humean view of personal identity. On this question, see Kagan 1986.
6. Mill (1861) 2003, 122.
7. Mill (1861) 2003, 98.
8. Mill's argument would not have garnered so much critical attention if it were wholly clear how it was supposed to go. But here is a fairly uncontroversial summary, using Mill's own words. The first part of the argument is given in the third paragraph of the proof chapter:

> (1) The sole evidence it is possible to produce that anything is desirable is that people do actually desire it.
>
> (2) Each person [...] desires his own happiness.
>
> Therefore (3) Each person's happiness is a good to that person.
> Therefore (4) The general happiness is a good to the aggregate of all persons.

As Mill himself acknowledges, this argument in itself shows only that the general happiness is *one of the things* that is desirable. It does not show, what he sets out to show, that the general happiness is *the only thing* that is desirable. To reach this conclusion, he supplements the argument of the third paragraph by spending the latter part of the proof chapter defending psychological hedonism, the claim that "there is in reality nothing desired except happiness."

Sidgwick offers three criticisms of the argument. Two of them are given in the discussion of Mill's proof at the end of III.XIII, pp. 387–88. First, though he emphasizes it much less than Moore does, Sidgwick criticizes the step in premise (1) from "desired" to "desirable." The criticism is suggested in the text, and made more explicit in footnote 2 on page 388. The second criticism, which Sidgwick emphasizes much more than he does the first criticism, is a criticism of the step from (3) to (4), from the desirability of individual happiness to the desirability of general happiness. Sidgwick's line is that Mill's procedure, of moving from what is desired to what is desirable, will only demonstrate the desirability of general happiness if there is a desire for general happiness. A desire for individual happiness won't do. Third, as we saw in Chapter 3, Sidgwick explicitly rejects psychological hedonism, siding with Butler against Mill.

Some more recent commentators have argued that the first two of these criticisms are not compelling. See for instance Sayre-McCord 2001.

9. Moore 1903, 98–99.
10. Mackie 1976, 322–23.
11. Nagel 1986, 152–53; italics in the original. As he explains, when he first made the distinction between two kinds of reasons in *The Possibility of Altruism* he used the terms "objective" and "subjective." But in his later work "objective" and "subjective" were used for another purpose so he adopted instead Parfit's terms "agent-neutral and "agent-relative."
12. Nagel 1970.
13. Nagel 1986.
14. Moore 1903; Broad 1930.
15. Schneewind 1977.
16. Crisp 2015; Hurka 2014a; Irwin 2009; Lazari-Radek and Singer 2014; Parfit 2011a.
17. Shaver 2003.
18. Phillips 2011.
19. Schneewind 1977, Chapter 7; Deigh 1992; Shaver 2003; Shaver 2006; Phillips 2020.
20. McGrath 2019, 12.
21. Rawls 1971.
22. Schneewind 1977.
23. Schneewind 1977, 262.
24. Singer 1974.
25. Singer suggests that reflective equilibrium allows for no distinction between knowledge and truth; but, as lots of later work shows, a reflective equilibrium conception of knowledge and justification is compatible with a correspondence conception of truth. And Singer also suggests that reflective equilibrium is necessarily a method for discovering factual truths

about our moral psychology rather than a method for discovering normative truths. Again, later work shows that this is not the case.
26. Sverdlik 1985; Skelton 2010.
27. Brink 1994.
28. Shaver 1999, Chapter 3.
29. Phillips 2011.
30. Sidgwick (1879) 2000.
31. Sidgwick (1879) 2000, 107.
32. Sidgwick (1879) 2000, 106.

10
Utilitarianism and Common-Sense Morality (*Methods* IV.III, IV.IV, and IV.V)

In the next three chapters of Book IV, Sidgwick completes the "proof" of utilitarianism against intuitionism by articulating the "positive relation" between utilitarianism and the morality of common sense. He goes on to consider the extent to which utilitarianism and common-sense morality can be brought together by combining the method of common-sense morality with the first principle of utilitarianism.

10.1. The Positive Relation Between Utilitarianism and the Morality of Common Sense

There is a good deal to unpack in Sidgwick's claim that there is a "positive relation" between utilitarianism and the morality of common sense. As we just saw, at the end of IV.II he writes:

> It remains to supplement this line of reasoning by developing the positive relation that exists between Utilitarianism and the Morality of Common Sense: by showing how Utilitarianism sustains the general validity of the current moral judgments, and thus supplements the defects which reflection finds in the intuitive recognition of their stringency; and at the same time affords

a principle of synthesis, and a method for binding the unconnected and occasionally conflicting principles of common moral reasoning into a complete and harmonious system. If systematic reflection upon the morality of Common Sense thus exhibits the Utilitarian principle as that to which Common Sense naturally appeals for that further development of its system which this same reflection shows to be necessary, the proof of Utilitarianism seems as complete as it can be made. (422)

We can here distinguish two general lines of thought. The first line of thought is that according to utilitarianism it is a good thing if people exhibit the character traits common sense takes to be virtues and follow the rules of common-sense morality. Sidgwick develops this first line of thought further at the start of IV.III with reference to Hume.

No one can read Hume's *Inquiry into the First Principles of Morals* without being convinced of this at least, that if a list were drawn up of the qualities of character and conduct that are directly or indirectly productive of pleasure to ourselves or others, it would include all that are commonly known as virtues [. . .] It is not necessary to prove that existing moral rules are *more* conducive to the general happiness than any others: but only to point out in each case some manifest felicific tendency which they possess. (424–25)

No advocate of dogmatic intuitionism in particular or of deontology more broadly need have any quarrel with this first line of thought: the idea that there are good utilitarian reasons to exhibit common-sense moral virtues and follow common-sense moral rules.

Sidgwick tends however to move seamlessly from this first line of thought to a second different line of thought. This second line of thought has it that common-sense morality is in various ways defective, and that utilitarianism is the right way to fix its defects. As Sidgwick articulates this second line of thought in an important passage towards the end of Section 1 of IV.III:

> [Utilitarianism] explains anomalies in the Morality of Common Sense, which from any other point of view must seem unsatisfactory to the reflective intellect; and moreover, where the current formula is not sufficiently precise for the guidance of conduct, while at the same time difficulties and perplexities arise in the attempt to give it additional precision, the Utilitarian method solves these difficulties and perplexities in general accordance with the vague instincts of Common Sense, and is naturally appealed to for such solution in ordinary moral discussions. It may be shown further, that it not only supports the generally received view of the relative importance of different duties, but is also naturally called in as an arbiter, where rules commonly regarded as co-ordinate come into conflict: that, again, when the same rule is interpreted somewhat differently by different persons, each naturally supports his view by urging its Utility, however strongly he may maintain the rule to be self-evident and known *a priori*: that where we meet with marked diversity of opinion on any point, in the same age and country, we commonly find manifest and impressive utilitarian reasons on both sides: and that finally the remarkable discrepancies found in comparing the moral codes of different ages and countries are for the most part strikingly correlated to differences in the effects of actions on happiness, or in men's foresight of, or concern for, such effects. (425–26)

This second line of thought is significantly more controversial. Even if, in the light of the arguments Sidgwick makes in III.XI, which we discussed in Chapter 6, dogmatic intuitionists have to acknowledge that their view does have defects, it is a significant further step to accept that utilitarianism provides the right way to fix these defects.

There is also a third line of thought which is naturally suggested by the idea that there is a positive relation between utilitarianism and common-sense morality. It is the idea that common-sense moral rules have an important role to play in utilitarian moral reasoning. This third line of thought is not emphasized in the key passages on the positive relation between utilitarianism and common-sense morality at the end of IV.II and the beginning of IV.III. But Sidgwick does articulate it elsewhere. At the end of the short intellectual autobiography in the Preface to the sixth edition, he says:

> Investigation of the Utilitarian method led me to see defects [in it]; the merely empirical examination of the consequences of actions is unsatisfactory; and being thus conscious of the practical imperfection in many cases of the Utilitarian calculus, I remained anxious to treat with respect, and make use of, the guidance afforded by Common Sense. (xxiii)

And the third line of thought is articulated more fully at the beginning of IV.IV:

> From the considerations that we have just surveyed it is but a short and easy step to the conclusion that in the Morality of Common Sense we have ready to hand a body of Utilitarian doctrine: that [. . .] the apparent first principles of Common Sense may be accepted as the "middle axioms" of Utilitarian method; direct reference being only made to utilitarian considerations, in order to settle points upon which the verdict of Common Sense is found to be obscure or conflicting. (461)

Like the first line of thought, with which it nicely fits, this third line of thought is not one with which dogmatic intuitionists or deontologists more generally have any obvious need to quarrel. They have no reason to deny that it might be best on utilitarian grounds for most or all people most or all the time to follow the rules of common-sense morality rather than to decide what to do by appeal to utilitarian calculations—by using what, as we saw, Sidgwick calls the method of "empirical hedonism."

The idea that there is a "positive relation" between utilitarianism and the morality of common-sense is thus complex and multifaceted.

In the remainder of IV.III Sidgwick develops this complex and multifaceted idea, giving the third of his three overviews of the morality of common sense in the *Methods*. As we saw in Chapter 6, the first two of these overviews are to be found in Book III. The first is the detailed account in Chapters III through X of Book III, where Sidgwick tells us his aim is "to throw the Morality of Common Sense into a scientific form" (p. 338). The second is the argument in III.XI that the principles of common-sense morality do not satisfy the four conditions to be self-evident axioms. Finally, here in IV.III, Sidgwick argues that there is this "positive relation" between utilitarianism and the various different elements of common-sense morality.

As in our discussion of the first two of Sidgwick's overviews of the morality of common sense in Chapter 6, we do not have space to consider his detailed claims about all its different elements. As we did there we will focus on his discussion of just one element of common-sense morality, promissory obligation.

Sidgwick develops his utilitarian account of promissory obligation on pages 442 through 444 of IV.III. We can find in this account particular versions of the first two lines of thought we distinguished above. Sidgwick first explains the utilitarian reasons that favor the keeping of promises. He does so by bringing them under

the general head of "normal expectations"[.] (442)[1]

And he argues that, once we do so, we can explain why in ordinary cases the duty to keep promises will seem absolute.

[The Utilitarian] will hold any disappointment of expectations to be *pro tanto* an evil, but a greater evil in proportion to the previous security of the expectant individual, from the greater shock thus given to his reliance on the conduct of his fellow-men generally: and many times greater in proportion as the expectation is generally recognised as normal and reasonable, as in this case the shock extends to all who are in any way cognisant of his disappointment. The importance to mankind of being able to rely on each other's actions is so great, that in ordinary cases of absolutely definite engagements there is scarcely any advantage that can counterbalance the harm done in violating them. (442–43)

As we saw in Chapter 6, in criticizing the dogmatic intuitionist view that there is a self-evident principle of promissory obligation Sidgwick argues that there are less ordinary circumstances in which common sense gives no clear answer as to whether a promise has been made or as to its degree of bindingness.

If we ask, (*e.g.*) how far our promise is binding if [...] circumstances have materially altered since it was given, and we find that the results of fulfilling it will be different from what we foresaw when we promised; or even if it be only our knowledge of the consequences which has altered, and we now see that fulfilment will entail on us a sacrifice out of proportion to the benefit received by the promisee; or perhaps see that it will even be injurious to him though he may not think so;- different conscientious persons would answer these and other questions (both generally and in particular cases) in different ways: and though we could perhaps obtain a decided majority for some of these qualifications and against others, there would not in any case be a clear *consensus* either way. (353–54)

Here what we above distinguished as the second line of thought comes into play: the idea that utilitarianism is the right way to remedy these defects in common-sense morality.

> [We] found that several exceptions and qualifications to the rule of Good Faith were more or less distinctly recognised by Common Sense: and most of these have a utilitarian basis, which it does not need much penetration to discern. To begin, we may notice that the superficial view of the obligation of a promise which makes it depend on the assertion of the promiser and not, as Utilitarians hold, on the expectations produced in the promise, cannot fairly be attributed to Common Sense: which certainly condemns a breach of promise much more strongly when others have acted in reliance on it, than when its observance did not directly concern others, so that its breach involves for them only the indirect evil of a bad precedent, - as when a man breaks a pledge of total abstinence. We see, again, how the utilitarian reasons for keeping a promise are diminished by a material change of circumstances, for in that case the expectations disappointed by breaking it are at least not those which the promise originally created [. . .] We saw, again, that when the performance would be injurious to the promisee, Common Sense is disposed to admit that its obligation is superseded; and is at least doubtful whether the promise should be kept, even when it is only the promiser who would be injured, if the harm be extreme;- both which qualifications are in harmony with Utilitarianism. And similarly for the other qualifications and exceptions: they all turn out to be as plainly utilitarian, as the general utility of keeping one's word in plain and manifest. (443–44)

10.2. A Rossian Response

We saw in Chapter 6 that Ross develops a new form of deontology distinct from the dogmatic intuitionism Sidgwick criticizes. The key to this new form of deontology is the concept of *prima facie* duty: deontological principles are not absolute and exceptionless but defeasible. And, as we also noted, though Ross did not have Sidgwick particularly in mind when he introduced the concept of *prima facie* duty, Broad independently introduced the concept in *Five Types of Ethical Theory*, published in the very same year as *The Right and the Good*.[2] And Broad did have Sidgwick in mind: he articulated the new form of deontology as a response to Sidgwick's critique of dogmatic intuitionism.

We focused in Chapter 6 on the Rossian response to the negative half of Sidgwick's treatment of common-sense morality: the claim that common-sense morality contains no genuinely self-evident principles. But Ross's work also provides resources for a response to Sidgwick's claim that there is a positive relation between utilitarianism and common-sense morality.

Ross agrees with Sidgwick that consequentialism is an important part of the truth about morality. As he puts it at one point:

> A great part of our duty [. . .] is to bring what is good into existence.[3]

But he denies that consequentialism is the whole truth about morality. He gives a general explanation why it isn't in a famous passage from *The Right and the Good*:

> The essential defect of the 'ideal utilitarian' theory is that it ignores, or at least does not do full justice to, the highly personal character of duty. If the only duty is to produce the maximum of good, the question who is to have the good—whether it is myself, or my benefactor, or a person to whom I have made a promise to confer that good on him, or a mere fellow man to whom I stand in no such special relation—should make no difference to my having a duty to produce that good. But we are all in fact sure that it makes a vast difference.[4]

Promissory obligation is Ross's go-to example in arguing against the consequentialist view.[5] Ross agrees with Sidgwick that promissory obligation is not absolute.

> If I have promised to meet a friend at a particular time for some trivial purpose, I should certainly think myself justified in breaking my engagement if by doing so I could prevent a serious accident or bring relief to the victims of one.[6]

But he also rejects the consequentialist view of promissory obligation.

> Suppose, to simplify the case by abstraction, that the fulfillment of a promise to A would produce 1,000 units of good for him, but that by doing some other act I could produce 1,001 units of good for B, to whom I have made no promise, the other consequences of the two acts being of equal value: should we really think it self-evident that it was our duty to do the second act and not the first? I think not. We should, I fancy, hold that only a much greater disparity of value between the total consequences would justify us in failing to discharge our *prima facie* duty to A. After all, a promise is a promise, and is not to be treated so lightly as the [consequentialist] theory [...] would imply.[7]

Pushed by a contemporary consequentialist critic,[8] Ross sketches a general view of promissory obligation.

> There appears to be no reason why one who does not take the utilitarian view of promises should consider the bindingness of all promises to be equal. In our natural thought about it, I believe we think of it as being, as it were, a product of two factors. *One* of these is the value of the promised service in the eyes of the promisee; we clearly think ourselves more bound not to fail another person in an important matter, than not to fail him in an

unimportant one [. . .] The *other* factor tending to increase the obligation to fulfil a promise depends on the way in which and the time at which the promise has been made. Any one would feel that a promise made casually in a moment of half-attention is less binding than one made explicitly and repeatedly [. . .] We may then, if we like to put the matter so, think of the responsibility for conferring a promised benefit as being n times as binding as the responsibility for conferring an exactly similar unpromised benefit, where n is always greater than 1, and, when the promise is very explicit, is much greater than 1. It will follow that it is always our duty to fulfil a promise, except when the uncovenanted benefit to be conferred is more than n times greater than the covenanted benefit. We are not able to assign a very definite value to n in any case, but I believe there is pretty general agreement that n is usually great enough to secure that when the alternative advantage to be conferred is not very different in amount, the promised advantage ought to be conferred.[9]

Ross here gives a positive account of promissory obligation that is neither absolutist nor utilitarian. If Ross's account is right, then Sidgwick is wrong that the best way to fix the defects in the dogmatic intuitionist approach to promissory obligation is by appeal to utilitarianism.[10]

10.3. A Comparison with Contemporary Treatments of the Debate Between Utilitarians and Their Critics

It is instructive to compare Sidgwick's treatment of the relation between utilitarianism and common-sense morality with the more contemporary debate between utilitarians and their critics.

That more contemporary debate standardly begins with critics introducing problem cases for utilitarianism—cases where, as it is sometimes put, utilitarianism tells us that one option is right, while moral common sense tells us instead that another is. There are many such problem cases. James and Stuart Rachels introduce a version of the most celebrated one, presented by the philosopher H. J. McCloskey:[11]

> In 1965, writing in the racially charged climate of the American civil rights movement, H. J. McCloskey asks us to consider the following case:
> Suppose a utilitarian were visiting an area in which there was racial strife, and that, during his visit, a Negro rapes a white woman, and that race riots occur as a result of the crime [...] Suppose too that our utilitarian is in the area of the crime when it is committed such that his testimony would bring about the conviction of [whomever he accuses]. If he knows that a quick arrest will stop the riots and lynchings, surely, as a utilitarian, he must conclude that he has a duty to bear false witness in order to bring about the punishment of an innocent person.[12]

In this case utilitarianism apparently says that the right thing to do is to testify falsely to bring about the punishment of an innocent person; moral common sense says that doing so would be wrong.

As the debate standardly proceeds, there are three broad kinds of way in which the utilitarian can respond to objections like this: (1) The utilitarian can deny that utilitarianism really says that the right thing to do is to testify falsely. When we take into account all the probable consequences, long-term as well as short-term, utilitarianism will agree with moral common sense; (2) The utilitarian can agree that the original version of utilitarianism—often at this point dubbed "act-utilitarianism"—does imply that the right thing to do is to testify falsely. But then the utilitarian can move to a new version of utilitarianism—often some form of "rule-utilitarianism"—which agrees with moral common sense that it would be wrong to testify falsely; (3) The utilitarian can accept that utilitarianism does indeed imply that it is right to testify falsely, and hold that utilitarianism is right about this and moral common sense wrong.[13]

This familiar contemporary debate is strikingly and instructively different from Sidgwick's discussion of the relation between utilitarianism and common-sense morality. In philosophy and other like intellectual endeavors it can matter a lot how a debate is shaped—who is the aggressor and who is on the defensive, who has the burden of proof. In the contemporary debate it is the critic of utilitarianism, the advocate of moral common sense, who is the aggressor. The critic presents a problem case. It is the utilitarian's job to respond. Common-sense intuitions about particular cases, like McCloskey's case, are taken initially as reliable data. The fact that utilitarianism initially seems not to be able to explain or account for this data is taken to be a problem for utilitarianism.

By contrast, in the *Methods* it is the utilitarian who is the aggressor. As we saw in Chapter 6, Sidgwick argues in Book III that the common-sense moralist does not present any genuine axioms—that the supposed axioms put forward by the common-sense moralist all fail to satisfy the four conditions. In addressing a "proof" to the common-sense moralist, the utilitarian is offering in effect to salvage something of the common-sense moralist's discredited theory. Moreover, Sidgwick's common-sense moralist is importantly different from the character sometimes described as a proponent of "moral common sense" in contemporary debates. The proponent of moral common sense in contemporary debates typically appeals to intuitions about specific problem cases (like McCloskey's case). As we saw in Chapter 4, Sidgwick thinks little of this "phase" or "version" of intuitionism, which he dubs "perceptional intuitionism": he dismisses it in a paragraph. The form of common-sense morality on which he spends much more time gives significant weight to intuitions about general principles or rules, not to intuitions about specific cases.

The contemporary debate between utilitarianism and its critics thus has a significantly different shape from the debate in Sidgwick.

One interesting thing to note in this connection is the relative recency of this, the most famous problem case objection to utilitarianism. As Stephen Sverdlik has shown, the earliest versions of cases like McCloskey's in philosophical literature date back only to about 1930.[14]

It is not that Sidgwick completely failed to envisage a strategy of objection to utilitarianism animated by problem cases. He says in I.VI that:

> Butler, I think, was our first influential writer who dwelt on the discrepancies between Virtue as commonly understood and "conduct likeliest to produce an overbalance of happiness." (86)

He refers in a footnote to Butler's *Dissertation of the Nature of Virtue*. And, as we saw, in discussing Butler in the short intellectual autobiography in the Preface to the sixth edition he remarks:

> I had no doubt that my conscience claimed authority, though it was a more utilitarian conscience than Butler's: for, through all this search for principles I still adhered for practical purposes to the doctrine I learned from Mill, *i.e.* I still held to the maxim of aiming at the general happiness as the supreme directive rule of conduct, and I thought I could answer the objections that Butler brought against this view [in the "Dissertation on Virtue" at the end of the *Analogy*]. (xx)

In *Dissertation* Butler offers objections to utilitarianism quite like the problem case objections familiar in contemporary discussions. But the debate between utilitarianism and moral common sense in the *Methods* isn't structured by requiring the utilitarian to respond to objections like those Butler made. Instead, in the *Methods* it is the utilitarian who is the aggressor and the common-sense moralist who is on the defensive. The key question is not how the utilitarian can respond to objections like Butler's; it is what to make of common-sense morality once its rules have been shown to fail to meet the conditions for being genuine ethical first principles.

10.4. Replacing Common-Sense Morality: Spencer and Stephen

The agenda for IV.IV and IV.V is set by what we distinguished above as the third line of thought in the complex, multifaceted idea that there is a positive relation between utilitarianism and the morality of common sense. The simple version of this third line of thought allows for a satisfying reconciliation between the two: utilitarianism is correct about first principles, but, except in hard cases, common-sense morality supplies the right method.

While acknowledging its attractions, Sidgwick rejects this simple version of the third line of thought.

> It is one thing to hold that the current morality expresses, partly consciously but to a large extent unconsciously, the results of human experience as to the effects of actions: it is quite another thing to accept this morality *en bloc*, so far as it is clear and definite, as the best guidance we can get to the attainment of maximum general happiness. However attractive this simple reconciliation of Intuitional and Utilitarian methods may be, it is not, I think, really warranted by the evidence. (463)

He goes on in Section 1 of IV.IV to present various arguments to show that

> the morality of Common Sense [is] a machinery of rules, habits, and sentiments, roughly and generally but not precisely or completely adapted to the production of the greatest possible happiness for sentient beings generally[.] (475)

Among the considerations he presents is an argument drawing on Hume and Adam Smith, that moral sentiments are derived from sympathy. If this is so, Sidgwick argues, then the limitations of sympathy make it unlikely that our moral sentiments always favor the same outcomes as are favored by impartial utilitarianism.

At this point some philosophers would argue on utilitarian grounds for a wholesale rejection of common-sense morality and its replacement by something new that is "precisely and completely adapted to the production of the greatest possible happiness for sentient beings generally." In the remainder of IV.IV Sidgwick argues that it is not possible in this way to replace common-sense morality wholesale. He raises general problems for the replacement project. One on which he lays significant stress has the form of a dilemma: Either when trying to carry out the replacement project we imagine human beings like ourselves, but without any of our current habits and moral sentiments. But those human beings are so unlike us that it is not clear what use a morality adapted for them will have. Or when trying to carry out the replacement project we imagine human beings who already have our current moral code. But then the current code cannot be set aside in trying to carry out the replacement project.

Sidgwick also offers specific arguments against two of his late Victorian contemporaries who endorsed something like this replacement project—Herbert Spencer and Leslie Stephen. Spencer and Stephen were the most prominent figures in a school of evolutionary ethicists who saw themselves as the intellectual heirs of Mill's naturalistic utilitarianism. While he shared their utilitarian sympathies, Sidgwick was always in other ways skeptical of the claims of the evolutionists. In IV.IV he argues against Spencer's idea in *The Data of Ethics*[15] that we can

> solve the problems of practical ethics by constructing the final perfect form of human society, towards which the process of human history is tending[.] (470)

Among the problems are that

> a society in which [...] there is no such thing as punishment, is necessarily a society so unlike our own, that it would be idle to attempt any close imitation of its rules of behavior. (470)

He also considers Stephen's suggestions in *The Science of Ethics*[16] that utilitarians should adopt

> as the *practically* ultimate end and criterion of morality, "health" or "efficiency" of the social organism, instead of happiness. (471)

Against Stephen, Sidgwick argues, first, that it is no easier to come up with a whole new set of moral rules to promote the health of the social organism than it is to come up with a whole new set of moral rules to promote happiness and, second, that there is no good reason to suppose that rules that promote the health of the social organism will maximize general happiness. These criticisms are persuasive.

10.5. Reforming Common-Sense Morality

In IV.V Sidgwick turns to the question: if utilitarians can neither unreservedly endorse common-sense morality nor completely replace it, what should their attitude to it be?

He emphasizes first that in general utilitarians will support it and conform to it, in a fine passage articulating a conservative approach to established and generally beneficial institutions:

> The Utilitarian must repudiate altogether that temper of rebellion against the established morality, as something purely external and conventional, into which the reflective mind is always apt to fall when it is first convinced that the established rules are

not intrinsically reasonable [... He] will naturally contemplate it with reverence and wonder, as a marvellous product of nature, the result of long centuries of growth, showing in many parts the same fine adaptation of means to complex exigencies as the most elaborate structures of physical organisms exhibit: he will handle it with respectful delicacy as a mechanism, constructed of the fluid element of opinions and dispositions, by the indispensable aid of which the actual *quantum* of human happiness is continually being produced; a mechanism which no 'politicians or philosophers' could create, yet without which the harder and coarser machinery of Positive Law could not be permanently maintained, and the life of man would become—as Hobbes forcibly expresses it—"solitary, poor, nasty, brutish, and short." (475–76)

Nonetheless, since common-sense morality is imperfect, utilitarians must be open to improving it. The only method that can be employed in considering possible improvements is the method of empirical hedonism: considering the gains and losses in happiness to be expected from the attempts to introduce such improvements. Sidgwick focuses mainly on possible improvements in rules of duty included in common-sense morality: rules of duty enforced by "penalties of social favor and contempt" (480) rather than by legal punishment. He considers first the case of new improved rules that conflict with old rules, rather than merely supplementing them. He notes various general reasons to worry that, even if the new improved rule would produce more utility if followed to the same extent as the old rule it replaces, the attempt to introduce the new rule would nonetheless be on balance bad: the reformer will face painful social disapprobation; the new rule might not get as well established as the old one was; the attempt at reform may weaken a beneficial general habit of adhering to moral rules. These considerations do not, however, apply in two other cases of reform: reforms that involve mere supplements to currently recognized rules, and reforms that involve promoting proper adherence to current rules respect for and adherence to which has decayed.

He turns in Section 3 of IV.V to the question not of reforming the current rules but of allowing exceptions to them. The latter part of this long and nuanced discussion contains the most famous passage in IV.V, concerning the possibility of (what usually gets referred to as) "esoteric morality":

> [The] Utilitarian may have no doubt that in a community consisting generally of enlightened Utilitarians [. . .] grounds for exceptional ethical treatment would be regarded as valid; still he may [. . .] doubt whether the more refined and complicated rule which recognises such exceptions is adapted for the community in which he is actually living; and whether the attempt to introduce it is not likely to do more harm by weakening current morality than good by improving its quality. Supposing such a doubt to arise [. . .] it becomes necessary that the Utilitarian should consider carefully the extent to which his advice or example are likely to influence persons to whom they would be dangerous: and it is evident that the result of this consideration may depend largely on the degree of publicity which he gives to either advice or example. Thus, on Utilitarian principles, it may be right to do and privately recommend, under certain circumstances, what it would not be right to advocate openly; it may be conceivably right to do, if it can be done with comparative secrecy, what it would be wrong to do in the face of the world; and even, if perfect secrecy can be reasonably expected, what it would be wrong to recommend by private advice or example. These conclusions are all of a paradoxical character: there is no doubt that the moral consciousness of a plain man broadly repudiates the general notion of an esoteric morality, differing from that popularly taught [. . .] Thus the utilitarian conclusion, carefully stated, would seem to be this; that the opinion that secrecy may render an

action right which would not otherwise be so should itself be kept comparatively secret; and similarly it seems expedient that the doctrine that esoteric morality is expedient should itself be kept esoteric. (489–90)

After quoting the end of this passage, Parfit wrote:

> This is what Williams calls 'Government House' Consequentialism, since it treats the majority like the natives in a colony. As Williams claims, we cannot welcome such a conclusion. Sidgwick regretted his conclusions, but did not think regret a ground for doubt.[17]

Though Sidgwick regretted these famous conclusions, they do not mean that there is anything distinctively problematic about his version of utilitarianism, and their importance should not be exaggerated. As we saw in Chapter 9, in order to respond to the familiar objection that utilitarianism is self-defeating because the attempt to act on utilitarian principles has worse results in utilitarian terms than would attempting to act on some other principle, Sidgwick distinguishes the idea that utilitarianism is the correct criterion of rightness from the idea that utilitarianism supplies the best decision procedure. Even if utilitarianism provides the criterion of rightness, it may be better on utilitarian grounds if we use some other decision procedure—like employing the rules of common-sense morality. The most obvious way to understand this response is to imagine a single individual, who both accepts the utilitarian criterion of rightness and adopts (at least in normal cases) some non-utilitarian decision procedure. But once the distinction between criterion of rightness and decision procedure has been made, the possibility of esoteric morality has in effect also been introduced. For then, as Sidgwick argues in IV.V, it might turn out that it would be best on utilitarian grounds if the distinction were institutionalized socially rather than individually: the select few knowing the criterion of rightness, the rest given the false impression that the decision procedure and the criterion of rightness are the same. That Sidgwick recognized this possibility is not a reason to think that there is something especially problematic about his own version of utilitarianism. Instead, what he recognized was a conceptual possibility inevitably opened up once the utilitarian makes the important distinction between criterion of rightness and decision procedure. And his recognizing this conceptual possibility at the end of a long and nuanced discussion does not mean that he thought it would be particularly significant in practice.

10.6. Overview Discussion: Sidgwick on Consequentialism versus Deontology

Given their importance, it is surprising that there has not been more discussion in the literature of Sidgwick's arguments for consequentialism as against deontology.

The most important twentieth-century treatments of the *Methods* are Broad 1930 and Schneewind 1977. As we saw in Chapter 6, Broad says that Sidgwick's arguments succeed against the Whewellian dogmatic intuitionist, but suggests that a revised version of deontology featuring a version of the concept of *prima facie* duty is invulnerable to Sidgwick's critique. As we saw at the end of Chapter 9, Schneewind gives a distinctive, complex account of Sidgwick's methodology, as featuring what Schneewind calls "the dependence argument" and "the subordination argument." Schneewind is primarily concerned to interpret rather than to evaluate Sidgwick's arguments. But Schneewind 1977, Chapters 9 through 11, certainly convey the impression that Schneewind thinks those arguments succeed. As we saw in Chapter 6, Alan Donagan dissents: he argues in Donagan (1977a) 1992 that the Whewellian dogmatic intuitionist can be defended against Sidgwick's criticisms.

More recently others have also criticized Sidgwick's arguments. Both I, in Phillips 2011, Chapter 4, and Thomas Hurka, in Hurka 2014a, Chapter 7, and Hurka 2014b, suggest that Sidgwick in some way equivocates between a stronger version of the maxim of benevolence that his argument requires but that he is not entitled to, and a weaker version which is more defensible but which will not do the argumentative work that needs to be done in defending consequentialism. We also both suggest that Sidgwick's arguments against deontology are open to charges of unfairness. Katarzyna de Lazari-Radek and Peter Singer defend Sidgwick against the charges of unfairness in Lazari-Radek and Singer 2014, Chapter 5, Section 5. Shaver 2014 gives a more positive take on Sidgwick's argument. Shaver does not defend Sidgwick against the charge of unfairness, but he does argue that the right interpretation of the maxim of benevolence is the weaker interpretation. And he gives a sympathetic reconstruction of Sidgwick's overall strategy of argument if the maxim of benevolence is so interpreted.

Notes

1. For a fuller treatment of Sidgwick on promissory obligation, see Shaver 2019.
2. Ross 1930; Broad 1930.
3. Ross 1939, 252.
4. Ross 1930, 22.
5. For a fuller treatment of Ross on promissory obligation, see Phillips 2019, Chapter 3.
6. Ross 1930, 18.
7. Ross 1930, 34–35.
8. Pickard-Cambridge 1932a, 1932b, and 1932c.
9. Ross 1939, 100–101.
10. There is a range of other possible views about the nature of promissory obligation. For a survey, see Habib 2021.
11. Rachels and Rachels 2012; McCloskey 1965.
12. Rachels and Rachels 2012, 112–13.

13. Elements of these different responses can also be combined, by claiming that though response (3) is correct about the criterion of rightness, response (2) is correct about the decision procedure we should adopt.
14. Sverdlik 2012.
15. Spencer 1879.
16. Stephen 1882.
17. Parfit 1984, 41, citing Williams 1973.

11
The Dualism of Practical Reason
(*Methods* Concluding Chapter)

The Concluding Chapter is the place where Sidgwick most fully articulates his most famous idea: that there is an unresolvable conflict between egoism and utilitarianism, the "dualism of practical reason." As we will see, Sidgwick's commentators are divided on how to interpret the dualism. Indeed, the two questions that have generated the most discussion in the secondary literature on Sidgwick are the question of how to understand his moral epistemology (which we talked about at the end of Chapter 9) and this question of how to understand the dualism.

11.1. The "Proofs" of Utilitarianism Versus Intuitionism and of Utilitarianism Versus Egoism

The title of the concluding chapter is "The Mutual Relations of the Three Methods." Characteristically, Sidgwick does not here focus on the relation between intuitionism and egoism. That is his focus in II.V, as we saw in Section 5.4. But usually, as here in the Concluding Chapter, Sidgwick's focus is instead on the relation between utilitarianism and intuitionism and on the relation between utilitarianism and egoism.

He begins with the relationship between utilitarianism and intuitionism, summarizing the conclusions reached at the end of Book III and in the earlier chapters of Book IV:

We have found that the common antithesis between Intuitionists and Utilitarians must be entirely discarded: since such abstract moral principles as we can admit to be really self-evident are not only not incompatible with a Utilitarian system, but even seem required to furnish a rational basis for such a system. (496)

He then reminds us that, by contrast, the "proof" of utilitarianism as against egoism fails, for reasons articulated in IV.II:

> In chap. ii. of this Book we have discussed the rational process (called by a stretch of language 'proof') by which one who holds it reasonable to aim at his own greatest happiness may be determined to take Universal Happiness instead, as his ultimate standard of right conduct. We have seen, however, that the application of this process requires that the Egoist should affirm, implicitly or explicitly, that his own greatest happiness is not merely the rational ultimate end for himself, but a part of Universal Good: and he may avoid the proof of Utilitarianism by declining to affirm this. (497–98)

11.2. The Argument for the Rationality of Egoism

At this point Sidgwick introduces something new, an argument for the rationality of egoism:

> It would be contrary to Common Sense to deny that the distinction between any one individual and any other is real and fundamental, and that consequently "I" am concerned with the quality of my existence as an individual in a sense, fundamentally important, in which I am not concerned with the quality of existence of other individuals: and this being so, I do not see how it can be proved that this distinction is not to be taken as fundamental

in determining the ultimate end of rational action for an individual. (498)

The setup in the late editions of the *Methods* makes it easy to miss the novelty and significance of this passage. It appears in the middle of a paragraph right after the already familiar material about why the "proof" of utilitarianism as against egoism fails. The casual reader might take the passage to contain merely an alternative explanation of this point. To see that the argument it contains has a different and greater significance, you need to look to Sidgwick's writings outside the *Methods*, specifically to his 1889 article "Some Fundamental Ethical Controversies." There he writes:

> I have not, therefore, seen cause to modify my view; but I admit that I put it forward without a sufficient rational justification, so far as Egoism is concerned. This objection was forcibly urged in a review of my book (2nd edition) by Prof. v. Gizycki [. . .] where it was pointed out that I had made no attempt to show the irrationality of the sacrifice of self-interest to duty. I will not pause to explain how the plan of my book—concerned as it was with 'methods' rather than 'principles—led to this omission: I quite agree with Prof. v. Gizycki that the missing argument, if demanded, ought to be supplied; and certainly the assumption on which the rationality of Egoism is based has been denied by philosophers; though the denial seems to Common Sense so absurd that a serious demand for its explicit statement is rather paradoxical. The assumption is simply that the distinction between any one individual and any other is real and fundamental, and that consequently 'I' am concerned with the quality of my existence as an individual in a sense, fundamentally important, in which I am not concerned with the quality of the existence of other individuals. If this be admitted, the proposition that this distinction is to be taken as fundamental in determining the end

of rational action for an individual cannot be disproved; and to me this proposition seems self-evident.[1]

This passage from "Some Fundamental Ethical Controversies" suggests that nothing that appeared in earlier editions of the *Methods* constitutes the argument for the rationality of egoism. But both a version of the material on the maxim of prudence in III. XIII (which we discussed in Chapter 7) and a version of the material explaining why the "proof" of utilitarianism as against egoism fails in IV.II (which we discussed in Chapter 9) did appear in those earlier editions of the *Methods*. So Sidgwick clearly indicates that this argument for the rationality of egoism, which (as we've just seen) was inserted almost verbatim into the Concluding Chapter in late editions of the *Methods*, is something new and important.

This new material adds to the significant difficulties we have already noticed in understanding Sidgwick on the principle of egoism. As we noticed in Chapter 5, in Book II on egoism (in sharp contrast to Book III on intuitionism) Sidgwick nowhere considers whether its first principle meets the four conditions for genuine self-evidence. As we saw in Chapter 7, the crucial paragraph on the maxim of prudence in III.XIII allows for three different candidates to be the principle of prudence: "hereafter as such is to be regarded neither less nor more than now," "there is a *prima facie* duty to aim at one's good on the whole," and "there is a duty proper to aim at one's good on the whole." As we saw in Chapter 9, in IV.II we get the first introduction of the distinction between (absolute) goodness and goodness-for in explaining why the "proof" of utilitarianism as against egoism fails. Finally, here in the Concluding Chapter, we get the further complication of the introduction of this new argument for the rationality of egoism. Anyone in the business of interpreting the dualism of practical reason needs to find a way to make all this fit together to generate a consistent view on the principle of egoism. The complexity of that task is one part of the explanation why there is—as we will see in Section 11.5—significant disagreement as to how best to understand the dualism.

Putting aside these more general interpretive issues, we should now ask how to understand the new argument for the rationality of egoism, and how strong an argument it is.[2] Begin with the question how to understand the argument. As we saw in **Chapters 3 and 4**, Sidgwick thinks that there is a basic distinction between factual and evaluative claims, and so that any good argument for an evaluative conclusion needs an evaluative premise. Keeping this lesson in mind, the obvious way carefully to formulate the argument is:

(1) The distinction between any one individual and any other is real and fundamental.

(2) If the distinction between any one individual and any other is real and fundamental, then I ought to be concerned with the quality of my existence as an individual in a sense, fundamentally important, in which I ought not to be concerned with the quality of the existence of other individuals.

Therefore, (3) I ought to be concerned with the quality of my existence as an individual in a sense, fundamentally important, in which I ought not to be concerned with the quality of the existence of other individuals.

In accordance with the lesson from earlier chapters, this formulation makes it explicit that the conclusion, (3), is evaluative, and that one of the premises is also evaluative: conditional premise (2). By contrast, premise (1) is a (extremely familiar and commonsensical) factual claim.

The next question is how strong the argument is. I think that, while it is a strong argument for a conclusion related to egoism, it is not a strong argument for egoism itself. A way to see this is to notice the difference between the conclusion of the argument, (3), and egoism. The conclusion of the argument is that I ought to be concerned with the quality of my existence in a way in which I ought not to be concerned with the quality of the existence of others. As we might rephrase this, the conclusion is that I ought to be *specially* concerned with the quality of my existence. According to rational egoism, by contrast, I ought to be *exclusively* concerned with the quality of my existence. But special concern need not take the form of exclusive concern. There are all sorts of other ways in which I might be specially concerned with the quality of my existence: I might give it three times, or six times, as much weight as I give the quality of others' existence. Once you begin thinking about this, it quickly becomes apparent that there are indefinitely many forms such special concern might take. Rational egoism involves the very strongest version of such special concern: giving exclusive weight to the quality of my existence and no weight at all to the quality of the existence of other individuals. The argument is a good argument for some kind of special concern for the quality of my existence. It is not a good argument for the exclusive concern for the quality of my existence that rational egoism involves.

11.3. Sanctions Again

The bulk of the Concluding Chapter is devoted to sanctions. As we saw in Chapter 9, if the "proof" of utilitarianism against egoism fails, if the egoist cannot be brought to accept the correctness of the utilitarian first principle, the fallback is an appeal to sanctions. As Sidgwick puts it on page 498:

> If an Egoist remains impervious to what we have called Proof, the only way of rationally inducing him to aim at the happiness of all, is to show him that his own greatest happiness can be best attained by so doing. (498)

Sidgwick draws first on II.V (which we discussed in Chapter 5). As we saw, he there concludes that three categories of sanction distinguished in the earlier utilitarian tradition, legal, social, and conscientious sanctions, do not make egoism and common-sense morality fully coincide. While it will usually be in an egoist's interest to follow common-sense moral rules, these sanctions do not make it always in an egoist's interest to do so. Noting that utilitarianism requires more in the way of self-sacrifice than does common-sense morality, Sidgwick concludes that it is even less likely that these sanctions will secure a perfect coincidence between utilitarianism and egoism than it is that they will secure a perfect coincidence between common-sense morality and egoism:

> It must be admitted that [...] whatever difference exists between Utilitarian morality and that of Common Sense is of such a kind as to render the coincidence with Egoism still more improbable in the case of the former. (499)

He then turns to consider two further sanctions: sanctions of sympathy and religious sanctions. His verdicts about these two further sanctions are different. His view about the sympathetic sanctions is the same as his view about the legal, social, and conscientious sanctions: while they will make it the case that it is usually in an egoist's interest to act as utilitarianism requires, they will not make it always in an egoist's interest to so act.

> It [...] seems to me as certain as any conclusion arrived at by hedonistic comparison can be, that the utmost development of sympathy [...] which is now possible to any but a few exceptional persons, would not cause a perfect coincidence between Utilitarian duty and self-interest. (501–2)

By contrast, the religious sanction would, all on its own, guarantee a perfect coincidence between utilitarianism and egoism.

> From this point of view the Utilitarian code is conceived as the Law of God, who is to be regarded as having commanded men to promote the general happiness, and as having announced

an intention of rewarding those who obey His commands and punishing the disobedient. It is clear that if we feel convinced that an Omnipotent Being has, in whatever way, signified such commands and announcements, a rational egoist can want no further inducement to frame his life on Utilitarian principles. (504)

The problem with the religious sanction is not its effectiveness in securing a perfect coincidence between utilitarianism and egoism. It is the difficulty of coming to know that there is the right kind of God or other cosmic setup.[3] Sidgwick says that such knowledge cannot be acquired in the way in which (as we've seen) he thinks knowledge of fundamental ethical principles can be acquired: through intuition.

I find that I undoubtedly seem to perceive, as clearly and certainly as I see any axiom in Arithmetic or Geometry, that it is 'right' and 'reasonable' for me to treat others as I should think that I myself ought to be treated under similar conditions, and to do what I believe to be ultimately conducive to general good or happiness. But I cannot find inseparably connected with this conviction, and similarly attainable by mere reflective intuition, any cognition that there actually is a Supreme Being who will adequately reward me for obeying these rules of duty, or punish me for violating them. (507)

11.4. Sidgwick's Characterizations of the Dualism

Sidgwick's most important characterizations of the dualism are to be found on page 508:

For the negation of the connexion [of Virtue and self-interest] must force us to admit an ultimate and fundamental contradiction in our apparent intuitions of what is Reasonable in conduct; and from this admission it would seem to follow that the apparently intuitive operation of the Practical Reason, manifested in these contradictory judgments, is after all illusory.

I do not mean that if we gave up the hope of attaining a practical solution of this fundamental contradiction, through any legitimately obtained conclusion or postulate as to the moral order of the world, it would become reasonable for us to abandon morality altogether: but it would seem necessary to abandon the idea of rationalizing it completely. We should doubtless still, not only from self-interest, but also through sympathy and sentiments protective of social wellbeing, imparted by education and sustained by communication with other men, feel a desire for the general observance of rules conducive to general happiness; and practical reason would still impel us decisively to the performance of duty in the more ordinary cases in which what is recognised as duty is in harmony with self-interest properly understood. But in the rarer cases of a recognised conflict between self-interest and duty, practical reason, being divided against itself, would cease to be a motive on either side; the conflict would have to be decided by the comparative preponderance of one or other of two groups of non-rational impulses.

If then the reconciliation of duty and self-interest is to be regarded as a hypothesis logically necessary to avoid a fundamental contradiction in one chief department of our thought, it remains to ask how far this necessity constitutes a sufficient reason for accepting this hypothesis. (508)

This passage, which stayed largely unchanged over the course of the revisions between the later editions of the *Methods*, is less dramatically phrased than the famous ending of the first edition:

The whole system of our beliefs as to the intrinsic reasonableness of conduct must fall, without a hypothesis unverifiable by experience reconciling the Individual with the Universal Reason, without a belief, in some form or other, that the moral order which we see imperfectly realised in this actual world is yet actually perfect. If we reject this belief, we may perhaps still find in the non-moral universe an adequate object for the Speculative Reason, capable of being in some sense ultimately understood. But the Cosmos of Duty is thus really reduced to a Chaos: and the prolonged effort of the human intellect to frame a perfect ideal of rational conduct is seen to have been foredoomed to inevitable failure.[4]

Two things are particularly worth noting in these passages. First, Sidgwick consistently treats the dualism as a fundamental and devastating problem. It is, as he says more than once in the passage from the end of the seventh edition, a "fundamental contradiction." To accept it would be, as he says at the end of the first edition, to reduce the cosmos of duty to a chaos. Second, Sidgwick is not committed to the view that there actually is a fundamental contradiction, that the cosmos of duty actually is a chaos. Rather, what he is committed to is a conditional. To borrow language from a passage we quoted earlier, the conditional is:

If there is not a Supreme Being who will adequately reward me for obeying the rules of duty, then there is a fundamental contradiction in practical reason.

This conditional can be part of two different arguments. In one argument, we affirm the antecedent, that there is indeed no such supreme being, and end up with the conclusion that there is a fundamental contradiction in our practical reason. In the other we deny the consequent, and end up with an argument for the existence of God. Sidgwick was torn between these different arguments. In his more pessimistic moods he was apt to believe that the cosmos of duty was a chaos. But, as we saw in Chapter 1, he devoted a great deal of intellectual energy to trying to find evidence for the existence of God. It was not for nothing that Keynes said of him:

> He never did anything but wonder whether Christianity was true and prove that it wasn't and hope that it was.[5]

So Sidgwick was of course tempted by the other way of appealing to the conditional: as part of an argument for the existence of God. The final paragraph of the *Methods* shows how seriously he took this possibility.

> Those who hold that the edifice of physical science is really constructed of conclusions logically inferred from self-evident premises, may reasonably demand that any practical judgments claiming philosophic certainty should be based on an equally firm foundation. If on the other hand we find that in our supposed knowledge of the world of nature propositions are commonly taken to be universally true, which yet seem to rest on no other grounds than that we have a strong disposition to accept them, and that they are indispensable to the systematic coherence of our beliefs, - it will be more difficult to reject a similarly supported assumption in ethics, without opening the door to universal scepticism. (509)

11.5. Overview Discussion: Interpretations of the Dualism

There has been much debate in the secondary literature as to how to interpret the dualism. And a significant number of interpreters deny that the dualism is best understood as a contradiction. After reading the passages just quoted this may be surprising: Surely Sidgwick is very explicit in these passages that the dualism is a contradiction. How could it then be reasonably understood as anything less? The answer, as we will see, is twofold. First, Sidgwick is much less clear than he might be as to what exactly the conflicting utilitarian and egoist principles say. Even the idea that the dualism is a contradiction comes in two importantly different forms. Second, what Sidgwick says elsewhere in the *Methods* can be taken to cut against what he says in the passages at the end of the Concluding Chapter. So, despite what he says in these passages, the best charitable interpretation of the *Methods* overall might indeed be that the dualism involves a kind of conflict that is something other and less than a contradiction.

To understand the interpretive options it is helpful to begin by recalling the ambiguities we noticed in Chapter 7 as to how to understand the maxim of prudence and the maxim of benevolence articulated in III.XIII. We there distinguished three different possible understandings of the maxim of prudence, which we can now number:

(P1) There is an absolute duty to aim at one's good on the whole.
(P2) There is a *prima facie* duty to aim at one's good on the whole.
(P3) Hereafter *as such* is to be regarded neither less nor more than now.

We also noticed two different possible understandings of the maxim of benevolence, corresponding to (P1) and (P2), which we can also now number:

(B1) There is an absolute duty to aim at universal good.
(B2) There is a *prima facie* duty to aim at universal good.

We said in Chapter 7 that (B1) is a stronger claim than (B2); and that therefore (B2) is a better candidate to be self-evident, to satisfy the four conditions from III.XI, than is (B1). Similarly (P1) is a stronger claim than (P2) and (P3); and therefore (P2) and (P3) are better candidates to be self-evident, to satisfy the four conditions from III.XI, than is (P1).

To complete the framework we need in order to understand the range of interpretations of the dualism we have to do two further things. First we need to add two claims, even stronger than (P1) and (B1) respectively, which we can number (P0) and (B0):

(P0) The only absolute duty is to aim at one's good on the whole.
(B0) The only absolute duty is to aim at universal good.

Second, in the light of our discussion in Section 11.2, of the argument for the rationality of egoism, we need to introduce yet one further claim, stronger than (P2) but weaker than (P1), which we can number (P1.5).

(P1.5) There is a specially strong *prima facie* duty to aim at one's good on the whole.

We are then in a position to understand the different interpretations of the dualism as the products of different readings of the competing egoist and utilitarian principles. Begin with the two interpretations according to which the dualism is a contradiction. The first of these we can call the "immediate contradiction" interpretation. This is the interpretation you get if you understand the competing egoist and utilitarian principles as (P0) and (B0). On this interpretation, the contradiction is generated simply by the two principles themselves. No additional claims are required to generate it. Though this interpretation has not been prominent in recent secondary literature, it is the interpretation offered by two early readers who certainly knew their Sidgwick: Moore and Broad. Moore thinks Sidgwick's discussion of the dualism is confused, but that the only proper interpretation of the dualism is as a matter of an immediate contradiction of the kind generated by (P0) and (B0):

That *each* man's happiness should be the *sole good* [...] and that it should also be true that the Happiness of all is the *sole good* [is a] contradiction. And that these propositions should all be true might well be called 'the profoundest problem in Ethics': it would be a problem necessarily insoluble. But they *cannot* all be true, and there is no reason, but confusion, for the suggestion that they are.[6]

Broad concurs, though his criticism of Sidgwick is less pointed:

There are two principles which are logically inconsistent with each other, and, on reflexion each seems to Sidgwick equally self-evident. No God, however powerful and however benevolent, can alter the fact that these two principles are logically incompatible and that therefore something which seemed self-evident to Sidgwick must in fact have been false.[7]

This interpretation tracks something important in Sidgwick. He has a commitment to theoretical unity, particularly clearly expressed in a passage from Book I Chapter III of the first edition of the *Methods*:

Conduct appears to us irrational, or at least imperfectly rational, not only if the maxims upon which it is professedly based conflict with and contradict one another, but also if they cannot be bound together and firmly concatenated by means of some one fundamental principle.[8]

To interpret the dualism as Moore and Ross do, as involving an immediate contradiction, is to think of the egoist and utilitarian principles as competing for a status that necessarily only one of them can have: the status of being the one fundamental principle of practical reason.

The passages from Moore and Broad also, however, point to a reason to explore a different interpretation. As we have just seen,

Sidgwick does think that the right kind of God or cosmic setup would resolve the dualism. We can ask: is there a way to understand the dualism as a contradiction, but one that the existence of an all-powerful and benevolent deity would resolve? The answer is that there is: what we can call the "mediate contradiction" interpretation. On the mediate contradiction interpretation, the competing egoist and utilitarian principles are (P1) and (B1). On their own (P1) and (B1) do not generate a contradiction. We get a contradiction only if we add to them a third claim, which we can call "No Moral Government":

> (No Moral Government) Sometimes the action we are required to take if we have an absolute duty to aim at our own good conflicts with the action we are required to take if we have an absolute duty to aim at universal good.

What we then get is a contradiction generated by the combination of three claims, (P1), (B1), and No Moral Government; put another way, (P1), (B1) and No Moral Government together form an inconsistent triad. This is a contradiction that the existence of the right kind of all-powerful and benevolent deity or other cosmic setup would resolve. If there is such a deity or cosmic setup then No Moral Government is false, and there is no contradiction.

This mediate contradiction interpretation thus has significant attractions. It fits very nicely with the text of the Concluding Chapter of the *Methods*, in that it makes the dualism a contradiction, but a contradiction that the religious sanction would eliminate. Unsurprisingly the mediate contradiction interpretation has a number of distinguished proponents. They include Jerome Schneewind in *Sidgwick's Ethics and Victorian Moral Philosophy*, the starting point for recent scholarship on Sidgwick;[9] William Frankena;[10] John Mackie (in his article "Sidgwick's Pessimism");[11] and Bart Schultz in his important biographical work on Sidgwick, both in *The Eye of the Universe* and *The Happiness Philosophers*.[12]

THE DUALISM OF PRACTICAL REASON 225

Given the clear attractions of the mediate contradiction interpretation, it is worth raising again the question why a significant number of readers should nonetheless be tempted to understand the dualism instead as something other and less than a contradiction. There are several potentially overlapping motivations. We can begin with one which has a very clear Sidgwickian pedigree. As we saw in Chapter 6, in III.XI Sidgwick articulates the four conditions that putatively self-evident principles have to satisfy. According to the third of them:

> The propositions accepted as self-evident must be mutually consistent. Here, again, it is obvious that any collision between two intuitions is a proof that there is error in one of the other, or in both. Still, we frequently find ethical writers treating this point very lightly. They appear to regard a conflict of ultimate rules as a difficulty that may be ignored or put aside for future solution, without any slur being thrown on the scientific character of the conflicting formulae. Whereas such a collision in absolute proof that at least one of the formulae needs qualification. (341)

Sidgwick, it can be argued, is in danger of making the same mistake he here accuses "ethical writers" of making. If the otherwise apparently self-evident formulae of egoism and utilitarianism contradict one another, this is "absolute proof that at least one of the formulae needs qualification." And, as we have already seen, there are ways to qualify or reinterpret the egoist and utilitarian principles so that they no longer contradict one another. If we understand the egoist and utilitarian principles as (P2) or (P1.5) and (B2), as principles of *prima facie* duty rather than absolute duty, then they no longer contradict one another.[13] Or if we understand the egoist principle as (P3), it no longer contradicts any of the utilitarian principles, even (B0).

This line of thought can be interestingly supplemented by reflecting on Schultz's work. Schultz emphasizes that Sidgwick was very committed to regarding the dualism as a contradiction, in part because doing so sets up an argument for the existence of God by which he was strongly tempted. If we further recall that Sidgwick is very concerned to assess the self-evidence of the putative axioms of the common-sense moralist, but strikingly reticent about similarly assessing the putative axiom of the egoist, we might suggest that this reticence is no accident. At some level, it can be suggested, Sidgwick doesn't want to subject the principle of egoism to careful scrutiny because he wants the dualism to come out as a contradiction and he fears that if he subjects the egoist principle to careful scrutiny the contradiction will disappear. In one way this point might be taken to support the contradiction interpretations of the dualism. But in another way it might not: the idea that the dualism is a contradiction might be something Sidgwick wants to believe in order to generate the argument for the existence of God, but something which he is not properly entitled to believe.

A final motivation for non-contradiction interpretations is an ethically constructive one. Some philosophers think that there is an important truth about practical reason that is captured by Sidgwick. An error theorist like Mackie can combine this thought with the idea that the dualism is a contradiction—indeed, one way of reading the article "Sidgwick's Pessimism" is as articulating an argument for error theory significantly different from the argument Mackie famously made in *Ethics*.[14] But anyone other than an error theorist who sees important truth in the dualism will be disposed to understand the dualism as something less than a contradiction.

Three different non-contradiction interpretations of the dualism have been articulated and defended in the philosophical literature. All involve in some way weakening or qualifying the egoist and utilitarian principles so they no longer contradict one another. The most common non-contradiction interpretation, which we can introduce as "the *prima facie* duty interpretation," weakens both the egoist and the utilitarian principles. It understands the egoist principle as (P1.5) or as (P2) and the utilitarian principle as (B2).

A second non-contradiction interpretation, defended by Robert Shaver in *Rational Egoism*, weakens only the egoist principle, understanding it merely as (P3).[15] We can call it "Shaver's egoism-deflating interpretation." A third non-contradiction interpretation, defended in two articles by David Brink, qualifies the egoist principle and the utilitarian principle not by weakening them but by restricting their scope. As Brink sees it, (P1) is Sidgwick's principle for the domain of practical reason, while (B1) is Sidgwick's principle for the domain of morality. We can call this "Brink's two domains interpretation."[16]

Philosophers who have suggested and explored something like the *prima facie* duty interpretation include Derek Parfit, Roger Crisp, myself, and Owen McLeod. Our provisional label for interpretations of this kind is, however, potentially misleading. For these philosophers by no means all employ the concept of *prima facie* duty. Instead they employ a range of concepts, including the concept of the (rationally) permissible and the ubiquitous contemporary concept of a normative reason.[17] But, though they differ in important details, all these interpretations have the same fundamental effect as Ross's introduction of the concept of *prima facie* duty: the effect of turning egoist and utilitarian principles formulated in terms of duty proper that contradict one another into egoist and utilitarian principles formulated in other terms that do not contradict one another.

We should begin our survey of interpretations of this kind with Parfit's extremely influential work. In Volume 1 of *On What Matters*[18] Parfit articulated a view as to how to understand Sidgwick's dualism that he had long held:

> Objective theories also differ in their claims about whose well-being we have reasons to promote. We can next consider three such theories. According to
> *Rational Egoism*: We always have most reason to do whatever would be best for ourselves. According to *Rational*

> *Impartialism*: We always have most reason to do whatever would be impartially best [. . .]
>
> In his great, drab book *The Methods of Ethics*, Sidgwick qualifies and combines these two views. According to what Sidgwick calls *The Dualism of Practical Reason*: We always have most reason to do whatever would be impartially best, unless some other act would be best for ourselves. In such cases, we would have sufficient reasons to act in either way. If we knew the relevant facts, either act would be rational.
>
> Of these three views, Sidgwick's, I believe, is the closest to the truth.[19]

Characteristically, Parfit does not here defend this non-contradiction interpretation of the dualism as against the contradiction interpretation. Also characteristically, he formulates the interpretation in terms of reasons and rationality rather than in terms of *prima facie* duty. And his project is ethically constructive: he sees the dualism as importantly close to the truth about practical reason.

There is significant further variety in the conceptual apparatus and terminology employed by others who develop interpretations of this kind. Roger Crisp prefers to think solely in terms of reasons.[20] Particularly in my 1998 article I think primarily in terms of rational permissibility, though I also moot something close to the concept of *prima facie* duty.[21] It is McLeod who most straightforwardly formulates his interpretation in terms, in effect, of the concept of *prima facie* duty.[22]

It is also tempting for those who think of the dualism as expressing an important truth about practical reason to employ other terminology popularized by Parfit and by Thomas Nagel which we introduced in Chapter 9:[23] to think that in his reluctant sympathy with egoism Sidgwick is recognizing the important fact that there are agent-relative reasons, while in his utilitarian sympathies he is recognizing the equally important fact that there are agent-neutral reasons. And once we frame things in this way it is natural to ask how the agent-relative and agent-neutral reasons weigh against one another. Everyone we initially characterized (potentially misleadingly) as embracing the *prima facie* duty interpretation raises in one form or another this question of weighting. The range of possible answers is wide, both about what view about weighting is best as an interpretation of Sidgwick, and about what view about weighting is closest to the truth about practical reason.

The other two non-contradiction interpretations have been each been developed by just one interpreter of Sidgwick. As we noted earlier in briefly introducing it, the key to the egoism-deflating interpretation Robert Shaver presents in *Rational Egoism* is an asymmetric weakening of the egoistic side of the dualism. He suggests, in effect, that the egoistic principle is simply (P3), the principle of temporal irrelevance. And that principle does not contradict any utilitarian principle. The distinctive worry about Shaver's interpretation, in addition to those faced by any non-contradiction interpretation, is about this asymmetry, about whether Sidgwick's commitment to egoism can really be a matter merely of a commitment to temporal irrelevance.

As we also noted in briefly introducing it, Brink's interpretation eliminates the contradiction not by weakening the competing utilitarian and egoist principles but instead by restricting their scope. He treats the egoist principle as the correct principle for the domain of practical reason and the utilitarian principle as the correct principle for the domain of morality. The distinctive worry about Brink's interpretation, in addition to those faced by any non-contradiction interpretation, is about whether these domain restrictions can really be grounded in the text of the *Methods*. The problem is not so much with the idea that egoism is not a principle of morality; there is textual evidence that can be adduced in support of it. The problem is rather in the restriction of the utilitarian principle to the moral domain. There is lots of countervailing evidence that Sidgwick instead consistently thinks of the utilitarian principle as competing with the egoist principle in the (for him more important) domain of practical reason.

A final important recent treatment of the dualism is to be found in the work of Katarzyna de Lazari-Radek and Peter Singer.[24] They are not primarily concerned with Sidgwick interpretation. Their aim rather is to resolve the dualism in a way of which Sidgwick would approve, by undermining egoism. Their key innovation is to employ resources famously deployed by Sharon Street. In "A Darwinian Dilemma for Realist Theories of Value"[25] and elsewhere, Street develops an evolutionary debunking argument: an argument that the powerful evolutionary influence on our evaluative thinking undermines our justification for accepting evaluative claims if these are construed as realists—like Sidgwick—construe them. Street's is a general debunking argument, targeting all evaluative beliefs. De Lazari-Radek and Singer's key innovation is to develop instead a selective variant of Street's argument: an evolutionary debunking argument that, they claim, undermines egoism but not utilitarianism. They give an updated three-condition variant of Sidgwick's four conditions:

1. Careful reflection leading to a conviction of self-evidence
2. Independent agreement of other careful thinkers
3. The absence of a plausible explanation of the intuition as a non-truth-tracking psychological process[26]

and they claim that while a debunking explanation for the self-interest principle can be given, "Sidgwick's axiom of universal benevolence passes [the] test."[27]

Their strategy is an interesting one. For it to succeed, they need to be able to debunk the egoistic principle without debunking the utilitarian principle. And they also need not to debunk hedonism. Critics have—of course—cast doubt on whether they can succeed in achieving all these aims. And if they do succeed, Sidgwick would get one thing he would certainly have liked—an argument for the truth of utilitarianism—at the cost of losing another thing he also very much wanted, an argument for the existence of God.

Notes

1. Sidgwick (1889) 2000, 44.
2. For a different take on the argument, see Shaver 2020.
3. In footnote 1 on page 507 Sidgwick makes it clear that "it is not necessary, if we are simply considering Ethics as a possible independent science, to throw the fundamental premiss of which we are now examining the validity into a Theistic form." In Buddhism "[the] notion of the rewards inseparably attaching to right conduct seems to have been developed in a far more elaborate and systematic manner than [. . .] in [. . .] Christianity. But, as conceived by enlightened Buddhists, these rewards are not distributed by the volition of a Supreme Person, but by the natural operation of an impersonal Law."
4. Sidgwick 1874, 473.
5. Quoted on p. 118 of Regan 1986.
6. Moore 1903, 103.
7. Broad 1930, 253.
8. Sidgwick 1874, 26.
9. Schneewind 1977, Chapter 13.
10. Frankena 1974.
11. Mackie 1976.
12. Schultz 2004; Schultz 2017.
13. As we noted in Chapter 7, Sidgwick regrettably did not have the concept of *prima facie* duty. So while the move from principles of duty proper to principles of *prima facie* duty can be justified by appeal to condition 3, Sidgwick himself did not envisage this way of qualifying principles which would otherwise contradict one another. As we suggested in Chapter 7, this is a reason to treat the *prima facie* duty interpretation as a specification of what Sidgwick *ought* to have thought rather than as a specification of what he *did* think.
14. Mackie 1976; Mackie 1977.
15. Shaver 1999.
16. Brink 1988; Brink 1992.

17. For a discussion of the relationship between Ross's concept of *prima facie* duty and the contemporary concept of a normative reason, see Phillips 2019, Chapter 2.
18. Parfit 2011a.
19. Parfit 2011a, 130–31.
20. Crisp 1996.
21. Phillips 1998; see also Phillips 2011, Chapter 5.
22. McLeod 2000.
23. Parfit 1984; Nagel 1986.
24. Lazari-Radek and Singer 2012; Lazari-Radek and Singer 2014, Chapter 7.
25. Street 2006.
26. Lazari-Radek and Singer 2014, 195.
27. Lazari-Radek and Singer 2014, 196.

Guide to Terminology

If the term was initially introduced and/or helpfully defined by Sidgwick or by one of the other philosophers whose work we have discussed I give their definition. Where terms are explained or discussed in specific places in this book, the entries include references to those places.

Axiom: A foundational, self-evident principle.

Benevolence, Maxim of: "Each one is morally bound to regard the good of any other individual at least as much as his own, except in so far as he judges it to be less, when impartially viewed, or less certainly knowable or attainable by him." (382) (Section 7.4)

Coherentism: The view in epistemology that justification involves sets of propositions which fit together and are mutually supporting. (Contrast with "Foundationalism") (Section 4.2; Section 9.6)

Common-Sense Morality: In the narrow sense, a synonym for "Dogmatic Intuitionism": the view that what are really self-evident are absolute, non-consequentialist moral rules. (However, the term is ambiguous between a narrow and a broad sense. In the narrow sense common-sense morality includes only the deontological principles common sense is disposed to accept. In the broad sense, common-sense morality includes the egoistic and utilitarian principles common sense is disposed to accept as well as the deontological principles common sense is disposed to accept.) (Section 6.1)

Consequentialism: "[Consequentialist] theories hold that the rightness or wrongness of an action is always determined by its tendency to produce certain consequences which are good or bad." (Broad 1930, 206–7. Broad does not call views of this kind "consequentialist." He calls them instead "teleological." The name "consequentialism" comes from Anscombe 1958.) (Contrast with "Deontology") (Section 4.1)

Deontology: "Deontological theories hold that there are ethical propositions of the form: "Such and such a kind of action would always be right (or wrong) in such and such circumstances, no matter what the consequences might be." (Broad 1930, 206) (Contrast with "Consequentialism"; see also

"Intuitionism," "Dogmatic Intuitionism (or Absolutist Deontology)"; Moderate Deontology) (Section 4.1)

Dogmatic Intuitionism (or Absolutist Deontology): The view that what are really self-evident are absolute, non-consequentialist moral rules. (Note that the definition is problematic. When Sidgwick introduces dogmatic intuitionism as the second "phase" of intuitionism it is introduced as the view that what are really self-evident are general moral rules. The classification scheme from which this definition comes distinguishes the different phases of intuitionism by reference to the particularity or generality of the claims that are really self-evident, and so should be neutral with respect to moral theory. Sidgwick nonetheless standardly treats dogmatic intuitionism as a deontological view.) (Contrast with "Perceptional Intuitionism" and with "Philosophical Intuitionism"; See also "Intuitionism," "Deontology," "Moderate Deontology") (Section 4.3)

Dualism of Practical Reason: The idea that there is an unresolvable conflict between egoism and utilitarianism. (Chapter 11)

Egoism (or Egoistic Hedonism): The theory, that the conduct which, under any given circumstances, is objectively right, is that which will produce the greatest amount of happiness for the agent.

Epistemic: To do with knowledge.

Epistemic Intuitionism: Fundamental moral truths are self-evident. (Section 4.1; see also "Intuitionism").

Epistemology: The theory of knowledge.

Ethical First Principle: An ethical first principle asserts that some property which acts may or may not possess is an ultimate reason for the rightness of acts. (Schneewind 1977, 194–95) (Section 2.4)

First Principle: A foundational, self-evident principle.

Foundationalism: The view in epistemology that justification is linear and has to begin with propositions that provide justification but do not themselves require justification from other propositions. (Contrast with "Coherentism") (Section 4.2; Section 9.6)

(The) Four Conditions: The conditions that supposedly self-evident axioms have to meet (Sidgwick 1907, 338–42). Here are brief expressions of them: (1) The terms of the proposition must be clear and precise; (2) The proposition must genuinely seem self-evident; (3) All the self-evident propositions must be consistent with one another; (4) There should be no disagreement between epistemic peers as to the truth of the proposition. (Section 6.3)

Hedonism (or Ethical Hedonism): Pleasure or Happiness is the only thing that is intrinsically good; pain or unhappiness is the only thing that is intrinsically bad. (Contrast with "Psychological Hedonism")

Intuitionism: A hybrid concept in Sidgwick with two quite distinct components, one epistemic and the other moral-theoretic. The epistemic component is the idea that fundamental moral truths are self-evident. The moral-theoretic component is the idea that the fundamental moral truths are absolute rules which do not take into account consequences. Noting the problems involved in using a single concept to cover these two quite distinct ideas, Broad introduced the term "Deontology" as the name for the moral-theoretic idea. The epistemic idea can then be called "Epistemic Intuitionism." (Broad 1930, 206) (Section 4.1)

Justice, Principle of: "It cannot be right for A to treat B in a manner in which it would be wrong for B to treat A, merely on the ground that they are two different individuals, and without there being any difference between the natures or the circumstances of the two which can be stated as a reasonable ground for difference of treatment." (Sidgwick 1907, 380) (Section 7.2)

Metaethics: "The philosophical study of questions about the nature of ethical judgment as distinct from questions of normative ethics, for example, whether ethical judgments state facts or express attitudes, whether there are objective standards of morality, and how moral judgments can be justified." (Collins English Dictionary)

Method of Ethics: "Any rational procedure by which we determine what individual human beings 'ought'—or what it is 'right' for them—to do, or to seek to realise by voluntary action." (Sidgwick 1907, 1) (Section 2.4)

Moderate Deontology: The view that deontological principles are principles of *prima facie* duty. (Contrast with "Dogmatic Intuitionism (or "Absolutist Deontology")"; see also "*Prima Facie* Duty") (Section 6.5)

Monistic Theory: A theory according to which there is just one thing of the relevant kind. (Hedonism, or Ethical Hedonism, is a monistic theory of the good because it says that happiness is the only thing that is intrinsically good.) (Contrast with "Pluralistic Theory")

Moral Theory (or Normative Ethics): The philosophical study of questions about what things are right/wrong, good/bad, virtuous/vicious, etc., and what makes them right/wrong, good/bad, virtuous/vicious etc. (Contrast with "Metaethics")

Naturalism: The metaethical view that in making moral judgments we are making statements that are true or false, and that moral judgments are a kind of factual judgment. (Contrast with "Non-Naturalism") (Section 3.1)

Non-Naturalism: The metaethical view that that in making moral judgments we are making statements that are true or false, and that moral judgments are fundamentally different from factual judgments. (Contrast with "Naturalism") (Section 3.1)

Perceptional Intuitionism: The view that the moral judgments that are self-evident are judgments about particular cases. (The first "phase" of intuitionism; contrast with "Dogmatic Intuitionism" and with "Philosophical Intuitionism") (Section 4.3)

Philosophical Intuitionism: The view that the moral principles that are self-evident are "of too abstract a nature, and too universal in their scope, to enable us to ascertain by immediate application of them what we ought to do in any particular case" (Sidgwick 1907, 379). (The third "phase" of intuitionism; contrast with "Perceptional Intuitionism" and "Dogmatic Intuitionism") (Section 4.3; Chapter 7)

Pluralistic Theory: A theory according to which there are multiple things of the relevant kind, rather than just one. (Ross's theory of the good, according to which virtue, knowledge, pleasure, and the allocation of pleasure to the virtuous are all intrinsically good, is a pluralistic theory of the good.) (Contrast with "Monistic Theory")

***Prima Facie* Duty:** "The characteristic (quite distinct from that of being a duty proper) which an act has, in virtue of being of a certain kind (e.g. the keeping of a promise), of being an act which would be a duty proper if it were not at the same time of another kind which is morally significant." (Ross 1930, 19) (Section 6.5)

"Proof" (in scare quotes): An argument in favor of a first principle. ("Proofs" are different from ordinary proofs. The impossibility of giving an ordinary proof of a first principle is a consequence of the nature of first principles. Giving an ordinary proof of anything else involves deducing it from a first principle. So first principles themselves cannot be the subject of ordinary proofs. In IV.II Sidgwick outlines the structure of the kind of "proofs" he considers: "A line of argument which on the one hand allows the validity, to a certain extent, of the maxims already accepted, and on the other hand shows them not to be absolutely valid, but needing to be controlled and completed by some more comprehensive principle.") (Sidgwick 1907, 420) (Section 9.3)

Psychological Hedonism: "Pleasure alone is the object of all our desires." (Moore 1903, 68) (Contrast with "Hedonism (or Ethical Hedonism)") (Section 3.2)

Reflective Equilibrium: A theory of epistemic justification most famously articulated in Rawls 1971. According to reflective equilibrium theory, the process of justification begins with initial considered judgments at all levels of generality. Some of these initial considered judgments will conflict with one another. There is then a process of mutual adjustment. At the end of that process, a stable point is reached. That point is reflective equilibrium. (Section 4.3; Section 9.6)

Sanctions: Incentives. "The pleasures consequent on conformity to moral rules, and the pains consequent on their violation [are] the 'sanctions' of these rules." (Sidgwick 1907, 164) (Section 5.4)

Self-Evident: Propositions are self-evident if they can be seen to be true by people who properly understand them. Like most philosophers who think moral intuitions are important, Sidgwick often appeals to mathematical knowledge as a model for moral knowledge. Fundamental moral truths are supposed to be self-evident in the way $1 + 1 = 2$ is self-evident. To know that $1 + 1 = 2$ you just need to understand the concepts involved. When you do, you see that it is true. (Section 4.1)

Utilitarianism (or Universalistic Hedonism): "The ethical theory, that the conduct which, under any given circumstances, is objectively right, is that which will produce the greatest amount of happiness on the whole." (Sidgwick 1907, 411)

Bibliography

Ancombe, G. E. M. 1958. "Modern Moral Philosophy." *Philosophy* 33:1–19.
Bentham, Jeremy. 1789. "Principles of Morals and Legislation," in Troyer, ed., 1–91.
Bradley, F. H. 1877. *Mr. Sidgwick's Hedonism*. London: Henry S. King.
Brink, David. 1988. "Sidgwick's Dualism of Practical Reason." *Australasian Journal of Philosophy* 66:291–307.
Brink, David. 1992. "Sidgwick and the Rationale for Rational Egoism," in Schultz, ed., 199–240.
Brink, David. 1994. "Common Sense and First Principles in Sidgwick's Methods." *Social Philosophy and Policy* 11:179–201.
Broad, C. D. 1930. *Five Types of Ethical Theory*. London: Kegan Paul.
Butler, Joseph. 2017. *Fifteen Sermons & Other Writings on Ethics*. Edited by David McNaughton. Oxford: Oxford University Press.
Crisp, Roger. 1996. "The Dualism of Practical Reason." *Proceedings of the Aristotelian Society* 96:53–73.
Crisp, Roger. 2015. *The Cosmos of Duty: Henry Sidgwick's Methods of Ethics*. Oxford: Clarendon Press.
Dancy, Jonathan. 2004. *Ethics Without Principles*. Oxford: Clarendon Press.
Daurio, J. 1997. "Sidgwick on Moral Theories and Common Sense Morality." *History of Philosophy Quarterly* 14:425–45.
Deigh, John. 1992. "Sidgwick on Ethical Judgement," in Schultz, ed., 241–58.
Donagan, Alan. 1977a. "Sidgwick and Whewellian Intuitionism: Some Enigmas," in Schultz, ed., 123–42.
Donagan, Alan. 1977b. *The Theory of Morality*. Chicago: University of Chicago Press.
Foot, Philippa. 1978. *Virtues and Vices*. Berkeley: University of California Press.
Frankena, William. 1939. "The Naturalistic Fallacy." *Mind* 48:464–77.
Frankena, William. 1974. "Sidgwick and the Dualism of Practical Reason," *Monist* 58:449–67.
Gibbard, Allan. 1990. *Wise Choices, Apt Feelings*. Cambridge, MA: Harvard University Press.
Habib, A. 2021. "Promises." *Stanford Encyclopedia of Philosophy*, Summer 2021 edition.
Hume, David. 1888. *A Treatise of Human Nature*. Edited by L. A. Selby-Bigge. Oxford: Clarendon Press.
Hurka, Thomas. 2003. "Moore in the Middle." *Ethics* 113 (3): 599–628.

Hurka, Thomas. 2014a. *British Ethical Theorists from Sidgwick to Ewing*. Oxford: Oxford University Press.
Hurka, Thomas. 2014b. "Sidgwick on Consequentialism and Deontology." *Utilitas* 26 (2): 129–52.
Irwin, T. 2009. *The Development of Ethics, Volume 3: From Kant to Rawls*. Oxford: Oxford University Press.
Kagan, Shelly. 1986. "The Present Aim Theory of Rationality." *Ethics* 96 (4): 746–59.
Lazari-Radek, Katarzyna de and Peter Singer. 2012. "The Objectivity of Ethics and the Unity of Practical Reason." *Ethics* 123 (1): 9–31.
Lazari-Radek, Katarzyna de and Peter Singer. 2014. *The Point of View of the Universe: Sidgwick & Contemporary Ethics*. Oxford: Oxford University Press.
Louden, Robert. 1996. "Towards a Genealogy of 'Deontology.'" *Journal of the History of Philosophy* 34 (4): 571–92.
MacIntryre, Alasdair. 1981. *After Virtue*. London: Duckworth.
Mackie, J. L. 1976. "Sidgwick's Pessimism." *Philosophical Quarterly* 26:317–27.
Mackie, J. L. 1977. *Ethics*. Harmondsworth: Penguin.
McCloskey, H. J. 1965. "A Non-Utilitarian Approach to Punishment." *Inquiry* 8:239–55.
McGrath, Sarah. 2019. *Moral Knowledge*. Oxford: Oxford University Press.
McLeod, O. 2000. "What is Sidgwick's Dualism of the Practical Reason?" *Pacific Philosophical Quarterly* 81:273–90.
Mill, J. S. 1861. "Utilitarianism," in Troyer, ed., 95–149.
Moore, G. E. 1903. *Principia Ethica*. Cambridge, UK: Cambridge University Press.
Moore, G.E. 1912. Ethics. London: Williams & Norgate.
Moore, G. E. 1942. "An Autobiography," in Schilpp, ed., 1–39.
Moore, G. E. 1993. *Principia Ethica*. Rev. ed. Cambridge, UK: Cambridge University Press.
Nagel, Thomas. 1970. *The Possibility of Altruism*. Oxford: Clarendon Press.
Nagel, Thomas. 1986. *The View from Nowhere*. New York: Oxford University Press.
Nakano-Okuno, M. 2011. *Sidgwick and Contemporary Utilitarianism*. Basingstoke: Palgrave MacMillan.
Parfit, Derek. 1984. *Reasons and Persons*. Oxford: Clarendon Press.
Parfit, Derek. 2011a. *On What Matters*. Vol. 1. Oxford: Oxford University Press.
Parfit, Derek. 2011b. *On What Matters*. Vol. 2. Oxford: Oxford University Press.
Paytas, Tyler, and Tim Henning, eds. 2020. *Kantian and Sidgwickian Ethics*. New York and London: Routledge.
Pereboom, Derk. 2001. *Living Without Free Will*. Cambridge, UK: Cambridge University Press.
Phillips, David. 1998. "Sidgwick, Dualism and Indeterminacy in Practical Reason." *History of Philosophy Quarterly* 15 (1): 57–78.

Phillips, David. 2011. *Sidgwickian Ethics*. New York: Oxford University Press.
Phillips, David. 2019. *Rossian Ethics: W. D. Ross and Contemporary Moral Theory*. New York: Oxford University Press.
Phillips, David. 2020. "Sidgwick's Kantian Account of Moral Motivation," in Paytas and Henning, eds., 84–104.
Pickard-Cambridge, W. A. 1932a. "Two Problems About Duty (I.)." *Mind* 41 (161): 72–96.
Pickard-Cambridge, W. A. 1932b. "Two Problems About Duty (II.)." *Mind* 41 (162): 145–72.
Pickard-Cambridge, W. A. 1932c. "Two Problems About Duty (III.)." *Mind* 41 (163): 311–40.
Price, Richard. 1974. *A Review of the Principal Questions of Morals*. Edited by D. D. Raphael. Oxford: Clarendon Press.
Prichard, H. A. 1912. "Does Moral Philosophy Rest on a Mistake?" *Mind* 21:21–37.
Rachels, James, and Stuart Rachels. 2012. *The Elements of Moral Philosophy*. 7th ed. New York: McGraw-Hill.
Rawls, John. 1971. *A Theory of Justice*. Cambridge, MA: Harvard University Press.
Regan, Tom. 1986. *Bloomsbury's Prophet: G. E. Moore and the Development of His Moral Philosophy*. Philadelphia: Temple University Press.
Riley, Jonathan. 2003. "Interpreting Mill's Qualitative Hedonism." *Philosophical Quarterly* 53 (212): 410–18.
Ross, W. D. 1930. *The Right and the Good*. Oxford: Clarendon Press.
Ross, W. D. 1939. *Foundations of Ethics*. Oxford: Clarendon Press.
Sayre-McCord, Geoffrey. 2001. "Mill's 'Proof' of the Principle of Utility: A More than Half-Hearted Defense." *Social Philosophy and Policy* 18 (2): 330–60.
Scanlon, Thomas. 1998. *What We Owe to Each Other*. Cambridge, MA: Harvard University Press.
Scanlon, Thomas. 2014. *Being Realistic About Reasons*. Oxford: Oxford University Press.
Schilpp, P. A., ed. 1942. *The Philosophy of G. E. Moore*. Chicago: Northwestern University Press.
Schneewind, J. B. 1963. "First Principles and Common Sense Morality in Sidgwick's Ethics." *Archiv fur Geschichte der Philosophie* 45 (2): 137–56.
Schneewind, J. B. 1977. *Sidgwick's Ethics and Victorian Moral Philosophy*. Oxford: Clarendon Press.
Schultz, Bart, ed. 1992. *Essays on Henry Sidgwick*. Cambridge, UK: Cambridge University Press.
Schultz, Bart. 2004. *Henry Sidgwick, Eye of the Universe: An Intellectual Biography*. Cambridge, UK: Cambridge University Press.
Schultz, Bart. 2017. *The Happiness Philosophers*. Princeton: Princeton University Press.

Shaver, Robert. 1997. "Sidgwick's False Friends." *Ethics* 107:314–20.
Shaver, Robert. 1999. *Rational Egoism: A Selective and Critical History*. Cambridge, UK: Cambridge University Press.
Shaver, Robert. 2003. "Sidgwick's Minimal Metaethics." *Utilitas* 12:261–77.
Shaver, Robert. 2006. "Sidgwick on Moral Motivation." *Philosopher's Imprint* 6:1–14.
Shaver, Robert. 2014. "Sidgwick's Axioms and Consequentialism." *Philosophical Review* 123 (2): 173–204.
Shaver, Robert. 2016 "Sidgwick on Pleasure." *Ethics* 126 (4): 901–28.
Shaver, Robert. 2019. "Promissory Obligation: A Sidgwickian View." *History of Philosophy Quarterly* 36 (2): 181–97.
Shaver, Robert. 2020. "Sidgwick's Distinction Passage." *Utilitas* 32 (4): 444–53.
Sidgwick, Arthur, and Eleanor Mildred Sidgwick. 1906. *Henry Sidgwick: A Memoir*. London: MacMillan.
Sidgwick, Henry. 1874. *The Methods of Ethics*. 1st ed. London: MacMillan.
Sidgwick, Henry. 1879. "The Establishment of Ethical First Principles," in Sidgwick 2000, 29–34.
Sidgwick, Henry. 1883. *The Principles of Political Economy*. London: MacMillan.
Sidgwick, Henry. 1886. *Outlines of the History of Ethics for English Readers*. London: MacMillan.
Sidgwick, Henry. 1889. "Some Fundamental Ethical Controversies," in Sidgwick 2000, 35–46.
Sidgwick, Henry. 1891. *The Elements of Politics*. London: MacMillan.
Sidgwick, Henry. 1902. *Lectures on the Ethics of T. H. Green, Mr. Herbert Spencer and J. Martineau*. London: MacMillan.
Sidgwick, Henry. 1903. *The Development of European Polity*. Edited by Eleanor Mildred Sidgwick. London: MacMillan.
Sidgwick, Henry. 1905. "Further on the Criteria of Truth and Error," in Sidgwick 2000, 166–70.
Sidgwick, Henry. 1907. *The Methods of Ethics*. 7th ed. London: Macmillan.
Sidgwick, Henry. 2000. *Essays on Ethics and Method*. Edited by Marcus G. Singer. Oxford: Oxford University Press.
Singer, Peter. 1974. "Sidgwick and Reflective Equilibrium." *The Monist* 58:490–517.
Singer, Peter. 1975. *Animal Liberation*. New York: Harper Collins.
Singer, Peter. 2011. *Practical Ethics*. 3rd ed. Cambridge, UK: Cambridge University Press.
Skelton, Anthony. 2008. "Sidgwick's Philosophical Intuitions." *Etica & Politica/Ethics and Politics* 10:185–209.
Skelton, Anthony. 2010. "Henry Sidgwick's Moral Epistemology." *Journal of the History of Philosophy* 48:491–520.
Smart, J. J. C., and Bernard Williams. 1973. *Utilitarianism: For and Against*. Cambridge, UK: Cambridge University Press.

Spencer, Herbert. 1879. *The Data of Ethics*. New York: Thomas Y. Crowell & Co.
Stephen, Leslie. 1882. *The Science of Ethics*. London: John Murray.
Street, Sharon. 2006. "A Darwinian Dilemma for Realist Theories of Value." *Philosophical Studies* 127 (1): 109–66.
Sverdlik, S. 1985. "Sidgwick's Methodology." *Journal of the History of Philosophy* 23:537–53.
Sverdlik, S. 2012. "The origins of The Objection." *History of Philosophy Quarterly* 29 (1): 79–101.
Troyer, John, ed. 2003. *The Classical Utilitarians*. Indianapolis: Hackett.
Williams, Bernard. 1973. "A Critique of Utilitarianism," in Smart and Williams.

Index

For the benefit of digital users, indexed terms that span two pages (e.g., 52–53) may, on occasion, appear on only one of those pages.

Anscombe, Elizabeth, 62
Aristotle
    common-sense morality and, 10, 96
    on ethics and practice, 99
    first principles and, 30–31
    intuitionism and, 10
    Parfit on, 12
    Prefaces to *Methods of Ethics* on, 7–8, 14
    virtue ethics and, 149

Bacon, Francis, 101–2
Balfour, Arthur, 1
benevolence
    absolute duty and, 137–38, 221–22
    canonical formulation of, 135–36
    consequentialism and, 63
    prima facie duty and, 137–40, 141–43, 221–22
    prudence and, 135
    self-evident moral principles and, 122, 135–38, 139–41, 146
    universal good and, 135, 136–38, 221–22
    utilitarianism and, 134, 139–40, 163
Benson, Edward White, 1–2
Bentham, Jeremy
    distributive justice and, 165–66
    happiness and, 83–85
    hedonism and, 33
    pleasure and, 88–89
    sanctions and, 92–93
    utilitarianism and, 6, 33, 89, 163–64
Bradley, F. H., 34–35, 88
Brink, David, 183, 226–27, 229–30
Broad, C. D.
    deontology concept introduced by, 61–62, 68–69, 78–79n.2
    dualism of practical reason and, 222–24
    non-naturalism and, 179
    prima facie duty and, 112–13, 194–95, 207
    Sidgwick's *Methods of Ethics* commended by, 11–13
    on teleological theories of morality, 62
Butler, Joseph
    dualism of practical reason and, 9
    goodness and, 76
    opposition between intuitionism and utilitarianism posed by, 34
    opposition between utilitarianism and common sense morality posed by, 200–1
    Prefaces to *Methods of Ethics* on, 7–8
    psychological hedonism and, 51–53
    Sidgwick and, 9–10, 50, 51–53, 76, 200–1

Cambridge Apostles, 3–4, 17n.2
Cambridge University, 1–5
Church of England, 2, 4–5
Clarke, Samuel, 136
coherentism, 65, 180–81, 183–84
common-sense morality. *See also* dogmatic intuitionism
  absolutist deontology and, 110–11, 114–15, 143
  Aristotle and, 10, 96
  clearness and precision of, 99–100
  egoism and, 98–99, 116–17, 125–26, 215–16
  esoteric morality and, 205–7
  first principles and, 116–17
  four conditions posited by Sidgwick and, 14, 100–11, 114, 117, 192
  hedonism and, 82–83, 204–5
  intuitionism and, 10, 98–99, 110, 125–26
  methods of ethics and, 116, 201
  moderate deontology and, 111–15
  promissory obligation and, 192–94
  sanctions and, 204–5
  self-evident moral principles and, 96–97, 120–21, 195, 225–26
  utilitarianism and, 10–11, 34, 98–99, 125–26, 177–78, 188–95, 197–207, 216
  virtue and, 146
consequentialism
  Anscombe's introduction of the term, 62
  benevolence and, 63
  defining characteristics of, 27
  deontology contrasted with, 61, 63, 207–8
  egoism and, 27, 80
  "Government House Consequentialism" and, 206
  promissory obligation and, 107, 196–97
  Ross and, 107, 195–97
  self-evident moral principles and, 142
  utilitarianism and, 27, 80
  virtue and, 28
contractualism, 28
Crisp, Roger, 179, 227, 228

Darwin, Charles, 2
The Data of Ethics (Spencer), 202–3
Deigh, John, 179
deontology. *See also* intuitionism
  absolutist deontology and, 27–28, 110–11, 114–15, 140, 143
  Broad's introduction of the concept of, 61–62, 68–69, 78–79n.2
  common-sense morality and, 110–15, 143
  consequentialism contrasted with, 61, 63, 207–8
  dogmatic intuitionism and, 69–70
  moderate deontology and, 111–15, 140
  monistic deontology and, 27–28
  prima facie duty and, 111–14, 130, 143, 194–95, 207
  self-evident moral principles and, 142–43
  utilitarianism and, 21
  virtue and, 28
Descartes, Rene, 101–2, 167
The Development of European Polity (Sidgwick), 5
Dissertation of the Nature of Virtue (Butler), 34, 200–1
dogmatic intuitionism. *See also* common-sense morality
  deontology and, 69–70
  first principles and, 94–95
  four conditions and, 67–68

methods of ethics and, 94–95
perceptual intuitionism compared to, 67, 68–69
philosophical intuitionism compared to, 68–69
self-evident general moral rules and, 67–68, 70–71, 98
Donagan, Alan, 110–11, 207
dualism of practical reason
absolute duty and, 222
agent-neutral *versus* agent-relative reasons and, 176, 228–29
arguments regarding existence of God and, 219–20, 223–24, 225–26, 230–31
Brink's two domains interpretation and, 226–27, 229–30
Broad and, 222–24
Butler and, 9
conflict between duty and self-interest in, 9, 217–18
conflict between egoism and utilitarianism in, 210, 220–21, 222, 225–27, 229–31
immediate contradiction and, 222
mediate contradiction and, 223–25
Moore and, 222
"No Moral Government" claim and, 223–24
non-contradictory interpretations of, 225–30
Parfit and, 176, 227–29
prima facie duty and, 222, 226–29
Sidgwick on the "fundamental contradiction" in, 218–19

egoism. *See also* hedonism
agent-relative reasons and, 175–76
authority and, 81
coherence questions regarding, 175–76

common-sense morality and, 98–99, 116–17, 125–26, 215–16
consequentialism and, 27, 80
criticisms of Sidgwick's treatment of, 174–75
deductive hedonism and, 82–83
empirical-reflective method of ethics and, 82, 91, 94
first principles and, 81–82, 116–17, 172, 175, 213–14
four conditions and, 213–14
goodness and, 37
Hobbes and, 81
intuitionism and, 32–33, 92, 210
Kant and, 8–9
methods of ethics and, 32–33, 81–82, 92, 116, 210
as moral theory, 21, 38–39
objective hedonism and, 82–83, 91
personal identity and, 167–68
pleasure at individual level and, 22, 23–24, 64–65, 80–81, 116–17, 153, 172–74
"proof" and, 172–73, 211–15
prudence and, 132–34, 174–75
rationality and, 8–9, 82, 211–15, 222, 227–28
Ross and, 37–39
sanctions and, 215–17
self-evident moral truths and, 175, 225–26
self-preservation and, 81
time preferences and, 166–67
universal good and, 211
utilitarianism and, 10–11, 22, 28–29, 32–33, 80, 92, 133, 162–63, 172, 176, 210–17, 220–21, 222, 225–27, 229–30
The Elements of Politics (Sidgwick), 5
epistemology
coherentism and, 65, 180–81, 183–84
first principles and, 31

epistemology (*cont.*)
   foundationalism and, 65, 180–81, 182–84
   intuitionism and, 14, 50, 60–65, 68–69, 179–81
   moral epistemology and, 180–85
   self-evident propositions and, 60
   utilitarianism and, 63–64
error theory, 43–44, 226
esoteric morality, 205–7
Essays on Ethics and Method (Singer), 104
"The Establishment of First Ethical Principles" (Sidgwick), 30–31
The Eye of the Universe (Schultz), 224

first principles
   Aristotle and, 30–31
   common-sense morality and, 116–17
   criteria for establishing, 183–85
   dogmatic intuitionism and, 94–95
   egoism and, 81–82, 116–17, 172, 175, 213–14
   epistemology and, 31
   excellence and, 25
   intuitionism and, 94–95, 117
   metaphysical significance of, 31
   methods of ethics and, 29, 30–32, 82
   Mill and, 30–31, 169–71
   "proof" of, 168–71
   right-making properties and, 31
   Ross and, 31
   Schneewind on defining qualities of, 30–31
   utilitarianism and, 168–69, 201
Five Types of Ethical Theory (Broad), 11–12, 61–62, 112–13, 194–95
foundationalism, 65, 180–81, 182–84
Foundations of Ethics (Ross), 112

the four conditions
   clarity and precision condition and, 67, 101–2, 106, 108, 114, 117, 122, 126–27, 152
   common-sense morality and, 14, 100–11, 114, 117, 192
   consensus condition and, 67, 103, 106, 108–9, 152, 225
   consistency condition and, 67, 103, 118n.14, 152
   De Lazari-Radek and Singer's update of, 230
   dogmatic intuitionism and, 67–68
   egoism and, 213–14
   exclusion of error and, 104
   genuinely self-evident appearance condition and, 67, 102–3, 106, 152
   hedonism and, 158
   intuitionism and, 67–68, 111, 117
   justice and, 126–27
Frankena, William, 224
free will, 53–57

Gibbard, Allan, 38
Gladstone, W. E., 1
God
   arguments regarding existence of, 2, 219–20, 223–24, 225–26, 230–31
   intuitionism and, 217
   moral duty and the will of, 25–26
   utilitarianism and, 216–17
Golden Rule, 123–24, 126
goodness
   desire and, 74–75, 88
   excellence and, 76–77
   "good on the whole" and, 75–76
   happiness and, 76–77, 145
   ideal goods and, 77–78
   intuitionism and, 36–37, 63
   monistic conception of, 145–46, 154, 157, 159n.1

Moore and, 36–37, 72, 73, 77–78, 154, 173–74
naturalism and, 74–75
non-naturalism and, 72, 73, 76
pleasure and, 73–74, 88–89
pluralistic conception of, 145, 149–54, 155–57
rightness and, 75–76
ultimate good and, 88–89, 127–28, 146, 148, 151, 153
virtue and, 145–48

happiness. *See also* pleasure
Bentham and, 83–85
duty and, 92–94
goodness and, 76–77, 145
hedonism and, 8, 63, 74
measurements of, 83–85
Mill and, 83–85
The Happiness Philosophers (Schultz), 224
hedonism. *See also* egoism
Butler and, 51–53
common-sense morality and, 82–83, 204–5
deductive hedonism and, 82–83
empirical hedonism and, 191–92, 204–5
individual happiness and, 8, 63, 74
intuitionism and, 63, 157–59
Mill and, 8–10, 33, 41–42, 51–52, 85
monistic alternative to, 145–46, 154, 157, 159n.1
Moore and, 24, 51, 78, 154–56
objective hedonism and, 82–83, 91
pleasure and, 50–51, 74, 90, 145
pluralistic alternative to, 145, 149–54, 155–57
psychological hedonism and, 50–53
qualitative hedonism and, 90
Ross and, 24, 154, 155–57
self-evident moral truths and, 64–65, 175, 225–26
utilitarianism and, 8, 145
Hobbes, Thomas, 34, 74, 81, 203–4
Hume, David, 45–46, 166–68, 189, 202
Hurka, Thomas, 6–7, 14, 159n.1, 179, 208

Inquiry into the First Principles of Morals (Hume), 189
intuitionism. *See also* deontology
absolute self-evident rules of ethics and, 8, 22, 37, 60–61, 63
aesthetic intuitionism and, 147, 159–60n.2
common-sense morality and, 10, 98–99, 110, 125–26
criticisms of Sidgwick's treatment of, 34–35, 39, 115–17, 207
egoism and, 32–33, 92, 210
epistemology and, 14, 50, 60–65, 68–69, 179–81
excellence and, 24–25
first principles and, 94–95, 117
four conditions and, 67–68, 111, 117
God and, 217
goodness and, 36–37, 63
hedonism and, 63, 157–59
moral-theoretic components of, 60–62, 68–69
plurality of intuitive ethical principles and, 10
a posteriori morality compared to, 64
reflective equilibrium theory and, 70–71
utilitarianism and, 9–11, 14, 28–29, 33–34, 59–60, 63–64, 120, 138–39, 145, 158–59, 171, 176–78, 201, 210–11
Whewell and, 8, 10, 59–60, 61, 64–65, 111, 207

Jones, E. E. Constance, 7–8, 50
justice
    facts that ground, 124–25
    the four conditions and, 126–27
    Golden Rule and, 123–24, 126
    Kant's universal law formulation and, 126
    self-evident moral principles and, 96–97, 99, 122–27, 141, 146
    unexplained ethical variation and, 124–25
    utilitarianism and, 165–66

Kant, Immanuel
    egoism and, 8–9
    free will and, 8–9, 41–42, 53
    monistic deontology and, 27–28
    Moore and, 7
    motivation and, 45–47
    Prefaces to *Methods of Ethics* on, 7–8, 14
    Sidgwick and, 8–10, 41–42, 53, 126
    universal law formula and, 8–10, 27–28, 126
Keynes, John Maynard, 2–3, 219–20

Lazari-Radek, Katarzyna de, 179, 208, 230–31

Mackie, J. L., 173–74, 224, 226
Martineau, Jacques, 160n.4
McCloskey, H. J., 197–200
McGrath, Sarah, 181
McLeod, Owen, 227–28
metaethics
    definition of, 8
    error theory and, 43–44
    Methods of Ethics and, 30, 42–44
    Moore and, 42–44
    naturalism/non-naturalism distinction and, 43, 178–79
    non-cognitivism and, 43–44
    Sidgwick's position within, 178–80

methods of ethics
    common-sense morality and, 116, 201
    dogmatic intuitionism and, 94–95
    egoism and, 32–33, 81–82, 92, 116, 210
    first principles and, 29, 30–32, 82
    individual human beings as emphasis in, 29–30
    "ought" and "right" considerations in, 29–30
    rational procedures and, 29–30
    Sidgwick's definition of, 29–30
The Methods of Ethics (Sidgwick)
    analytical table of contents in, 13
    initial publication (1874) of, 1, 5
    long sentences of, 13
    organizational challenges of, 15–16
    overall aims of book outlined, 20–21
    potential omission of moral theories from, 21–29
Mill, John Stuart
    first principles and, 30–31, 169–71
    on happiness, 83–85
    hedonism and, 8–10, 33, 41–42, 51–52, 85
    on higher pleasures, 85
    naturalism and, 43
    Prefaces to *Methods of Ethics* on, 7–8, 14
    Sidgwick and, 8–10, 41–42, 50, 170–71, 185–86n.8, 200
    utilitarianism and, 6, 8–9, 33, 59–60, 64–65, 89, 163–64, 185–86n.8
Moore, G.E.
    dualism of practical reason and, 222
    on egoism and "one's own good," 173–75

goodness and, 36–37, 72, 73, 77–78, 154, 173–74
happiness and, 85
hedonism and, 24, 51, 78, 154–56
Kant and, 7
metaethics and, 42–44
non-naturalism and, 43–45, 72, 73, 179
rightness and, 73
Sidgwick and, 6–7, 14, 42, 72, 77–78, 154–55, 173–75, 222
moral epistemology, 180–85
Moral Knowledge (McGrath), 181
moral theory. *See* methods of ethics

Nagel, Thomas, 44, 167, 175–76, 228–29
naturalism
 fundamental moral concept definitions under, 47–50
 goodness and, 74–75
 Mill and, 43
 moral judgments viewed as similar to factual judgments under, 43, 178–79
Newman, John Henry, 2
Nicomachean Ethics (Aristotle), 96
non-cognitivism, 43–44, 48, 178–79
non-consequentialist moral theories, 27–28
non-naturalism
 goodness and, 72, 73, 76
 indefinite nature of fundamental moral concept in, 43–44, 46–47, 65, 72
 Moore and, 43–45, 72, 73, 179
 moral judgments viewed as different from factual judgments under, 43, 178–79
 reason and desire's roles within, 179
 recent resurgence in, 44
 rightness and, 72–73, 179

Sidgwick and, 43–45, 46–47, 50, 72, 73, 179
simplicity and, 72–73
normative ethics, 8, 30

On What Matters (Parfit), 6–7, 12, 28–29, 227–28
Oxford Movement, 2

Palladino, Eusapia, 6
Parfit, Derek
 dualism of practical reason and, 176, 227–29
 egoism and, 167–68, 175–76
 on "Government House Consequentialism," 206
 on Moore and Sidgwick, 7
 non-naturalism and, 44, 179
 population ethics and, 164
 Sidgwick's *Methods of Ethics* commended by, 12
 "triple theory" of, 28–29
perceptional intuitionism, 66–67, 68–70, 71, 159–60n.2, 199
Pereboom, Derk, 57
Phillips, David, 179, 183–85, 207, 227–28
philosophical intuitionism, 68–71
pleasure. *See also* happiness
 changes in judgments about, 91
 comparisons regarding types of, 90, 91, 94
 desirability and, 86–88, 90
 desire and, 86, 149
 distinctiveness of, 86–87
 goodness and, 73–74, 88–89
 hedonism and, 50–51, 74, 90, 145
 higher pleasures and, 85, 87–88
 non-human animals and, 89
 prudence and, 127–28
The Possibility of Altruism (Nagel), 167, 176
Price, Richard, 57n.1, 118n.9

prima facie duty
  benevolence and, 137–40, 141–43, 221–22
  Broad and, 112–13, 194–95, 207
  deontology and, 111–14, 130, 143, 194–95, 207
  dualism of practical reason and, 222, 226–29
  prudence and, 130–31, 133–34, 213–14, 221–22
  Ross and, 27–28, 111–14, 130, 194–95
  tendencies and, 113
Principia Ethica (Moore), 6–7, 36–37, 42–45, 72–73
Principles of Political Economy (Sidgwick), 5
"proof"
  coherentism and, 180–81
  egoism and, 172–73, 211–15
  first principles and, 168–71
  sanctions and, 171
  Schneewind on, 182–83
  utilitarianism and, 171, 176–78, 180, 182–83, 188, 199, 211–15
prudence
  absolute duty and, 131–32, 221–22
  benevolence and, 135
  egoism and, 132–34, 174–75
  one's own good on the whole and, 127–34, 137, 213–14, 221
  pleasure and, 127–28
  prima facie duty and, 130–31, 133–34, 213–14, 221–22
  self-evident moral principles and, 122, 127–34, 141, 146
  time preferences and, 127–30, 131–33, 213–14, 221
  utilitarianism and, 133–34

Rachels, James and Stuart, 197–98
Rational Egoism (Shaver), 183, 226–27, 229

Rawls, John, 181–83
Reasons and Persons (Parfit), 164, 167–68
reflective equilibrium theory, 70–71, 181–83, 186–87n.25
The Right and the Good (Ross), 6, 37, 112–13, 194–95
rightness
  as attribute of means, 47
  goodness and, 75–76
  Moore and, 73
  non-naturalism and, 72–73, 179
  Ross and, 37
Ross, W.D.
  consequentialism and, 107, 195–97
  egoism and, 37–39
  first principles and, 31
  hedonism and, 24, 154, 155–57
  moderate deontology and, 111, 113–14, 143
  pluralistic conception of the good, 154, 155–57
  prima facie duties and, 27–28, 111–14, 130, 194–95
  on promissory obligations, 115, 196–97
  rightness and, 37
  self-evident moral principles and, 141–43
  Sidgwick and, 6, 14, 141–44, 154, 156–57, 194–95, 197

sanctions, 92–93, 171–73, 215–17
Scanlon, T. M., 44, 70–71
Schneewind, J. B., 30–31, 179, 182–83, 207, 224
Schultz, Bart, 224–26
The Science of Ethics (Stephen), 203
self-evident moral principles
  common-sense morality and, 96–97, 120–21, 195, 225–26
  consequentialism and, 142

deontology and, 142–43
dogmatic intuitionism and, 67–68, 70–71, 98
egoism and, 64–65, 175, 225–26
epistemology and, 60
hard cases and, 107–9
hedonism and, 64–65, 175, 225–26
intuitionism and, 8, 22, 37, 60–61, 63
justice and, 96–97, 99, 122–27, 141, 146
promissory obligation and, 97, 106–9, 111, 114–15, 130, 148–49, 193
Ross and, 141–43
tautology problem and, 120–22
utilitarianism and, 96–97, 120
Shaver, Robert, 179, 183, 208, 226–27, 229
Sidgwick, Arthur, 1–2
Sidgwick, Eleanor "Nora," 5–6
Sidgwick, Henry
   Butler and, 9–10, 50, 51–53, 76, 200–1
   Cambridge Apostles and, 3–4
   Church of England and, 2, 4–5
   education of, 1–4
   Kant and, 8–10, 41–42, 53, 126
   as Knightsbridge Professor of Moral Philosophy, 1, 4–5
   Mill and, 8–10, 41–42, 50, 170–71, 185–86n.8, 200
   Moore and, 6–7, 14, 42, 72, 77–78, 154–55, 173–75, 222
   non-naturalism and, 43–45, 46–47, 50, 72, 73, 179
   Ross and, 6, 14, 141–44, 154, 156–57, 194–95, 197
   Society for Psychical Research and, 5–6
   Whewell and, 7–8
   women's higher education promoted by, 5

Sidgwick, Mary, 1–2
Sidgwick, William, 1–2
Sidgwickian Ethics (Phillips), 179, 183–85
Sidgwick's Ethics and Victorian Moral Philosophy (Schneewind), 182, 224
Singer, Marcus, 104
Singer, Peter, 163–64, 179, 182–83, 186–87n.25, 208, 224
Skelton, Anthony, 183
Smith, Adam, 202
Society for Psychical Research, 5–6
"Some Fundamental Ethical Controversies" (Sidgwick), 212–13
Spencer, Herbert, 82–83, 86, 202–3
Stephen, Leslie, 202–3
Street, Sharon, 230
Sverdlik, Stephen, 183, 199–200

Ten Commandments, 22, 60–61
Tennyson, Alfred Lord, 1
A Theory of Justice (Rawls), 181–82
The Theory of Morality (Donagan), 111
Treatise of Human Nature (Hume), 167

utilitarianism
   act-utilitarianism and, 198–99
   benevolence and, 134, 139–40, 163
   Bentham and, 6, 33, 89, 163–64
   common-sense morality and, 10–11, 34, 98–99, 125–26, 177–78, 188–95, 197–207, 216
   consequentialism and, 27, 80
   deontology and, 27
   distribution of happiness and, 165–66
   egoism and, 10–11, 22, 28–29, 32–33, 80, 92, 133, 162–63, 172, 176, 210–17, 220–21, 222, 225–27, 229–30

utilitarianism (*cont.*)
  epistemology and, 63–64
  esoteric morality and, 205–7
  experience as means of knowing ethical correctness in, 8, 64–65
  first principles and, 168–69, 201
  greatest happiness for greatest number as goal of, 8, 10, 22, 23–24, 31, 33, 64–65, 80, 153, 162–65, 167
  hedonism and, 8, 145
  intuitionism and, 9–11, 14, 28–29, 33–34, 59–60, 63–64, 120, 138–39, 145, 158–59, 171, 176–78, 201, 210–11
  justice and, 165–66
  Law of God and, 216–17
  Mill and, 6, 8–9, 33, 59–60, 64–65, 89, 163–64, 185–86n.8
  non-human animals and, 89, 163–64
  philosophical intuitionism and, 69–70
  population ethics and, 164–65
  promissory obligation and, 192–94, 197
  "proof" of, 171, 176–78, 180, 182–83, 188, 199, 211–15
  prudence and, 133–34
  rule-utilitarianism and, 198–99
  sanctions and, 171–73, 215–17
  self-evident moral principles and, 96–97, 120
  universal good and, 139–40, 145
Utilitarianism (Mill), 170

Victoria (queen of England), 1
The View from Nowhere (Nagel), 176
virtue
  common-sense morality and, 146
  consequentialism and, 28
  deontology and, 28
  goodness and, 145–48
  virtue ethics and, 28, 148–49, 160n.4

Whewell, William
  anti-utilitarianism and, 8
  common-sense morality and, 98, 110
  intuitionism and, 8, 10, 59–60, 61, 64–65, 111, 207
  Sidgwick and, 7–8